The AI Optimization Playbook

Drive business success with proven AI strategies,
best practices, and responsible innovation

Dr. Chun Schiros

Supreet Kaur

Rajdeep Arora

Dr. Usha Jagannathan

‹packt›

The AI Optimization Playbook

Copyright © 2025 Packt Publishing

Portfolio Director: Gebin George
Relationship Lead: Gebin George
Project Manager: Prajakta Naik
Content Engineer: Aditi Chatterjee
Technical Editor: Rahul Limbachiya
Copy Editor: Safis Editing
Indexer: Pratik Shirodkar
Proofreader: Aditi Chatterjee
Production Designer: Ponraj Dhandapani
Growth Lead: Nimisha Dua

First published: November 2025

Production reference: 1261125

Published by Packt Publishing Ltd.
Grosvenor House
11 St Paul's Square
Birmingham
B3 1RB, UK.

ISBN 978-1-80611-511-2

www.packtpub.com

To Matt, Olivia, Adaline, Luke, Juju, Mom and Dad: Without your support and love, none of this would have been possible, nor would it matter.

– Chun

To my family, for their patience and unwavering support throughout this work.

– Supreet

To my wife, Ekta, sister, Avi, and parents, for their constant love and encouragement. And to my precious daughter, Mannat, whose laughter made every late night worth it.

– Rajdeep

To my super-supportive husband, Venkatesh, my loving children, Shreya, Akshaya, and Shashvath, and my dear parents, for being a constant source of love, unwavering support, and encouragement.

– Usha

Foreword

What does it mean to optimize the use of **Artificial Intelligence (AI)**?

Regarding "AI" in quotes because the term encompasses a range of architectures and methodologies, there are myriad books and principles designed to help users maximize the benefits or **return on investment (ROI)** of any form of AI.

Based on my work authoring *Heartificial Intelligence* (2016) and leading the IEEE Global Initiative on Ethics of Autonomous and Intelligent Systems, which resulted in the Ethically Aligned Design documents and the large IEEE 7000™ series of standards, it is clear that optimization starts at the outset of design.

This logic stems from a simple fact: where no formal, pragmatic metrics of success beyond GDP-oriented values of finance and productivity exist, harms to human mental health and nature are a given. You cannot avoid harming what you don't account for at the outset and throughout your AI Systems design.

This playbook provides the comprehensive roadmap necessary for this kind of rigorous, human-centric optimization with an end-to-end framework that weaves the critical components of the AI life cycle across five distinct parts. The authors, Dr. Chun Schiros (Strategy and Leadership), Supreet Kaur and Rajdeep Arora (Execution, Architecture, and MLOps), and Dr. Usha Jagannathan (Responsible AI and Governance), have addressed the full organizational life cycle, starting with AI Maturity Assessment, Data Strategy, and MLOps execution, where steps are designed to drive positive business value and measurable human flourishing, right from the initial strategic decision.

This is why *The AI Optimization Playbook* offers what most other treatises on Artificial Intelligence do not – a definition of 'optimization' stemming from and driven by **Responsible AI (RAI)**.

As noted throughout *The AI Optimization Playbook*, from the initial strategic design to final governance, the pillars of RAI (**Fairness, Ethics, Accountability, and Transparency (FEAT)**) establish that RAI is essential for true optimization. The true proof of optimization comes from clarity and connection to the metrics of success, proving increased positive flourishing for people and planet.

RAI as the basis and proof of optimization for AI, especially regarding **Generative AI (GenAI)**, where hallucinations, sycophancy, and anthropomorphism by design are attributes of most LLMs, will center design efforts using any AI architecture in a relationship of trust and agency with users, stakeholders, and the public at large.

It has been my pleasure to know Usha Jagannathan for several years and to witness her expertise in applying RAI from concept to execution at IEEE SA and in corporate environments. The collective knowledge of the authors, which includes this holistic, end-to-end framework, is matched only by their shared commitment to the human-centric mission of this book. I am excited for the 'optimization' your efforts will produce, bringing increased positive flourishing for people and planet based on your learning and increased success upon reading and completing *The AI Optimization Playbook*.

John C. Havens,

Founding E.D., The IEEE Global Initiative on Ethics of Autonomous and Intelligent Systems, Author, Heartificial Intelligence: Embracing Our Humanity to Maximize Machines

Contributors

About the authors

Dr. Chun Schiros is an award-winning technology and AI thought leader and field CTO at a leading cloud computing company, where she serves as a trusted advisor to the boards of directors and senior executives leading enterprise cloud, data, and AI transformations.

With decades of experience across financial services, healthcare, and technology, Dr. Schiros has built a distinguished career bridging the gap between business vision and technological execution. She helps organizations optimize the value of AI through the alignment of business initiatives with modern data architecture, scalable operating models, and effective change management.

Her leadership has earned industry-wide recognition, including the following:

- *Data Leader of the Year* by Corinium Global Intelligence (2022)
- *Most Powerful Women in Banking: Next* by American Banker (2023)
- *Global Top 100 Innovators in Data and Analytics* (2023 and 2024)

Dr. Schiros is known for her ability to translate complex AI and data strategies into business impact, guiding organizations to embed AI into their DNA, responsibly, efficiently, and at scale. She holds a Ph.D. in electrical engineering, with advanced training in probability, statistics, and data science.

Her work continues to influence executives and industry leaders seeking to unlock AI's full potential, not just as a technology, but as a strategic enabler of business excellence.

Supreet Kaur is a senior AI cloud solutions architect at Microsoft, enabling financial institutions to scale generative AI solutions from proof of concept to production while evangelizing the latest advancements in AI. Previously at Morgan Stanley, she spearheaded the development of a large-scale machine learning-based personalization engine and earned a patent for an innovative evaluation strategy. A recognized thought leader, Supreet has delivered talks at 50+ global events, authored over 30 thought leadership articles, been named a LinkedIn Top Voice for AI content, and featured in more than 10 media outlets.

Rajdeep Arora is a principal data scientist and machine learning architect at a Fortune 1 company, where he leads innovation in personalization and recommendation systems that shape the online customer journey. With a career spanning startups, consulting, and Fortune 100 companies, Rajdeep has driven cutting-edge machine learning initiatives across domains, including knowledge graphs, supply chain optimization, large-scale recommendation systems, causal inference, and generative AI, with a central mission of creating deeply personalized and human-centered digital experiences. A thought leader and innovator, Rajdeep has contributed to the field through patents, technical publications, and interviews that explore the evolving intersection of AI and personalization. His work reflects a passion for translating complex machine learning systems into scalable, business-driven solutions that transform how people experience technology.

Dr. Usha Jagannathan is a globally recognized leading voice in Responsible AI, serving as the Director of AI Products at a globally recognized standards body. She specializes in accelerating AI productization, driving solutions from PoC and pilots to scalable, trustworthy enterprise systems. She holds a Ph.D. (Technology and E-learning in engineering education) with advanced training in AI for Business and Ethics. Leveraging over 20 years of product engineering and IT experience across leading firms (McKinsey, Marsh) and major institutions (ASU, Purdue Global), Dr. Jagannathan brings deep expertise in data/AI engineering, governance, and risk management.

Dr. Jagannathan's thought leadership has earned industry recognitions, including Responsible AI Leader of the Year 2023 (Women in AI) and AI & Data Science Leader of the Year 2024 (WomenTech), along with global finalist recognition as AI Trailblazer of the Year 2025 for her thought leadership. She is deeply passionate about mentoring, having empowered over 1,000 young professionals to pivot their diverse backgrounds into high-impact engineering and product roles, fostering the next generation of responsible tech leaders.

About the reviewers

Jatindeep (Jatin) Singh is an applied artificial intelligence/machine learning lead in global financial services. He designs and deploys production AI systems that blend time-series modeling, large language models, reinforcement learning, deep learning, and classical machine learning to tackle high-impact problems in risk, payments, and forecasting. Previously, he worked in American Express's Decision Science team, where he built, launched, and monitored credit decisioning models at scale. Jatin holds an M.S. in financial engineering from Columbia University and a B.Tech. from IIT Gandhinagar. His current interests include AI agents for operations, robust forecasting, and trustworthy machine learning in regulated environments.

Raman Deep Singh is an AI thought leader and full-stack data scientist. He is passionate about turning data into impact. A former management consultant, he now helps Google Ads' largest clients with AI transformation by blending machine learning with strategic insight.

Saurabh S. Vaichal is a senior machine learning engineer specializing in large language models, retrieval-augmented generation, and agentic AI systems. He builds production-scale machine learning pipelines that power generative and conversational intelligence at The Home Depot, focusing on contextual retrieval, evaluation frameworks, and fine-tuning small language models for enterprise reliability. His work integrates deep learning, semantic search, and experimentation to drive scalable, data-driven decision systems.

Subscribe for a free eBook

New frameworks, evolving architectures, research drops, production breakdowns—*AI_Distilled* filters the noise into a weekly briefing for engineers and researchers working hands-on with LLMs and generative AI systems. Subscribe now and receive a free eBook, along with weekly insights that help you stay focused and informed.

Subscribe at https://packt.link/80z6Y or scan the following QR code:

Table of Contents

Part II: Aligning Projects with Business Impact   41

Chapter 3: Selecting High-Impact AI Projects   43

Chapter 4: Beyond the Build: Gaining Leadership Support for AI Initiatives   65

Chapter 7: From Model to Market: Operationalizing ML Systems   111

Chapter 8: From Metrics to Measurement: Experimentation and Causal Inference   159

Part IV: Emerging Topics: Generative AI and AI Agents   177

Chapter 9: Generative AI in the Enterprise: Unlocking New Opportunities   179

Chapter 10: Understanding GenAI Operations   193

Preface

The AI Optimization Playbook aims to train business leaders, data scientists, and AI engineers to achieve transformative business value throughout the entire AI project lifecycle. It covers not only the technical aspect of model optimization but also the crucial elements of strategy, leadership, project selection, AI/MLOps, and responsible AI governance required for putting AI into production successfully. The book introduces several key frameworks, such as the AI project lifecycle (from strategy to prototype to production to iteration), to provide proven approaches for consistently producing high-quality, high-impact output.

This book guides you on how to formulate an AI strategy, select high-impact projects, and navigate the entire lifecycle from pilot to production. It also details how to operationalize these systems using MLOps and, more recently, LLMOps for generative AI, to ensure solutions are scalable and reliable. Taking a practical, hands-on approach using real-world case studies, the book also dives deeper into the concepts behind why AI projects fail. This ensures that you will not only learn how to build something but also understand why strategic alignment and responsible governance are critical for producing scalable business outcomes. Learning to effectively manage this entire lifecycle is an empowering skill set in the quickly evolving field of artificial intelligence.

The book is structured into five parts:

- *Part 1, Laying the Groundwork for AI Success*, establishes the strategic foundation necessary for any successful AI initiative. We will begin by examining why most AI projects fail, showing that these are overwhelmingly strategy, execution, and integration failures, not technology failures. We will analyze common pitfalls, such as misaligned goals (chasing technical "surrogate metrics" instead of business value), siloed development, weak data foundations, and a misunderstanding of AI's iterative and non-deterministic nature. Having established what goes wrong, this part translates these lessons into a practical framework for building a mature AI strategy. This includes using evaluation processes such as the ICE framework to prioritize a project roadmap, building robust governance and compliance using established models such as the NIST AI RMF, and designing a modern data strategy that treats data as a product. Finally, we cover the need for a scalable AI platform, a principled algorithm selection strategy, and a hybrid "hub-and-spoke" organizational structure to manage change.

- *Part 2, Aligning Projects with Business Impact,* provides a practical blueprint for bridging the gap between strategy and execution, beginning with the selection of high-impact AI projects. We will first detail how to analyze and prioritize initiatives, moving beyond just technical novelty to focus on factors such as business impact, end-user definition, and comprehensive feasibility analysis covering data, the tech stack, and talent. This includes quantitative methods for opportunity sizing, such as T-shirt sizing and bottom-up comparables, as well as rigorous cost-benefit analysis to justify the potential ROI. Once a project is identified, we will cover the critical next step of gaining leadership support, offering a guide to crafting a compelling narrative by engaging stakeholders early, focusing on the "so-what" of business value, presenting a phased roadmap, and setting realistic expectations. With sponsorship secured, we will present a playbook for building an effective **Proof of Concept (PoC)** as a small-scale, low-risk experiment to test feasibility, detailing the critical post-PoC decisions: whether to refine, pivot, or proceed to an MVP. Finally, we will introduce a comprehensive framework for measuring the PoC's performance beyond just technical model metrics, covering the essential system, business, and safety metrics needed to prove its value and secure a clear path to production.

- *Part 3, Deploying and Proving ML Value,* provides a comprehensive guide to the complete, end-to-end lifecycle of an ML system, moving from defining its purpose to proving its causal impact on the business. We will start with the foundational framework for success, moving beyond simple accuracy to define multi-dimensional, business-aligned goals, essential guardrail metrics to prevent unintended harm, and surrogate metrics to track long-term objectives. Next, we will dive into "productization," which is the critical process of operationalizing models from experimental notebooks into robust, production-grade systems, exploring MLOps best practices, the importance of reproducible pipelines for code and data, and the architectural choices for model serving. Finally, we will explore the science of causal inference to answer the critical question, "Did the system do what it was intended to do?", covering the "gold standard" of A/B testing (RCTs), as well as advanced observational techniques and optimization methods such as multi-arm bandits.

- *Part 4, Emerging Topics: Generative AI and AI Agents,* explores the new frontier of AI technologies that are transforming enterprises. We will begin by explaining generative AI and LLMs in business-friendly terms, covering key use cases across various functions, from marketing and customer service to code generation, as well as practical adoption considerations. Following this, we will define LLMOps and detail how it extends traditional MLOps to handle the unique operational lifecycle of large language models, including prompt orchestration, fine-tuning, and specialized monitoring. Finally, we will explore the emerging world of AI agents, discussing what they are, their potential to automate complex multi-step tasks, and the frameworks for building and governing these autonomous systems safely.

- *Part 5*, *Responsible AI and Governance*, provides a crucial framework for ensuring AI solutions are ethical, fair, compliant, and sustainable, starting by defining **Responsible AI (RAI)** and its core pillars (FEAT). It then provides a practical guide to operationalizing these principles through governance committees, risk assessment checklists (Risk Score = Likelihood * Impact), and strategic **Human-in-the-Loop (HITL)** approaches. The part also addresses the unique challenges of trustworthy LLMs, such as "hallucinations," and surveys the evolving global regulatory landscape, including the EU AI Act, before concluding with a look at future trends such as quantum computing and a vision of the fully optimized, AI-driven enterprise of 2030.

Who this book is for

This book is designed for the key individuals and teams responsible for driving business value from artificial intelligence. It is written for the following:

- **Senior leaders and C-suite executives (CXOs, CDOs, CDAOs)**: If you are responsible for setting the enterprise AI strategy, fostering an AI-first culture, or making critical sponsorship and resource decisions, this book provides the frameworks to align technology initiatives with tangible business outcomes.

- **AI scientists and technical practitioners**: If you are a data scientist or applied AI scientist, this book will guide you not only in building models but also in learning the crucial and often-overlooked skill of "selling" your proposed AI solutions to senior leadership and end users. It provides practical tips on how to frame problems, conduct cost-benefit analyses, and demonstrate value to gain buy-in.

- **AI product managers and strategists**: If you are tasked with developing the go-to-market strategy for an AI product, managing the project roadmap, or keeping teams on track, this book offers a complete lifecycle view, from project selection and opportunity sizing to measuring success.

- **Machine Learning Engineers (MLEs)**: For those who specialize in deploying viable PoCs to production, this book provides the crucial context around strategy, governance, and business alignment needed to build systems that are not just technically sound but also scalable, reliable, and impactful.

- **Business leaders and stakeholders:** If you are a business-side leader who collaborates with technical teams, this book will demystify the AI lifecycle. It will equip you to ask the right questions, participate in the selection of high-impact projects, and understand your vital role in the development and adoption process.

What this book covers

Chapter 1, Understanding the Perils of AI Products, describes the common patterns of how AI projects fail. It makes a case that most breakdowns are not technology failures but are a result of poor strategy, execution, and integration. It explores specific pitfalls such as misaligned goals, siloed development, weak data foundations, and a lack of production-readiness.

Chapter 2, Building the Enterprise AI Strategy, outlines the structural elements of a mature AI strategy. It provides a step-by-step guide to align business initiatives with technical development, using frameworks such as ICE for roadmap prioritization. The chapter covers the essential pillars of a comprehensive AI strategy, including governance, a modern data strategy, a scalable AI platform, and organizational change management.

Chapter 3, Selecting High-Impact AI Projects, provides a practical guide for choosing AI initiatives that deliver optimal returns. It details how to perform a feasibility analysis by evaluating data, the tech stack, and talent. The chapter also introduces quantitative methods for opportunity sizing and a framework for conducting a cost-benefit analysis.

Chapter 4, Beyond the Build: Gaining Leadership Support for AI Initiatives, describes the critical step of securing sponsorship from senior leadership. It makes a case that technical teams must "sell" their solutions by crafting a compelling narrative. The chapter provides tips such as engaging stakeholders early, justifying the investment with the "so-what," and setting realistic expectations.

Chapter 5, Building an AI Proof of Concept and Measuring Your Solution, details how to execute a successful PoC as a low-risk experiment to test feasibility. It provides a five-step "PoC playbook" and covers the critical post-PoC decisions: whether to refine, pivot, or build a minimum viable product. Finally, it introduces a framework for measuring performance using a 360-degree view of model, system, business, and safety metrics.

Chapter 6, Beyond Accuracy: A Guide to Defining Metrics for Adoption, explains why simple accuracy is a sufficient measure of success for an ML model. It is a framework for defining holistic, multi-dimensional metrics that align with business goals, including the use of guardrail metrics to prevent unintended harm. The chapter also covers how to link technical model performance to business value, use surrogate metrics for long-term goals, and balance trade-offs using multi-objective optimization.

Chapter 7, From Model to Market: Operationalizing ML Systems, details the process of "productiza-tion," from turning an experimental model into a scalable and maintainable production-grade system. It emphasizes that modern ML requires managing an entire reproducible pipeline (for data, code, and infrastructure), not just a static model file. The text explores the MLOps practices, infrastructure choices (such as IaaS versus PaaS), and model-serving strategies (such as REST APIs or streaming) required to successfully deploy and monitor ML systems.

Chapter 8, From Metrics to Measurement: Experimentation and Causal Inference, focuses on causal inference, the science of proving that an ML system *caused* a specific business outcome, moving beyond simple correlation. It provides a comprehensive guide to randomized control trials (A/B testing) as the "gold standard" for measuring impact, covering hypothesis-driven design and statistical analysis. The chapter also explores advanced methods, such as multi-arm bandits for optimization, and observational techniques, such as uplift modeling, for when A/B tests aren't possible.

Chapter 9, Generative AI in the Enterprise: Unlocking New Opportunities, explores the transformational impact of GenAI, detailing key enterprise use cases such as enhancing customer engagement with chatbots and democratizing enterprise intelligence with copilots. The chapter provides best prac-tices for implementation and measuring ROI through metrics such as cost savings and employee experience. Critically, it also outlines when not to consider GenAI, such as for purely mathematical analysis or high-stakes, reliable decision-making where traditional tools are more appropriate.

Chapter 10, Understanding GenAI Operations, defines GenAI Ops as the essential process to accelerate and optimize the LLM system lifecycle, highlighting how it differs from traditional MLOps in areas such as metrics, talent, and training. The chapter details the "building" phase by explaining the three core optimization techniques: RAG for grounding models with external data, fine-tuning for specializing models on specific tasks, and prompting for instructing the model. It concludes with the "operationalization" phase, which covers critical production practices such as offline and online evaluations, continuous logging and monitoring, and cost management.

Chapter 11, AI Agents Explained, introduces AI agents as autonomous programs that use plan-ning, tool interaction, and memory to automate complex, repetitive tasks. It provides critical guidance on when to apply them, such as for dynamic workflows, and when to avoid them in low-error-tolerance or low-latency situations. The chapter also reviews single versus multi-agent systems, popular agentic frameworks such as LangChain and AutoGen, and the necessity of agent observability for evaluation and monitoring.

Chapter 12, Introduction to Responsible AI, defines RAI as the practical framework for aligning AI with ethical goals, distinguishing it from ethical AI (moral principles) and trustworthy AI (reliability). It introduces the core pillars of **Fairness, Ethics, Accountability, and Transparency (FEAT)** and establishes that RAI is essential for true optimization, as it builds user trust and ensures models are optimized for equitable outcomes, not just technical metrics.

Chapter 13, Implementing RAI Frameworks, Metrics, and Best Practices, provides a practical roadmap for operationalizing RAI. It details establishing governance structures such as RAI committees, using ethical risk assessment checklists (Risk Score = Likelihood * Impact), and strategically integrating **Human-in-the-Loop (HITL)** for high-stakes decisions. The chapter also covers mandatory documentation, such as model and system cards, and specific metrics to quantify fairness, explainability, and safety.

Chapter 14, Building Trustworthy LLMs and Generative AI, explores the unique ethical challenges of LLMs, amplifying potential societal biases, and privacy risks such as data leakage. It details strategies for transparency using explainability methods, outlines fairness metrics to mitigate bias, and provides application-level guidelines such as content filters and user disclosures to build trust.

Chapter 15, Regulatory and Legal Frameworks for Responsible AI, compares the evolving global approaches to AI regulation, contrasting the EU's comprehensive, risk-based AI Act with the US's flexible, sectoral approach. It introduces the **Know Your AI (KYAI)** process for identifying and assessing AI risk and details new GenAI-specific risks such as "shadow AI" data leakage. The chapter provides actionable compliance strategies, including conducting **AI Impact Assessments (AIIAs)** and establishing AI governance boards.

Chapter 16, The Future of AI Optimization: Trends, Vision, and Responsible Implementation, concludes the book by exploring emerging trends, emphasizing that true optimization requires pairing innovation with responsibility. It discusses the impact of scaling laws, quantum computing, the rise of autonomous agentic AI, and the necessity of **Explainable AI (XAI)** for building trust. The chapter examines the profound societal impact on the future of work and sustainability, culminating in a vision of the "AI-driven Enterprise of 2030."

To get the most out of this book

Following along will be easier if you bear the following in mind:

- **Use the frameworks as hands-on tools**: When prioritizing your own initiatives, actively score them using the **Impact, Confidence, Ease (ICE)** framework. When planning a project, use the cost-benefit analysis framework and the five-step PoC playbook to guide your process.

- **Align business and tech**: Before you build, use the factors in *Chapter 3* as a checklist to conduct a feasibility analysis of your data, tech stack, and talent. Use the alignment questions in *Chapter 1* to "force" the critical conversation between your business and data teams.

- **Embed responsibility from day one**: Do not treat ethics and governance as an afterthought. Use the pillars of RAI and the implementation frameworks, such as Model Cards and System Cards, as mandatory steps in your development process. Proactively consider the unique risks of LLMs and the evolving regulatory landscape to build trust.

- **Learn from the case studies**: Study both the successful and the failed case studies. Use the lessons from the failed predictive maintenance of PoC (such as unclear problem definition and poor data quality) as a diagnostic checklist to avoid the same pitfalls in your own organization.

- **Think end-to-end lifecycle**: A successful PoC is only the beginning. Reflect on how a project will move from prototype to a scalable, production system using the MLOps, LLMOps, and AI agent principles. Consider how these optimized, repeatable processes connect to your long-term enterprise strategy and enhance your organization's entire AI maturity and governance model.

Disclaimer on images

Some images in this title are presented for contextual purposes, and the readability of the graphic is not crucial to the discussion. Please refer to our free graphic bundle to download the images.

Download the color images

We also provide a PDF file that has color images of the screenshots/diagrams used in this book. You can download it here: https://packt.link/gbp/9781806115112.

Conventions used

There are a number of text conventions used throughout this book.

Bold: Indicates a new term, an important word, or words that you see on the screen, for example, in menus or dialog boxes. For example: "The primary models considered are **Infrastructure as a Service (IaaS)**, **Platform as a Service (PaaS)**, **Software as a Service (SaaS)**, and **Container as a Service (CaaS)**. Each of these models presents a unique set of trade-offs in terms of operational effort, flexibility, and cost."

Warnings or important notes appear like this.

Tips and tricks appear like this.

Disclaimer on AI usage

The authors acknowledge the use of cutting-edge AI, such as ChatGPT, OpenAI API, Gemini, Claude, and GitHub Copilot, with the sole aim of enhancing the language and clarity within the book, thereby ensuring a smooth reading experience for readers. It is important to note that the content itself has been crafted by the authors and edited by a professional publishing team.

Get in touch

Feedback from our readers is always welcome!

General feedback: Email feedback@packtpub.com and mention the book's title in the subject of your message. If you have questions about any aspect of this book, please email us at questions@packtpub.com.

Errata: Although we have taken every care to ensure the accuracy of our content, mistakes do happen. If you have found a mistake in this book, we would be grateful if you reported this to us. Please visit http://www.packtpub.com/submit-errata, click **Submit Errata**, and fill in the form.

Piracy: If you come across any illegal copies of our works in any form on the internet, we would be grateful if you would provide us with the location address or website name. Please contact us at copyright@packtpub.com with a link to the material.

If you are interested in becoming an author: If there is a topic that you have expertise in and you are interested in either writing or contributing to a book, please visit http://authors.packtpub.com/.

Share your thoughts

Once you have read *The AI Optimization Playbook*, we would love to hear your thoughts! Scan the QR code below to go straight to the Amazon review page for this book and share your feedback.

https://packt.link/r/1806115115

Your review is important to us and the tech community and will help us make sure we're delivering excellent quality content.

Free Benefits with Your Book

This book comes with free benefits to support your learning. Activate them now for instant access (see the "*How to Unlock*" section for instructions).

Here's a quick overview of what you can instantly unlock with your purchase:

PDF and ePub Copies   **Next-Gen Web-Based Reader**

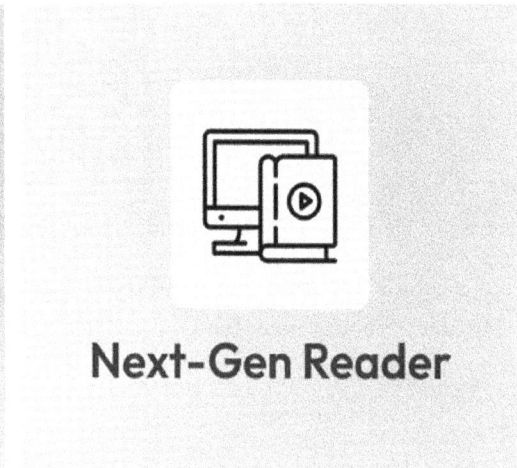

Free PDF and ePub versions

Next-Gen Reader

Access a DRM-free PDF copy of this book to read anywhere, on any device.

Multi-device progress sync: Pick up where you left off, on any device.

Use a DRM-free ePub version with your favorite e-reader.

Highlighting and notetaking: Capture ideas and turn reading into lasting knowledge.

Bookmarking: Save and revisit key sections whenever you need them.

Dark mode: Reduce eye strain by switching to dark or sepia themes

How to Unlock   **UNLOCK NOW**

Scan the QR code (or go to packtpub.com/unlock). Search for this book by name, confirm the edition, and then follow the steps on the page.

Note: Keep your invoice handy. Purchases made directly from Packt don't require an invoice.

Join our Discord and Reddit space

You're not the only one navigating fragmented tools, constant updates, and unclear best practices. Join a growing community of professionals exchanging insights that don't make it into documentation.

Stay informed with updates, discussions, and behind-the-scenes insights from our authors. Join our Discord space at `https://packt.link/z8ivB` or scan the QR code below:	Connect with peers, share ideas, and discuss real-world GenAI challenges. Follow us on Reddit at `https://packt.link/0rExL` or scan the QR code below:

Part 1

Laying the Groundwork for AI Success

In *Part 1* of this book, we will establish the strategic foundation necessary for any successful AI initiative. We will begin by examining why most AI projects fail, showing that these are overwhelmingly strategy, execution, and integration failures, not technology failures. We will analyze common pitfalls such as misaligned goals (chasing technical "surrogate metrics" instead of business value), siloed development, weak data foundations, and a misunderstanding of AI's iterative, non-deterministic nature. Having established what goes wrong, this part translates these lessons into a practical framework for building a mature AI strategy. This includes using evaluation processes such as the ICE framework to prioritize a project roadmap, building robust governance and compliance using established models such as the NIST AI RMF, and designing a modern data strategy that treats data as a product. Finally, we will cover the need for a scalable AI platform, a principled algorithm selection strategy, and a hybrid "hub-and-spoke" organizational structure to manage change.

This part contains the following chapters:

- *Chapter 1, Understanding the Perils of AI Products*
- *Chapter 2, Building the Enterprise AI Strategy*

1

Understanding the Perils of AI Products

Artificial intelligence (**AI**) has rapidly become a force multiplier for business and technology. Global investment in AI is projected to reach $360 billion in 2025, accounting for nearly one-third of all global venture funding and growing more than 60% year over year.

However, despite massive investments pouring into AI experiments, the reality is that most AI projects fail to deliver meaningful business outcomes. According to the recent *State of AI in Business 2025* report published by MIT, fewer than 5% of enterprise AI projects have produced measurable business returns. Adoption is high; most firms have pilots and prototypes, but almost all of this activity remains stuck in a productivity experiment, rather than a P&L-level transformation.

Why is that?

Over years of deploying AI systems, a consistent lesson has emerged: most failures are not caused by limitations in technology itself, although continuous improvements in the algorithm architecture, as well as storage and computing capabilities, could make outcomes more accurate. The failure is almost always a result of poor strategy, execution, and integration. Most breakdowns stem from a disconnect between business objectives and technical approaches, compounded by issues such as bad data and fragmented operational processes. The real challenge is not building more sophisticated algorithms but ensuring that AI solutions are designed and implemented to capture value for the organization that is secure, reliable, and scalable.

This chapter draws from real-world experiences and hard-learned lessons to examine patterns of how AI projects fail. We'll examine the practical challenges of aligning AI initiatives with business goals, establishing robust data foundations, and building systems that can scale beyond pilot phases. Whether you're overseeing your organization's first AI implementation or working to improve existing systems, understanding these fundamental challenges is critical for driving successful outcomes.

We will cover the following key topics:

- Some key definitions
- How AI products fail

Free Benefits with Your Book

Your purchase includes a free PDF copy of this book along with other exclusive benefits. Check the *Free Benefits with Your Book* section in the Preface to unlock them instantly and maximize your learning experience.

Some key definitions

Here are some important definitions to help you navigate through this book:

- **Artificial intelligence (AI)**: The overarching field of creating intelligent machines that can perform tasks typically requiring human intelligence, such as problem-solving, learning, and decision-making

- **Machine learning (ML)**: A subset of AI that enables machines to learn from data and improve at a task without being explicitly programmed for every step

- **Deep learning**: A subset of ML that uses artificial neural networks with multiple layers to identify complex patterns in data

- **Generative AI**: A type of deep learning model that generates new, original content such as text, images, or code based on the patterns it learned from its training data

- **AI agents**: A software system that automatically perceives its environment, makes decisions, and takes actions to achieve specific goals with minimal human intervention

- **Agentic AI**: A group of AI agents that can orchestrate, plan, reason, collaborate and perform actions for complex problems

How AI products fail

In the following sections, let's dive deep into some common patterns of failure.

Misaligned goals

Too often, AI and data teams chase after accuracy scores, losing sight of the business goal. Does a better metric always mean better business? Not necessarily.

Take the banking world. An attrition warning system might define the target as account closure. An AI system looks for signals right before someone closes their account. But what about customers who quietly move most of their money out and keep the account open? Focusing only on account closures misses the bigger goal: building trust and a lasting customer relationship.

Or consider e-commerce. Many recommendation systems are set up to maximize the **click-through rate (CTR)**. The result? More users click, at least for a while. But when people see low-quality or irrelevant suggestions, they get annoyed. Eventually, they visit less or stop using the site entirely. In these cases, more clicks do not equal more loyalty.

Fraud detection models present a different twist. If you tune the model to flag every unusual transaction, it may stop fraud but also catch too many legitimate purchases. Loyal customers face declined payments and businesses lose sales. In the rush to maximize technical success, customer experience suffers.

Retailers and manufacturers use forecasting models to predict demand. These models often strive for the lowest mean squared error, a classic accuracy measure. But just being "accurate on average" can be misleading. If the system underestimates sudden spikes, such as during special promotions, stores can run out of stock or sit on unsold inventory. The technical metric says the model is good, yet business results prove otherwise.

Hospitals encounter a similar dilemma. Triage AI tools aim for diagnostic accuracy to predict critical illnesses. But is accuracy alone enough? Not if patient wait times increase or costs grow because of too many unnecessary tests. Even a high-performing AI system can't solve business challenges if it loses sight of what matters to patients and providers.

These challenges only deepen in the world of generative AI and autonomous AI agents. Imagine a customer support chatbot powered by generative AI. Management tracks "chats handled" and "messages sent" as indicators of success. The bot produces plenty of activity, but does it actually solve issues? Sometimes, it may just spin in circles with customers, churning out long or repetitive responses. Thus, satisfaction drops, even if dashboard numbers look good.

The same misalignment can appear with agentic AI in marketing workflows. An online retailer might use an autonomous agent to send marketing emails with the single goal of maximizing open rates. The agent starts crafting attention-grabbing subject lines and sends emails frequently. For a short time, open rates surge. Soon, though, customers tire of the onslaught. They begin flagging emails as spam and unsubscribe in large numbers. The AI seems successful at first glance, but it's harming long-term trust and engagement.

So, why do these gaps between technical metrics and business goals show up so often?

- **Not everything that can be counted counts**

  "Not everything that can be counted counts, and not everything that counts can be counted."

  – William Bruce Cameron

  This quote describes one of the fundamental tensions in AI development: the broader, more abstract aims of a business, such as increasing revenue, improving customer satisfaction, or reducing operational costs, rarely translate neatly into a single, clearly defined model target. In practice, models tend to focus on specific, measurable outputs (e.g., classification accuracy or mean squared error), called the surrogate metrics.

  What are surrogate metrics?

  Surrogate metrics (also known as proxy metrics) are stand-in measurements used when direct business outcomes are hard to track or take too long to measure. Surrogate metrics provide a more immediate signal than the ultimate business outcome.

  For example, CTR is often used as a surrogate proxy for revenue in online advertising, and email open rates may stand as a substitute for actual sales conversions in marketing campaigns. Because the data for surrogate metrics is readily available and can be collected in real time, models can be trained and evaluated rapidly.

  However, they do not always capture the enduring factors behind long-term profitability, brand loyalty, or customer lifetime value. By contrast, these longer-term outcomes may not manifest for months or years, and attributing changes to a single intervention can be complex, requiring advanced tracking and modeling capabilities.

The key challenge in balancing short- and long-term considerations is that business goals are often broader or more abstract than any single AI target. Consequently, teams risk delivering local model improvements without advancing the actual strategic objectives of the business. As such, frameworks such as **Cross-Industry Standard Process for Data Mining (CRISP-DM**, Chapman et al., 2000) remain relevant, emphasizing aligning business understanding with technical work. Similarly, Provost and Fawcett (2013) discuss how proxy metrics can easily become ends in themselves, diverting attention from the more holistic measures of success that drive real value.

- **Correlation is not causality**

Another risk is misalignment: a surrogate that is only weakly correlated with the real target can yield suboptimal or even harmful outcomes. An excessive focus on CTR, for instance, might spur clickbait-like content, raising clicks in the short term while eroding user trust over time. This over-optimization of a proxy metric can create local maxima, that is, ideal results that look good on paper but do not translate into true business value. In addition, externalities arise when a single metric takes precedence over equally important but less quantifiable considerations, such as user experience or brand perception (Kleinberg et al., 2018).

Reminder: Correlation is not causality

Two variables moving together does not mean one causes the other. Always investigate the underlying factors before making decisions or drawing business conclusions. Causality requires deeper analysis, experimentation, or additional data to establish a true cause-effect link.

Classical ML typically excels at discovering correlations, that is, predictive patterns that can tell you who might churn next month or how many units you'll sell next quarter. In many business applications, this correlation-based approach is perfectly adequate, because simply knowing what's likely to happen is enough to make operational decisions or allocate resources. But if your core question becomes "What action should I take to reliably change this outcome?" then correlations alone won't cut it. You need to assess causality, that is, whether a specific factor actually *causes* the outcome you want to influence. For example, a grocery chain might discover that people who buy diapers also often buy beer. While fascinating (and frequently cited), it's just a correlation. If you wanted to alter consumer behavior, say, by rearranging store aisles, you can't be certain that the correlation indicates a causal relationship.

Here are some scenarios where differentiating correlation and causality is critical:

- **Marketing campaigns**: If your ML model says "customers who see ads in the morning are more likely to convert," you might interpret that as "morning ads cause higher sales." But perhaps morning customers were already more committed or had fewer distractions, making them more likely to purchase regardless of the ads.

- **Pricing strategies**: Lowering prices might correlate with increased sales, but is the price cut causing the higher volume, or are you simply experiencing an overall upswing in demand due to a competitor's shortage?

- **Churn reduction**: Offering a retention discount to customers labeled "high churn risk" might raise retention, but you need causal evidence to ensure the discount itself made the difference, rather than some unrelated seasonal effect.

Despite these nuances, most everyday ML applications remain predictive in nature. Forecasting monthly revenue, spotting potential churners, or identifying suspicious transactions generally revolves around "Who or what is likely to do X?" rather than "Which action definitely caused Y?" As you mature your data science practice, keep one guiding question in mind: *Am I simply predicting what might happen, or do I need to prove a certain action will make it happen?*

- **Business priorities don't stay the same**

Business priorities may change and adapt to market conditions. Models are often tuned for last quarter's goal, but the company's focus has already shifted. Unless there is active conversation, the two sides quickly drift apart. Plus, technical metrics are sometimes just proxies for real impact. Metrics such as CTR or number of chats handled are easy to track but don't always tell the full story. Over-optimizing these stand-ins can actually hurt the business.

Many teams default to standard technical measures because they're convenient, not because they're right. In doing so, hidden costs and unique business needs get missed. And finally, technical results show up fast, while business outcomes take time. Naturally, attention goes to the quick feedback, even if it isn't what really matters.

For these reasons, it is easier for AI products to look impressive on paper but still fail in the real world. The way to prevent this is by ensuring the right alignment of goals and metrics. This alignment may not always be achieved through precise math alone. If the alignment is unclear to begin with, we should start with a hypothesis about which measures are likely to drive the desired outcomes, then test and refine that hypothesis through the development and implementation cycle.

To force this alignment, the business and AI/data teams should challenge each other with questions such as the following:

Dimension	Business clarifying questions	AI/data team clarifying questions
True goal versus proxy metrics	What is the business outcome we care about (retention, trust, margin, or risk)? If the proxy metric improves, does it guarantee the business outcomes improve?	Is our target metric a proxy or a true representation of the business outcome? Is it possible that we are optimizing the metric but hurting the business outcome unintentionally?
Cost of being wrong	What are the business consequences of false positives versus false negatives (lost revenue, churn, compliance, or customer experience harm)?	Do we weight errors differently based on the business cost? Should we incorporate asymmetric loss or constraints?
Customer and operational impact	If the model behaves "correctly" by the metric, could it frustrate customers or employees (alerts, declines, privacy, or spam)?	Are there guardrails or human-in-the-loop checkpoints to prevent harm while optimizing?
Time horizon of impact	Is the objective short-term lift (open rate, for example) or long-term relationship (trust, lifetime value, etc.)?	Are our metrics short horizon but ignoring long-horizon effects?
Business context drift	Have priorities changed since the project started? Will the same metric still matter next quarter?	How often should we revisit target definition and KPIs? Do we need versioned KPI alignment as the product evolves?
Integration with decision and workflow	If the model works, who will act on it? How? In what process?	Is the model embedded into an actual decision loop, or only delivering a score/dashboard?
Hypothesis and validation	What is the explicit hypothesis that ties this metric to value?	How will we test, disprove, or refine the hypothesis during development cycles?

Table 1.1: Alignment questions and considerations

Siloed development

Another common reason why AI products struggle is siloed development. When teams operate separately, important context is lost, communication breaks down, and practical problems become much harder to solve.

When AI teams work independently from product, engineering, or business teams, they can easily miss the actual needs or goals of the project. This leads to models that may be technically sound but do not address real business problems or user needs.

From a business perspective, stakeholders often struggle to trust AI recommendations if they have not been involved in the development process. Without a clear understanding of how or why the model works, they may be skeptical or hesitant to use its results in decision-making.

Engineers face a different challenge. Integrating a model into existing systems is difficult if they have not been consulted along the way. This disconnect can result in long delays, technical mismatches, or even abandoned projects.

The reality is that AI products succeed when everyone is involved. These projects require close collaboration between data scientists, engineers, and business leaders. By working together from the beginning, teams are more likely to build solutions that meet real needs, gain the trust of decision-makers, and fit smoothly into operations.

Lack of a strong data foundation

Data is your organization's differentiator. Great AI needs a large amount of data. However, most organizations struggle with a strong data foundation. Data has missing values, biased samples, or inconsistent formats. Silos, delays, and messy pipelines make it even harder to get reliable input. Big data alone is not enough. The quality, freshness, and integration of that data are what turn models into meaningful solutions.

Is your data available?

One of the first considerations is whether you even have enough of the "right" data. Organizations may collect large volumes of logs, transactional records, or customer interactions, yet these data points might not capture the necessary signals for a particular use case. A churn-prediction project, for example, demands historical data about user interactions, subscription timelines, and user profiles. If these details are unavailable or incomplete, the resulting model has only a limited view of the factors driving user attrition. CRISP-DM (Chapman et al., 2000) addresses this early in its "Data Understanding" phase, emphasizing the importance of identifying gaps in the data and deciding how to fill or work around them.

Is your data consistent?

Equally important is whether your dataset is clean and consistent. Real-world data often includes missing values, incorrect entries, or duplicate records that stem from manual data entry, system migrations, or inconsistent logging processes. These anomalies can introduce biases, distort patterns, and, ultimately, confuse a learning algorithm. In many cases, extensive data-cleaning and feature-engineering steps can occupy the bulk of an ML practitioner's time (Provost & Fawcett, 2013). High-quality data, while more laborious to obtain, lays a strong foundation for model reliability and interpretability.

Is your data representative?

Even if your dataset is well structured, it may fail to represent all relevant segments of your problem domain. For instance, a next-best-product recommendation model trained solely on historical purchases from a specific age group could struggle to generalize to users outside that demographic. Underrepresentation or overrepresentation of certain groups can also lead to discriminatory outcomes, which might pose not only ethical concerns but also legal risks in regulated industries. Documenting and auditing the demographic and behavioral coverage of your dataset is therefore essential, as emphasized in recent literature on fairness in ML (Barocas et al., 2019).

Do you have ground truth?

Supervised learning tasks, whether classification, regression, or some form of ranking, depend heavily on labeled examples that accurately reflect the target concept. For image recognition, this can involve manually annotating large sets of images; for fraud detection, it may require extensive investigation to confirm which transactions were indeed fraudulent. If the labeled data is incomplete or incorrect, the model will learn patterns that diverge from reality. Active learning techniques, in which the model selectively queries which examples to label, can reduce the labeling burden, but obtaining a sufficiently robust ground truth remains a key challenge (Settles, 2009).

Data readiness is not a one-time concern

Business contexts, user behaviors, and external market conditions can shift over time, leading to "concept drift." The patterns learned by a model trained on last year's data may not apply to today's environment, especially in fast-moving sectors such as e-commerce or finance. Organizations need to monitor performance and periodically refresh the training data or retrain models to adapt to these shifts, a process sometimes aided by automated model monitoring and "online learning" systems (Sutton & Barto, 2018).

Infrastructure and governance

Lastly, data pipelines and governance structures play a pivotal role in ensuring that high-quality, relevant data arrives reliably for AI development. Siloed or inaccessible data prevents teams from gaining the full picture of the problem space, while a lack of versioning or lineage tracking can make it difficult to reproduce results or conduct thorough audits. Well-defined processes for data ingestion, transformation, and storage, supported by clear documentation, help organizations maintain the long-term viability of their ML pipelines.

Taken together, these factors show that preparing data for AI is rarely trivial. Before an organization can tackle any sophisticated algorithmic challenge, it must ensure that its data sources cover the necessary ground truth, maintain adequate quality standards, and remain representative of the population of interest.

AI is not deterministic

In traditional software, developers define rules that remain consistent. For instance, a loan application system may calculate interest income based on a predefined formula, such as principal balance times interest rate. An e-commerce platform may apply a unique coupon code according to programmed logic. These outputs are predictable because they're based on predefined instructions.

AI systems, however, work differently. For instance, a FICO credit risk rating model, designed to assess a borrower's creditworthiness, doesn't use a single formula. Instead, it analyzes various data points, such as debt-to-income ratio, income, and bankruptcy status, to predict default risk. This prediction is based on patterns in past data, meaning the model's performance can change if the data changes or if new features are introduced.

Why iteration matters in AI

The uncertainty of AI outcomes necessitates experimentation. Each model configuration or dataset adjustment provides insights into the model's performance, leading to a cycle of adjustments and improvements. Therefore, AI development is highly iterative, with each cycle addressing unexpected challenges that arise as models evolve, as illustrated in the following figure.

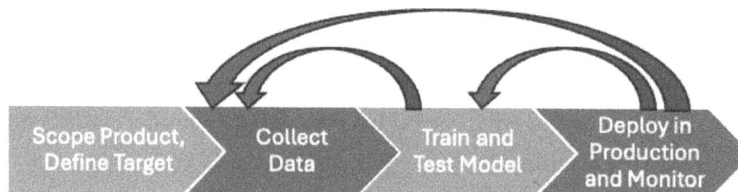

Figure 1.1: Iterative AI development cycle

A great example of this experimental nature is hyperparameter tuning in ML, a subset of AI.

> A **hyperparameter** in ML is a configuration variable that you set *before* training
> a model, which controls how the learning process unfolds and how the model is
> structured. Unlike model parameters, which are learned automatically from data
> during training (such as the weights in a neural network or the coefficients in linear
> regression), hyperparameters are chosen by the practitioner and remain fixed during
> the actual learning process.
>
> **Hyperparameter tuning** is the process of systematically searching for the best con-
> figuration of hyperparameters for an ML model.

Data scientists use methods such as grid search, random search, and Bayesian optimization to
try different hyperparameter combinations, looking for the best setup for a model's performance.
Adjustments to parameters, such as learning rate or tree depth, in models often result in varied
outcomes, and each tweak provides new information that can potentially improve or impair the
model's performance.

As James Bergstra and Yoshua Bengio explain in *Random Search for Hyper-Parameter Optimization*
(2012), hyperparameter tuning can "make the difference between a model that performs well and
one that fails to generalize." In other words, finding the right settings often requires an iterative,
trial-and-error approach.

Even after finding the best model configuration, models need to be re-evaluated as data shifts
post-production, a phenomenon known as **data drift**. For instance, the FICO credit model may
lose accuracy if consumer borrowing patterns or financial policy change over time. As Gama et
al. discuss in *A Survey on Concept Drift* (2014), ML models need regular monitoring and updates
to keep up with changing patterns in the data.

While iteration is essential, it can easily lead to scope creep if it isn't managed carefully. For
instance, when developing a customer service chatbot, it's easy to fall into the trap of endlessly
tuning the model to handle every possible query variation. Without clear objectives for each
round of experiments and establishing the balance between cost and accuracy, teams can spend
excessive time and resources fine-tuning without significant gains. In their *Cross-Industry Standard
Process for Data Mining (CRISP-DM) Guide* (2000), Chapman et al. emphasize that "structured
processes help teams avoid scope creep by clearly defining deliverables at each stage."

Setting specific objectives and knowing when to stop is crucial to keeping ML projects on track. If a model aimed at predicting customer churn achieves 85% accuracy, this might be "good enough" to make informed business decisions without pushing for an extra few percentage points that might require a significant increase in computational resources and time spent. However, a model aimed at capturing fraud will require a 98% true positive capture rate at a 95% false negative rate.

The key takeaway here is that recognizing the iterative nature of AI development is critical because of the uncertain outcomes that define ML. Each round of experimentation and adjustment helps navigate the unpredictability that comes with data-driven predictions. Iterative experimentation should be executed in a structured process.

This naturally brings us to the heart of the challenge: managing and understanding uncertainty in AI outcomes.

Uncertainty in outcomes

The iterative nature of AI development is largely a response to the unpredictable outcomes that characterize AI models. AI models, especially ML models, are essentially pattern-recognition tools, and they can only recognize the patterns present in the data used to train them. A model trained on historical data is limited by the quality and representativeness of that data. When the data changes, the model's performance can change too, which means that outcomes are harder to guarantee.

As highlighted by Halevy, Norvig, and Pereira in *The Unreasonable Effectiveness of Data* (2009), "more data often trumps better algorithms," showing how dependent ML models are on data. However, the world doesn't stand still, and neither does data. As data patterns shift due to changes in customer behavior, the economy, or other factors, the model may no longer perform as expected.

Take stock price prediction, for example. A model trained on historical market data and economic indicators might initially work well, but financial markets are highly sensitive to unexpected events, such as economic downturns or political instability. When these events occur, the model's accuracy can drop significantly, because it was trained on data that didn't include those new patterns.

Another source of uncertainty is the complexity of many advanced AI/ML models, especially in deep learning. Unlike simpler algorithms that follow clear decision paths, deep learning models can learn highly complex patterns in large datasets, but this complexity makes them harder to interpret. With multiple layers of non-linear transformations, deep learning models often function as "black boxes," where it's almost impossible to interpret how specific inputs will translate to outputs.

James Bergstra and Yoshua Bengio's work on hyperparameter optimization discusses this uncertainty. In their paper *Random Search for Hyper-Parameter Optimization* (2012), they argue that slight changes in model parameters can yield very different results, making it hard to reproduce consistent outcomes across environments or datasets.

Given these sources of unpredictability, both from the nature of the data and the growing complexity of modern models, it's important to consider the broader implications for project teams and stakeholders.

What are the implications?

This iterative characteristic and uncertainty in outcomes have real implications for project planning and stakeholder expectations. Traditional software projects often come with clear timelines and milestones, but AI development is less predictable. From data mining to training, development is never straightforward. Instead, it may need reworking or extended timelines if the model performance doesn't initially meet expectations.

Business leaders who are used to traditional waterfall project planning and timelines might question why AI models require ongoing refinement. As Davenport and Harris explain in *Competing on Analytics*, "data science projects often face skepticism from business leaders due to their experimental nature and unpredictable timelines."

This is also why data science work does not cleanly fit inside traditional Agile assumptions. Agile expects that requirements can be defined up front, that increments are predictable, and that "done" can be clearly stated before building. AI breaks those assumptions. Success can't be promised in advance, learning happens through iteration, and values emerge only after cycles of testing and refinement. As a result, AI may live inside an Agile delivery structure, but it can't behave like a standard Agile feature build. It is critical that organizations understand AI's iterative nature, and its need for fine-tuning can help manage these expectations and build trust.

Lack of production-readiness

Real business value comes from putting the model into production and delivering insights or automation at scale, reliably, and sustainably. But for many organizations, this step is where AI projects fizzle out.

Being too quick to put a model into production, without an appropriate amount of testing, is a common problem. We need to strike a balance.

Too often, there's no concrete plan for how models will be deployed, monitored, or retrained. Teams focus on building a technically impressive solution but stop short of operationalizing it. The result is a model that works in a development sandbox but never makes an impact in the real world.

Yet, bridging the gap between ML research and real-world deployment remains a significant challenge. Unlike traditional software, ML models degrade over time due to data drift and changing real-world conditions. Without automated retraining and monitoring, models quickly become outdated, leading to performance deterioration. A study by Breiter & Keane (2022) found that only 20% of companies have a mature AIOps pipeline, meaning most organizations lack the infrastructure to continuously update, monitor, and optimize their AI products. This limitation hinders AI scalability and can increase operational risks.

Think of developing a model in a Jupyter notebook as being in a laboratory or factory prototype shop. It's a creative, flexible space where ideas can be tested and refined quickly. But bringing a product to market and commercializing it requires careful design, manufacturing, and quality control. Operationalizing AI is no different. The leap from experimentation to production is not trivial and demands as much attention as the modeling itself.

Many AI initiatives fail here, not because the science falls short but because the engineering and operational plans never get the focus they deserve. Building for production from the start, with clear paths for testing, deployment, monitoring, and maintenance, is essential for transforming AI from an experiment into a lasting source of business value.

Lack of explainability and trust

Many AI models, particularly deep learning architectures, operate as black boxes, meaning they produce predictions without clear explanations. This lack of interpretability poses risks in regulated industries such as finance, healthcare, and criminal justice, where decision transparency is essential.

Lipton (2018) warns that misaligned interpretability expectations create misunderstandings between data scientists and business leaders. Regulators are now demanding greater transparency in AI-driven decisions. For example, the *EU AI Act* (2023) and GDPR's Article 22 require that AI models affecting individuals, such as credit scoring or hiring algorithms, must provide explainable reasoning for their predictions.

Even the most accurate AI model is useless if people don't trust it enough to use it. Nowhere is this more true than in highly regulated industries such as banking, finance, and healthcare. Here, black-box AI systems, whose decisions are hard to interpret, often meet resistance from business leaders and regulators alike.

Deep neural networks are a classic example. These models can deliver impressive predictions, but their reasoning is nearly impossible for a human to trace. There's no easy way to follow the logic from a specific input to a particular output. This "black-box" nature mirrors the complexity of the human brain, where millions of small decisions combine to produce a result.

While this kind of complexity might be acceptable for tasks such as image recognition or recommendation systems, it becomes a critical liability in high-stakes domains. In criminal justice, healthcare, and finance, every decision can affect lives, livelihoods, or compliance with the law. Stakeholders need to know not just what the answer is but why the model made that choice. Without that transparency, models face skepticism, lack of accountability, and sometimes outright rejection.

Building trust requires more than just technical performance. It means making AI systems more understandable and more transparent, so business leaders, regulators, and customers can see and trust the reason behind each decision. Without explainability, even the smartest AI can end up sitting on the shelf.

Changing business conditions and model degradation

AI models are built on the data available when they are developed. But the world is always changing. Business priorities shift. Customer behaviors evolve. Regulations get updated. If a model is not kept current, it quickly loses its value.

There are clear examples of this in recent history. Supply chain models trained before COVID-19 rapidly became inaccurate when the pandemic radically changed demand patterns worldwide. Time-series forecasting models built on pre-2008 data failed to anticipate the massive disruptions of the global financial crisis. Even today, AI-powered chatbots that rely on outdated product information end up frustrating users with incorrect or missing answers.

The lesson is simple: AI and ML are never finished. They are living processes that require ongoing investment and care. Yet, many organizations overlook the need for maintenance. They treat models as one-time projects rather than continuous programs. The result is predictable: performance slips, trust erodes, and business impact disappears.

Other challenges: compute, resources, and skill gaps

Businesses also contend with challenges in computational power, infrastructure, resource constraints, talent shortages, and operationalization. These factors determine whether ML initiatives remain experimental or successfully scale into production.

Compute and infrastructure challenges

Training ML models, especially training deep learning architectures, requires immense computational resources. Large models demand high-performing GPUs and TPUs, which can be prohibitively expensive. A study by Patterson et al. (2021) found that training a single large transformer model can emit as much carbon as five cars in their lifetime, underscoring the financial and environmental costs.

Organizations could choose between cloud services and on-premises infrastructure. Cloud solutions offer scalability but come with recurring costs and potential vendor lock-in. On-premises setups provide more control but require significant upfront investment and maintenance. These trade-offs impact how quickly and efficiently companies can build and deploy ML solutions.

Resource and budget constraints

Organizations often underestimate post-deployment costs when budgeting for ML projects. Beyond training, models require ongoing monitoring, retraining, and infrastructure maintenance. Sculley et al. (2015) describe this as "technical debt in ML," where companies focus on model accuracy but fail to plan for the hidden costs of operationalization.

Scaling ML across multiple business units introduces additional expenses, such as distributed computing and network bandwidth costs. A 2023 study from MIT AI Research found that 80% of ML project costs occur after deployment, emphasizing the need for cost-efficient model life cycle management.

Skill gaps and talent shortages

AI adoption is outpacing the availability of skilled professionals. The *LinkedIn AI Talent Report* (2023) (`https://economicgraph.linkedin.com/research/future-of-work-report-ai`) noted a 74% year-over-year increase in demand for AI/ML engineers, but hiring for specialized roles takes an average of 6–9 months. The biggest shortages exist in MLOps, data engineering, and model deployment roles, which are essential for production-ready AI systems.

Successful AI products require expertise across multiple disciplines. Data engineers manage large-scale data pipelines, AI engineers build and fine-tune models, and AIOps specialists ensure efficient deployment and monitoring. Many companies invest in upskilling existing employees, but the interdisciplinary nature of AI makes hiring the right talent a persistent challenge.

Summary

In this chapter, we have unpacked how so many AI initiatives have failed. Most AI failures are not technical; they come from a misalignment of goals, vague values, or poor integration into the business workflow. Optimizing for technical metrics alone can create solutions that "work" mathematically but hurt the business. AI is probabilistic and iterative; it should not be managed like a fixed-scope IT project.

Real success depends on getting the foundation right: a clear business objective and value hypothesis; a strong data foundation; secured, scalable, and automated AIOps; and shared ownership between business and AI/data teams.

What's next?

Now that we understand the failure patterns and the unique nature of AI work, we can shift from "what goes wrong" to "how to do it right."

In the next chapters, we will translate these lessons into a practical, repeatable framework for building and executing an AI strategy that aligns with business values, prioritizes the right opportunities, and builds for scalable and measurable impact.

References

- Barocas, S., Hardt, M., & Narayanan, A. (2019). *Fairness and Machine Learning: Limitations and Opportunities*. MIT Press. https://fairmlbook.org/

- Bergstra, J., & Bengio, Y. (2012). Random Search for Hyper-Parameter Optimization. *Journal of Machine Learning Research*, 13, 281–305. https://www.jmlr.org/papers/volume13/bergstra12a/bergstra12a.pdf

- Breiter, M., & Keane, M. (2022). *The State of AIOps Pipelines and Scalability*. [Industry Report].

- Cameron, W. B. (1963). *Informal Sociology: A Casual Introduction to Sociological Thinking*. *Random House.*

- Chapman, P., Clinton, J., Kerber, R., Khabaza, T., Reinartz, T., Shearer, C., & Wirth, R. (2000). CRISP-DM 1.0: *Step-by-step data mining guide*. https://public.dhe.ibm.com/software/analytics/spss/documentation/modeler/14.2/es/CRISP-DM.pdf

- Davenport, T. H., & Harris, J. G. (2007). *Competing on Analytics: The New Science of Winning*. Harvard Business Review Press.

- European Union. (2016*). Regulation (EU) 2016/679 (General Data Protection Regulation)*. Official Journal of the European Union. https://eur-lex.europa.eu/eli/reg/2016/679/oj

- European Union. (2023). *The Artificial Intelligence Act.* European Commission. https://artificialintelligenceact.eu/

- Gama, J., Žliobaitė, I., Bifet, A., Pechenizkiy, M., & Bouchachia, A. (2014). A Survey on Concept Drift Adaptation. *ACM Computing Surveys*, 46(4), 1–37. https://doi.org/10.1145/2523813

- Halevy, A., Norvig, P., & Pereira, F. (2009). The Unreasonable Effectiveness of Data. *IEEE Intelligent Systems*, 24(2), 8–12. https://doi.org/10.1109/MIS.2009.36

- Kleinberg, J., Lakkaraju, H., Leskovec, J., Ludwig, J., & Mullainathan, S. (2018). Human Decisions and Machine Predictions. *The Quarterly Journal of Economics*, 133(1), 237–293. https://doi.org/10.1093/qje/qjx032

- LinkedIn. (2023, August). *Future of Work Report: AI.* LinkedIn Economic Graph. https://economicgraph.linkedin.com/research/future-of-work-report-ai

- Lipton, Z. C. (2018). The Mythos of Model Interpretability. *Queue*, 16(3), 31–57. https://doi.org/10.1145/3236386.3241340

- MIT AI Research. (2023). *Study on Machine Learning Project Lifecycle Costs.* Massachusetts Institute of Technology.

- MIT Sloan Management Review. (2025, November). *The Gen AI Divide: State of AI in Business 2025.* MIT.

- Patterson, D., Gonzalez, J., Le, Q., Liang, C., Munguia, L-M., Rothchild, D., So, D., Texier, M., & Dean, J. (2021). *Carbon Emissions and Large Neural Network Training.* arXiv. https://arxiv.org/abs/2104.10350

- Provost, F., & Fawcett, T. (2013). Data Science for Business: *What You Need to Know about Data Mining and Data-Analytic Thinking.* O'Reilly Media.

- Sculley, D., Holt, G., Golovin, D., Davydov, E., Phillips, T., Ebner, D., Chaudhary, V., Young, M., Crespo, J.-F., & Dennison, D. (2015). Hidden Technical Debt in Machine Learning *Systems. Advances in Neural Information Processing Systems (NIPS)*, 28. https://proceedings.neurips.cc/paper/2015/file/86df7dcfd896fcaf2674f757a2463eba-Paper.pdf

- Settles, B. (2009). *Active Learning Literature Survey.* University of Wisconsin-Madison. http://burrsettles.com/pub/settles.activelearning.pdf

- Sutton, R. S., & Barto, A. G. (2018). *Reinforcement Learning: An Introduction (2nd ed.). MIT Press.* http://incompleteideas.net/book/the-book-2nd.html

Get This Book's PDF Version and Exclusive Extras

UNLOCK NOW

Scan the QR code (or go to packtpub.com/unlock). Search for this book by name, confirm the edition, and then follow the steps on the page.

Note: Keep your invoice handy. Purchase made directly from packt don't require one.

2

Building the Enterprise AI Strategy

Chapter 1 showed that most AI failures are not technology failures; they are strategy failures. Products collapse when they chase algorithms without the supporting data foundations and operational excellence, as well as having incomplete data pipelines, missing key skills, unclear ownership and accountability, or misalignment with business priorities. Fixing this requires a deliberate enterprise AI strategy.

To capture durable business values, organizations must deliberately align the business initiatives, people and culture, technology, and operating model around how AI will be used. In the pages ahead, through the following key topics, we outline the structural elements of a mature AI strategy:

- Aligning business initiatives with technical development and project selection
- Governance and compliance
- Data strategy – the differentiator for your AI systems
- AI platform – scalable infrastructure for experimentation and deployment
- AI algorithms/pattern selection strategy
- Organizational structure and change management

Connecting strategy to technical development

Before debating model architectures, leaders must first be clear on the business outcomes and whether AI is the right lever to achieve it. Not every problem is an AI problem.

Roadmap prioritization

Not all AI projects warrant immediate attention. So, a structured evaluation process, for example, the **Impact, Confidence, Ease (ICE)** framework, could help separate high-potential concepts from less urgent pursuits:

- **Impact**: Does the project address a top-line business priority (e.g., reducing churn, boosting revenue, or improving user experience)?
- **Confidence**: How certain are we that a model-based solution will work? Do we have the right data, domain knowledge, and staff expertise?
- **Ease**: How technically challenging is the project? Is the data already in good shape, or do we need extensive collection/cleaning efforts?

Score each project on these dimensions, then rank them. This ensures focus goes to initiatives with the greatest upside and likelihood of success, rather than dispersing resources across an unfiltered backlog of "cool ideas."

Let's take banking as a case study.

A mid-sized super-regional bank is launching an AI strategy with six potential use cases:

- Credit card fraud detection
- **Next-best product (NBP)** recommendations for consumer marketing
- Branch-staffing optimization via demand forecasting
- Deposit churn prediction and retention
- GenAI-powered customer service agent
- Commercial loan understanding assistant

The leadership team needs to decide what to deliver first. They apply the ICE framework to score each use case on impact, confidence, and effort. The following table illustrates the potential outcomes:

Use case	Impact	Confidence	Effort	ICE score	Notes
Credit card fraud detection	5	4	3	6.7	Existing pipeline and clear ROI, moderate effort
NBP recommendations for consumer marketing	4	3	2	6.0	Strong business pull, fast to pilot in app
Branch-staffing optimization via demand forecasting	3	4	2	6.0	Operational savings, easy data sourcing
Mortgage churn prediction and retention	5	2	4	2.5	High value but low confidence and heavy effort
GenAI-powered customer service agent	3	3	3	3.0	Good for productivity and experience, unclear ROI
Commercial loan understanding assistant	4	2	5	1.6	High governance friction and integration risk

Table 2.1: Use case scoring based on ICE framework (scale 1–5, ICE = Impact x Confidence ÷ Effort)

Based on the analysis, the bank can make an informed decision on what the first three initiatives to start with are, based on the highest ICE score:

- **Fraud model uplift**: Immediate economic impact and measurable risk reduction
- **NBP recommendation**: Revenue and engagement with low incremental effort
- **Branch staffing optimization**: Cost savings and efficiency win with high feasibility

Mortgage churn and loan-underwriting assistant products are deferred until data-, pipeline-, and organization-readiness improve. The GenAI agent is staged as an experiment, not a top-three initiative.

Start small, scale fast

A major hurdle when pushing many AI programs is justifying investment and convincing stakeholders that these initiatives will deliver real results. This is where proof-of-concept projects play a critical role. Rather than launching a full-scale deployment from the start, organizations run a proof of concept by focusing on a specific, well-defined use case, such as predicting churn for a subset of customers or automating a single step of a larger workflow. The purpose is to start small, show measurable benefits quickly, using a limited scope and manageable resources, then scale fast.

The process begins by starting small: select just one or two key metrics that have a strong connection to an important business outcome, such as using support ticket volume as a signal in a churn pilot. The main goal is to achieve a tangible **return on investment** (**ROI**) in a short time frame. For instance, if the pilot improves customer retention by 5% or reduces operating costs in one department, it offers clear evidence of value for stakeholders and decision-makers.

Beyond demonstrating outcomes, getting to a stage where stakeholders are aligned so that a pilot can be launched can be challenging. The best way to overcome this challenge is to build trust by sharing the journey from the beginning with the business, receiving feedback, and iterating to a version that achieves internal alignment.

Once a proof of concept demonstrates its impact, the next step is to iterate and scale. This could mean adding more features to the model, applying the approach to new business areas, or gradually automating more of the workflow. Proofs of concept help organizations build confidence, refine their approach, and set the stage for sustainable, enterprise-wide AI adoption.

With a clear AI vision and strategy, it's crucial to establish strong governance and compliance practices to ensure your AI systems are trustworthy, transparent, and aligned with legal requirements.

Governance and compliance

The regulatory landscape in 2025 is fragmented and rapidly evolving. Laws such as the EU AI Act have set new global standards, while the US, China, and other jurisdictions are rolling out sector-by-sector rules, causing overlapping requirements and uncertainty about what's expected and how enforcement will play out.

The following is a list of established frameworks for AI. Organizations should use these frameworks as a reference point and extract the principles and controls that map to their business, risk profile, and operating model:

Framework	Source/Focus	How it helps
NIST AI Risk Management Framework (AI RMF)	US NIST (2023)	Provides a structured approach for risk identification, mitigation, and monitoring
EU AI Act – risk-tiered model	EU Legislation (2024)	Introduces risk-based obligations and is useful for classifications and oversight tiers
OECD AI principles	Global policy body	Offers high-level responsible AI principles aligned across governments
ISO/IEC 23894:2023	ISO standard on AI risk	Provides standardized vocabulary and life cycle risk guidance
Model Risk Management (SR 11-7 adaptation)	Banking precedent	Extends the mature model governance discipline to an AI/GenAI context

Table 2.2: A list of established frameworks for AI

A modern AI governance strategy should lead with value creation. The goal is to build a system that starts with business value, not regulation for its own sake; sets guardrails that allow innovation without constant escalation; pushes decision rights and account stability to the teams doing the work, rather than centralizing all decisions; and establishes clear ownership, a clear escalation path, and self-service controls so compliance becomes built in, not bolted on. Consider the following four-layer operating model:

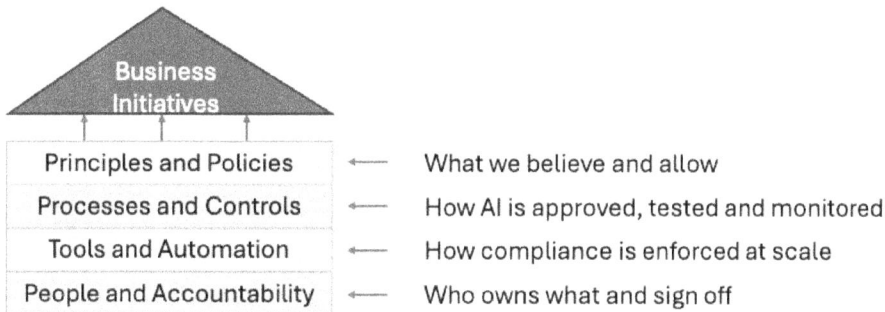

Figure 2.1: A four-layer AI governance operating model

Establishing AI governance and ensuring compliance can feel overwhelming, and it's no surprise. This is something that even experienced organizations struggle to navigate. The accelerated pace of AI innovation, especially in agentic AI and GenAI, only intensifies the challenge. Many business leaders and legal teams admit that it's hard to keep up and feel pressure balancing the excitement of new AI capabilities with the need for guardrails and public trust. Many organizations also lack in-house experts who can bridge technical and legal domains, making it hard to know where to even begin.

Given this reality, it's important to start with practical, manageable steps. Begin by identifying and cataloging exactly where AI is being used in your organization, especially in areas that handle sensitive data or make high-impact decisions. Assign clear responsibility for AI oversight. This might mean forming a cross-functional group that brings together compliance, risk, technology, and business stakeholders. Document your policies and processes, even if they feel basic at first, and make sure you can explain in plain language how key models are built, tested, and monitored.

Transparency and regular review are critical. Even as standards shift, keeping records of how decisions are made and problems handled will go a long way during audits or when questions arise. Don't be afraid to automate wherever possible; tools that can flag bias, track model drift, or update compliance alerts are increasingly available and designed for non-specialists. Most importantly, foster a culture where reporting issues or uncertainties about AI's behavior is seen as a strength, not a weakness.

Finally, expect this work to be ongoing. Regulations will change and new risks will emerge, and your policies should evolve in response. By taking small, steady steps and building good habits, organizations not only reduce risk but also develop the confidence to innovate responsibly even as the rules of AI keep changing.

With governance and compliance foundations in place, the next priority is to design a clear data strategy that ensures your AI systems are driven by relevant, high-quality, and well-managed information.

Data strategy — the differentiator for your AI systems

Creating a data strategy that enables AI is often the biggest hurdle for organizations.

A modern data strategy for AI should be value-driven, productized, governed, semantic, and using a multi-modal architecture that makes trusted data continuously usable by **machine learning (ML)**, GenAI, and agentic systems in production.

Below are the key pillars of a modern data strategy for AI:

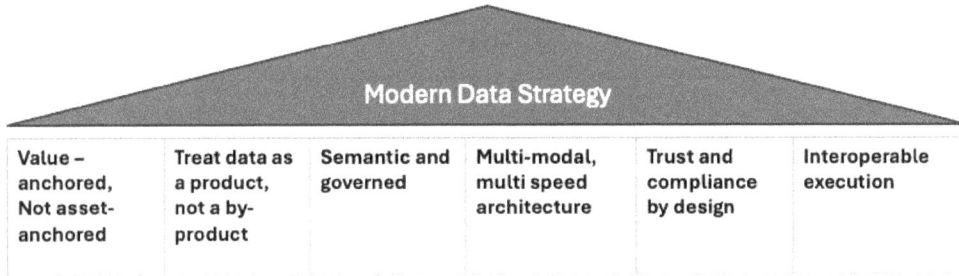

Modern Data Strategy					
Value – anchored, Not asset-anchored	Treat data as a product, not a by-product	Semantic and governed	Multi-modal, multi speed architecture	Trust and compliance by design	Interoperable execution

Figure 2.2: The modern data strategy

- **Value-anchored, not asset-anchored**: A modern data strategy for AI should begin with clarity of purpose: what business decisions or processes are we trying to improve, and how will we know if it works? Anchoring to value means translating business objectives into an explicit value hypothesis before any modeling effort begins, defining the target population, the business action expected to follow, and the economic signal that will validate the impact in production. When the data strategy is anchored to explicit business outcomes, prioritization becomes disciplined, execution becomes aligned, and success is measurable.

- **Treat data as a product, not a by-product**: In most organizations, data is still treated as something that is left over from applications, a by-product of transactions, logs, or operations. When data is treated this way, it's nobody's responsibility to ensure it is accurate, usable, documented, or trusted. AI systems built on such data will inherit the mess.

  Treating data as a product flips the paradigm. A data product is not data sitting in storage. It is a maintained, documented, trusted, and consumable asset with a defined purpose, defined users, and defined service expectations. Just like any product, it has an owner, a roadmap, quality standards, and a support model.

  A data product could take many forms: a curated customer-360 table, a feature store for modeling, a fraud detection model score, an embeddings catalog for GenAI, or a metric layer exposed to the finance reporting team. Treating data as a product requires several shifts:

  - Someone must own it
  - It must be discoverable and interpretable by others
  - It must be versioned and governed

- It must be built to serve a known use case or consumer
- It must be monitored, supported, and eventually retired through its life cycle

- **Semantic and governed**: Historically, organizations believed that once data was centralized or piped into a lake/warehouse, it was "ready." AI has now exposed the flaw in that assumption: integrated data without meaning is not useful intelligence. ML, GenAI, and especially agentic AI need to understand not just the format of the data but the business meaning, its intent, its constraints, and its appropriate use.

  Semantics provide shared meaning, such as what a customer is, what counts as attrition, what an active balance is, and what "churn" means in wealth versus retail banking. Without enforcing this logical business model on the AI systems, they could produce conflicting answers to the same questions.

  Governance ensures the right data is being accessed by the right people to perform the right tasks. It defines who can access what, which fields are sensitive, which models need review, and how AI decisions are monitored and justified.

- **Multi-modal, multi-speed architecture**: Legacy data strategies were built around structured, slow-moving data, such as quarterly finances, monthly risk reports, and daily warehouse refreshes. Modern AI systems, especially GenAI and agentic AI systems, learn from and act upon many kinds of signals moving at different speeds.

  "Multi-modal" means the system can consume more than rows and tables: text (notes, chats, and policies), audio (calls), documents (PDFs and contracts), images (checks and IDs), events (clickstreams), logs, vectors, embeddings, knowledge graphs, and more.

  "Multi-speed" means the architecture must support both slow and fast decisions at once: some use cases (marketing, forecasting, and capital planning) tolerate daily or weekly refresh, while others (payment fraud, personalization, and agentic responses) require real-time or near-real-time streaming.

  Practically, a multi-modal, multi-speed strategy means the following:

  - Designing the platform to handle structured + unstructured + vectorized embeddings
  - Supporting batch + micro-batch + streaming, depending on the business decision horizon
  - Using specialized stores where needed, for example, document stores, vector databases, feature stores, or knowledge graphs, rather than pushing everything into one warehouse pattern

- Treating latency as a business design choice, not a technical afterthought

- **Trust and compliance by design**: It goes without saying that building a trustworthy and transparent data platform is critical. Trust is not earned after deployment; it should be engineered into the life cycle. That means privacy, fairness, transparency, monitoring, and human oversight should be built into design, data preparation, modeling, validation, and ongoing operations.

  A "trust-by-design" data strategy in practice could look as follows:

  - Classification, sensitivity tagging, and quality assurance at ingestion
  - Row-/column-/attribute-level access controls built into the fabric
  - Policy-aware data products, containing usage bounds, lineage, and disclaimers
  - Automated audit trails, lineage, access logs, and transformation recorded as data moves

  Remember, AI does not fix bad data governance; it amplifies it. A data strategy that embeds trust at the source is required to enable more AI work with less friction and more agility.

- **Interoperable execution**: As organizations adopt AI across multiple clouds, SaaS platforms, and agent ecosystems, data can't live in isolated environments. Models, GenAI systems, and autonomous agents must be able to work off the same facts, reason over the same entities, and act within the same constraints, regardless of where they run or who built them.

  Note the following about data interoperability:

  - Customer, account, claim, and transaction means the same thing across clouds, systems, and platforms.
  - Policies on data usage, privacy, retention, and lineage travel with the data, not within the infrastructure that hosts it.
  - Systems can reference, not replace—that is, moving meaning, not copying raw data everywhere.
  - A data strategy that ensures interoperability is critical. Interoperability is what allows models, GenAI systems, and agents to operate consistently across clouds and platforms, turning data into a reusable enterprise asset instead of a set of disconnected silos.

Consider these six pillars when building a modern data strategy that is AI-ready.

The next step is to build an AI platform that can support experimentation, development, and reliable deployment at scale.

AI platform — scalable infrastructure for experimentation and deployment

A modern AI platform is the engine that powers innovation across all stages of the AI life cycle, from experimentation to production scale. Leading organizations and major cloud providers agree: moving from isolated pilot models to reliable, business-critical AI requires more than powerful algorithms. It demands an infrastructure that's modular, robust, and built for both rapid prototyping and enterprise stability.

Today, the core challenge is balancing speed of innovation with security, reliability, and compliance. The most effective AI platforms, whether on-premises, hybrid, or fully cloud-native, are designed as modular systems. They separate key functions such as data ingestion, feature engineering, model training, testing, and production serving. Modular design allows teams to update or scale individual components, such as rolling out a new model or swapping in a better data pipeline without risk to the entire system. This blueprint is regularly cited by major cloud platforms and industry leaders such as Netflix, Uber, and Airbnb.

A well-architected platform draws a clear line between sandboxed environments (where data scientists iterate and test with flexibility) and hardened production pipelines (where business continuity, compliance, and security take priority). This separation ensures innovation remains fast but doesn't put live services or sensitive data at risk. Many advanced teams run "shadow mode" tests: new models operate in parallel with production models, letting teams measure real-world performance and spot problems before a full rollout.

Scheduling and orchestration patterns also matter. Event-driven workflows power real-time systems, such as fraud detection, content personalization, or agentic AI, that adapt instantly to user interactions. Batch processes handle periodic retraining or large-scale analytics, offering efficiency for tasks that don't need immediate results. The best platforms blend both, automatically routing tasks to the right pipeline based on latency and cost needs.

AI operations (AIOps) has become the backbone for managing complexity at scale. Automated tools track models from initial build through testing and into production, with version control, reproducibility, and rollback capabilities as standard features. **Continuous integration/continuous deployment (CI/CD)** pipelines allow frequent, controlled updates backed by automated testing, minimizing the risk of pushing flawed models into production.

Monitoring and observability are now non-negotiable. Beyond basic accuracy scores, platforms need to track model drift, latency, user outcomes, and even fairness metrics, with triggers to re-train or roll back as soon as anomalies appear. Full stack observability, recommended by Google and Azure, means capturing not just system logs but operational metrics that actually matter to business performance.

Governance and compliance should be built directly into the platform, not handled after deployment. Enterprise-grade platforms now automate audit trails, access controls, model documentation, and approval workflows to stay ahead of evolving regulations (such as the EU AI Act and NIST frameworks). Steering committees and documented review processes maintain oversight.

In summary, a mature AI platform is critical to enable agility and scalability for enterprise innovation.

AI algorithms/pattern selection strategy

Choosing the right AI algorithm isn't a simple matter. Today's enterprise environments deal with complex, mixed data and must meet requirements set by compliance, security, cost, and explainability, which are often more decisive than raw accuracy or novelty. Research and experience show that the best results come from a principled, business-first process that blends experimentation, clear evaluation criteria, and continuous collaboration between technical and business stakeholders. For example:

- **Start with business and compliance requirements**: Algorithm choices should always begin with a clear understanding of the problem domain. Regulatory needs, interpretability demands, and operational constraints often rule out entire model classes before technical performance is even considered. For example, in heavily regulated sectors, such as financial services, healthcare, and government, explainability, transparency, and documented risk controls are essential. For other contexts, high-throughput or low-latency use cases may shape method selection as much as predictive power.

- **Align model types with data and use cases**: For structured, tabular data or problems requiring transparent decision paths (such as risk scoring or operational analytics), classical ML methods remain reliable. Tree-based models, linear models, and generalized boosting strike a strong balance between performance, interpretability, and ease of deployment.

  Deep learning excels with large, unstructured datasets, such as images, natural language text, or multimodal sensor feeds. However, the higher demands for data, compute, and monitoring must be measured against cost and maintenance realities.

Transfer learning sits between these two extremes and is particularly valuable when labeled data is scarce or time to production matters. Rather than training models from scratch, organizations adapt pre-trained models, for example, fine-tuning foundation models or reusing pre-trained embeddings, to dramatically reduce cost, training data requirements, and development time while still achieving high accuracy.

GenAI is a subset of deep learning, having the new capabilities for language, image, and code generation, as well as **retrieval-augmented generation** (**RAG**) for search and automation workflows. These models introduce powerful capabilities but bring added risk around unpredictability, high compute costs, and greater oversight for safety and ethical compliance.

Reinforcement learning and agentic architectures address dynamic, sequential decision problems, such as autonomous vehicles or adaptive supply chain systems, but require users to conduct careful reward design, simulation, and robust monitoring to avoid unintended outcomes in complex environments.

- **Evaluate, experiment, and combine approaches**: Enterprises rarely succeed by committing to a single model type from the outset. Instead, running structured experiments, via AutoML tools, cloud-based pilot platforms, and benchmark competitions, allows teams to compare classical, deep, and generative approaches early in the process. Increasingly, hybrid architectures are adopted: for instance, using gradient boosting to summarize tabular business data, followed by a transformer for document analysis, or combining a knowledge graph with a foundation model for enterprise search.

- **Consider deployment and life cycle impacts**: Performance in development rarely guarantees success in the field. As such, algorithm selection should account for downstream factors such as the following:

  - Ease of monitoring, interpretability, and retraining (especially as regulations shift or new data arrives)
  - Total compute and storage demand, at both training and inference time
  - Technical support, integration with existing MLOps stacks, and the ability to meet business KPIs by scaling
  - Risk of "technical debt" as over-complex models may look impressive but prove brittle, hard to govern, or too costly to maintain

- **Test, validate, and reassess regularly**: Organizations don't succeed by picking the "perfect" model right away. Instead, they treat model selection as an ongoing, step-by-step process. They rely on pilot tests, A/B comparisons, and regular performance checks. Business feedback helps keep solutions on track as needs change. Thorough documentation, version control, and audit trails are now essentials for compliance and trust. Here are the key considerations:

Application domain	Preferred approaches	Key considerations
Credit risk scoring	Tree-based, interpretable	Must be explainable, low latency, and compliant
Document summarization	GenAI + RAG	Context, quality control, and auditability
Image analysis	Deep learning (CNNs)	High data/compute, GPU scaling, and privacy
Real-time recommendations	Hybrid (classic + deep)	Cost, retraining frequency, and continuous feedback
Fraud detection	Ensemble/hybrid	Balance accuracy, explainability, and cost
Dynamic control/ agents	Reinforcement learning, agentic	Complex monitoring and risk of unintended action
Low-data domain adaptation (medical NLP, legal AI, etc.)	Transfer learning/fine-tuning	Limited labeled data, ability to reuse pre-trained models, and domain shift risks

Table 2.3: Model selection in enterprise context

Algorithm selection is not a one-off technical exercise but a dynamic, business-critical process. Organizations that see real impacts from AI routinely revisit model choices, prioritize operational clarity, and ground decisions in real-world constraints, using hybrid setups and pilot-driven validation whenever possible.

Organizational structure and change management

Launching AI initiatives is as much about people and processes as technology. Whether you've built an advanced data strategy or a sophisticated AI architecture, success depends on how teams are organized, motivated, and guided through change. Below are some proven best practices:

- Team structure matters:

    - AI touches both technical and business areas, so a clear team structure is key.

    Common models include the following:

        - **Centralized**: A single **center of excellence (CoE)** steers ML for the whole company. This drives consistency and deep expertise, but risks alienating frontline teams.
        - **Embedded**: Each business unit has its own ML staff, allowing for quick domain-specific solutions, but risking duplicated work and inconsistent standards.
        - **Hybrid**: A core platform team handles governance and tooling, while domain teams manage local projects. This "hub-and-spoke" approach offers balance but needs strong communication to avoid confusion.

    Choosing the best approach depends on the organization's size and needs, but most mature organizations lean toward hybrid to combine shared knowledge with business context.

- Build collaboration and shared goals:

    - Form cross-functional "tiger teams" that unite data, tech, and business experts on high-priority projects.
    - Use shared objectives (such as OKRs) so technical and business staff work toward the same outcomes, not isolated targets.

    Invest in ongoing training. Leaders should learn ML basics, and technical staff should deepen their business context. Regular internal workshops and upskilling programs help teams stay adaptable.An open, learning-focused culture, one that invites hands-on feedback and celebrates both successes and failures, keeps AI teams engaged and resilient.

- Manage change and align incentives:

    - Set shared metrics and rewards that reflect both business value and ML performance, such as revenue growth or customer retention, not just technical benchmarks.
    - Ensure strong executive sponsorship. Senior leaders should champion ML, clear obstacles, and communicate the "why" behind the transformation.

- Use structured change management frameworks, such as Kotter's eight steps or ADKAR, to support new workflows, roles, and mindsets. Start with small, focused pilots instead of wide-scale rollouts to build trust and momentum.

Successful AI organizations see change as ongoing, not one-time. They encourage ownership at all levels, keep communication open, and regularly review progress to adapt quickly as business and technology needs evolve.

Summary

In this chapter, we outlined the structural elements of a mature AI strategy. We showed that organizations with high-performing AI systems do not start with algorithms but with business alignment, structure, and repeatable patterns.

Key takeaways include the following:

- Business alignment should come first. AI must be tied to defined business initiatives and measured against real outcomes, not technical proxies.

- Governance is an enabler, not a brake. Policies, guardrails, and compliance must be built into the life cycle so innovation can scale safely and repeatedly.

- Data is the foundation and your organization's differentiator. Reliable, ethical, interoperable, and well-governed data products make AI trustworthy and reusable across use cases.

- Platform thinking replaces one-off projects. A modular AI platform enables fast iteration in the lab and hardened execution in production.

- The right family of algorithms depends on context, constraints, and value. Having a hammer should not mean everything looks like a nail.

- The operating model is what makes all elements work efficiently. AI succeeds when incentives, roles, and collaboration paths are designed for cross-functional delivery.

When these elements are in place, AI stops being experimental and starts becoming a durable business capability.

What's next?

Now that we have a foundation for how to build AI effectively, the next question is what to build first. The next chapter will show how to identify, rank, and select AI projects with the highest business impact.

References

- Board of Governors of the Federal Reserve System. (2011, April 4). *Supervisory Guidance on Model Risk Management (SR 11-7)*. Federal Reserve. https://www.federalreserve.gov/supervisionreg/srletters/sr1107.htm

- Ellis, S. (2010). *The ICE Score (Impact, Confidence, Ease)*. [Growth Hacking Framework].

- European Union. (2024). *Regulation laying down harmonised rules on artificial intelligence (Artificial Intelligence Act)*. Official Journal of the European Union. https://artificialintelligenceact.eu/

- Hermann, J., & Balso, M. (2017). *Meet Michelangelo: Uber's Machine Learning Platform*. Uber Engineering Blog. https://eng.uber.com/michelangelo-machine-learning-platform/

- Hiatt, J. M. (2006). *ADKAR: A Model for Change in Business, Government and our Community*. Prosci Learning Center Publications.

- International Organization for Standardization (ISO). (2023). ISO/IEC 23894:2023 *Information technology — Artificial intelligence — Guidance on risk management*. ISO. https://www.iso.org/standard/81230.html

- Karbhari, V. (2021, April 14). Airbnb's End-to-End ML Platform. Medium. https://medium.com/acing-ai/airbnbs-end-to-end-ml-platform-8f9cb8ba71d8

- Kotter, J. P. (2012). *Leading Change*. Harvard Business Review Press.

- National Institute of Standards and Technology (NIST). (2023, January). *Artificial Intelligence Risk Management Framework (AI RMF 1.0)*. U.S. Department of Commerce. https://www.nist.gov/itl/ai-risk-management-framework

- Netflix Technology Blog. (2020). *Machine Learning Platform at Netflix*. Netflix TechBlog. https://netflixtechblog.com/

- Organization for Economic Co-operation and Development (OECD). (2019, May). *OECD AI Principles*. OECD. https://oecd.ai/en/ai-principles

Subscribe for a free eBook

New frameworks, evolving architectures, research drops, production breakdowns—AI_Distilled filters the noise into a weekly briefing for engineers and researchers working hands-on with LLMs and GenAI systems. Subscribe now and receive a free eBook, along with weekly insights that help you stay focused and informed.

Subscribe at `https://packt.link/80z6Y` or scan the QR code below.

Part 2

Aligning Projects with Business Impact

In *Part 2*, we will provide a practical blueprint for bridging the gap between strategy and execution, beginning with the selection of high-impact AI projects. First, we will detail how to analyze and prioritize initiatives, moving beyond technical novelty to focus on factors such as business impact, end user definition, and comprehensive feasibility analysis. Next, we will cover the critical step of gaining leadership support, offering a guide to crafting a compelling narrative by engaging stakeholders early, focusing on the "so what" of business value, presenting a phased roadmap, and setting realistic expectations. With sponsorship secured, we will present a playbook for building an effective **proof of concept (PoC)**, detailing the critical post-PoC decisions: whether to refine, pivot, or proceed to a minimal viable product. Finally, we will introduce a comprehensive framework for measuring the PoC's performance beyond just technical model metrics.

This part contains the following chapters:

- *Chapter 3, Selecting High-Impact AI Projects*
- *Chapter 4, Beyond the Build: Gaining Leadership Support for AI Initiatives*
- *Chapter 5, Building an AI Proof of Concept and Measuring Your Solution*

3

Selecting High-Impact AI Projects

In today's rapidly evolving business landscape, organizations are turning to AI as a critical tool for driving efficiency, improving decision-making, and maximizing revenue. While companies can rapidly prototype AI solutions, the challenge lies in optimizing these solutions to achieve maximum benefits for their respective organizations. Building AI solutions is essential, but widespread adoption and sustained momentum are what truly give meaning to these solutions.

This chapter serves as a guide for companies interested in creating impactful AI solutions. *Impactful* may mean different things for each organization, but ultimately, it relates to delivering a 5-star experience to end users. In this chapter, we will explore the reasons behind building optimized and impactful AI solutions and provide a practical blueprint for steps you can take to achieve this optimization. Please note that we are not discussing model optimization in this chapter, but rather how to use AI most effectively to obtain the optimal return on investment.

We will cover the following key topics:

- Why is selecting high-impact AI projects important?
- Case study – choosing the right battle

Why is selecting high-impact AI projects important?

Selecting high-impact AI projects is important but difficult. It takes a village to determine the right use case at the right time. Hence, it is important to build optimized AI solutions. **AI optimization** refers to using AI algorithms and technologies to improve systems and processes effectively and efficiently to get the required business value. It is the framework that businesses can leverage to use AI most efficiently. Let's discuss a few reasons why this is important:

- Creating AI solutions and products is an expensive undertaking. Before investing millions of dollars in development, it's crucial to assess all factors, such as impact, end users, total cost, and more. Defining these factors helps you determine the solution's value and secure the necessary momentum and resources.

- AI is the new shiny object, and there is a strong urge to build solutions using AI. However, it's time to flip the script. Instead of using AI for a solution, it might be more effective to decide on the use case first and then determine whether AI can enhance it. This approach can save time and resources.

- Building AI solutions is a team effort, and assembling an A-team is essential. Getting buy-in from different teams and senior leaders before starting the development process ensures that everyone is fully engaged and provides their critical inputs to the AI project.

- By optimizing AI solutions, organizations can identify and address potential risks early in the development process. This proactive approach helps minimize the likelihood of costly errors or failures.

Now, let's dive deep into some of the factors that you could analyze before building an AI solution.

Key factors in developing effective AI solutions

Factors to consider before building an AI solution are as follows:

- **Business impact**: The problem you aim to solve should drive significant value for the business. Businesses should leverage AI to positively impact their operations, not just because it's a trending topic. Common examples of business value include generating new revenue streams, acquiring new users, retaining existing customers, and creating new assets. However, the impact isn't limited to customer value; it can also include improving internal operations, such as increasing employee productivity through tools such as AI copilots or streamlining processes such as recruitment or legal workflows using RAG-based solutions to access internal knowledge. Additionally, if you are a start-up, AI can provide you with a competitive edge in the market, which can help you secure funding from venture capitalists or angel investors.

Pro tip

Business impact/value should be defined by consulting appropriate business stake-holders. As a data scientist, feel free to propose the metrics, but also be flexible to incorporate feedback from business SMEs.

- **End users**: Defining your AI solution's end users is critical for tracking **return on investment (ROI)** once the AI product is launched. This will help you create an **optimized feedback loop mechanism**. This feedback loop is essential for measuring the ongoing success of the AI solution, enabling continuous improvement. The technical team should have a clear communication line with the end users so that they can understand the pain points and tailor the solution accordingly.

  Defining the end users also helps in defining the impact of your AI solution. For example, if the end users are internal employees, the impact is often measured in terms of productivity gains, efficiency improvements, or time saved per employee. On the other hand, if the solution targets external customers, the focus shifts to metrics such as user retention, revenue growth, customer acquisition, and increasing **customer lifetime value (CLV)**.

  Identifying the right end users ensures that you can tailor the solution to business goals and establish a dynamic system for capturing and acting on feedback, ensuring long-term success.

  Pro tip

  Ensure that your end users, especially if they are internal, are part of the development process and set realistic expectations with them. While you cannot include all the end users, you can identify a few power users who can provide critical feedback.

- **Choosing the right use case for AI**: Defining an impactful business problem is essential, but determining whether it's suitable for AI is an entirely different challenge. To put this in context, AI and **machine learning (ML)** excel in solving problems that involve identifying patterns, trends, or processing large volumes of data to predict or classify outcomes. However, not all use cases require the sophistication of AI. When considering the appropriate AI use case, it's crucial to first identify the business problem and then assess whether AI can enhance or solve it, rather than aimlessly searching for an AI application.

Let's explore three case studies that demonstrate when AI is a great fit, when it's overkill, and when it falls into a gray area.

Case study 1 (AI is overkill)

Suppose a company aims to calculate basic descriptive statistics, such as average sales over a given period or simple trend analysis. These tasks are well within the capabilities of standard statistical methods or tools such as Excel and dashboards. Introducing AI or ML here would add unnecessary complexity without adding value.

Solution: Simple statistical tools are more efficient in this case.

Word of caution: If, in the future, the size and complexity of the data change, then this should be revisited to see whether simple statistical methods such as linear regression can add more value than simple trend analysis.

Case study 2 (AI is a gray area)

Consider a company using a rule-based engine to recommend the next best marketing action for its users based on fixed parameters. The actions could look like recommending a newlywed couple to apply for a home loan. Basically, the marketing team sends promotions based on the customer's life events and/or other parameters. If these parameters (life events) can be coded in a static and predictable way, such as 1 if someone gets married and 0 if they don't, AI techniques might not be necessary. You can very well build a rules-based engine. However, if the user base grows significantly and you want your solution to be dynamic enough to decide the important parameters, transitioning to an AI-driven approach could be beneficial.

Solution: Advanced techniques such as deep neural networks might be able to solve the problem better here, as they can handle the complex relationship between a large user base with their preference over a simple rules-based engine. Deep neural networks are great at capturing large user preferences and relationships over time. They are also great for the cold start problem – basically, new customers/users that join the company, as they will be able to find similar users with similar interests and recommend them optimally.

Case study 3 (AI can be high impact)

Leveraging AI often benefits high-impact use cases, such as diagnosing rare diseases or detecting fraud. These scenarios typically involve massive datasets and complex patterns, which rule-based systems or manual processes might not be able to derive at scale. AI's predictive capabilities can significantly enhance accuracy and speed in such use cases.

Solution: Implementing AI would provide tangible benefits by processing vast data and identifying anomalies more effectively. Let's take an example of fraud detection using AI techniques.

To build a fraud detection solution, you need multiple data points, such as transaction records, user behavior logs, customer profiles, and maybe even external data sources such as credit bureau information. Now, all this vast amount of data can be efficiently handled by neural networks or reinforcement learning for adaptive fraud detection strategies. If you also had unstructured data, such as any kind of documents, you could also leverage advanced reasoning **large language models (LLMs)** to process structured and unstructured data and efficiently flag fraudulent transactions. With the advent of LLMs, it is also possible to alert users in real time without human intervention. You can deploy an agent to send that message or email to the user.

Now that we have defined the use cases that could leverage AI for the end users of the solution and determined the business impact, the next thing to consider is that just because AI can be beneficial, it doesn't mean it can be implemented immediately. In the next sections, let us explore other business constraints to AI implementation.

Feasibility analysis

In an enterprise setting, there might be additional constraints such as talent, resources, budget, and more. Therefore, to perform the due diligence, there are a few additional analyses to conduct before starting the build of the AI solution.

Conduct a comprehensive feasibility analysis to evaluate technical and business viability before implementing AI. This ensures that the solution that is built can deliver measurable business value. This can be performed on the following variables: data, tech stack, and talent.

Data

Data is the fuel of AI solutions. Your AI solution is as good as the data you provide. Even the most sophisticated techniques fail if the data is not of high-quality or if it is incorrect. Hence, it is important to pay attention to the data within your organization. Here are the factors to consider pertaining to data:

- **Availability of high-quality data**: AI/ML requires a significant amount of data to learn patterns and trends and generalize on those patterns. Once you have identified the right data sources, it is important to ensure that the data is cleaned before being ingested into AI algorithms. All models, including LLMs, require high-quality data.

For example, let's say you are building a chatbot for your employees to get information on all things HR, such as leave policy, benefits, and so on. The data supplied to the LLM has to be clean and updated so that employees can get relevant information. Otherwise, they might think they are adhering to company rules but could land in trouble because of outdated information.

Similarly, if you are building a simple prediction model, it is essential to ensure that the data doesn't have unnecessary characters or too many missing values, as these can be misleading for the model.

- **Limited amount of data**: Companies may have high-quality data limited to a few rows, such as data on only 100 users. The limited availability might be because of several reasons, such as the company just launched a new product and only has data for early adopters. In such cases, to augment the data, using synthetic data generation techniques such as a **generative adversarial network (GAN)** can be highly powerful.

For example, let's say a company is working on the launch strategy for a potential blockbuster drug. In this case, you might not have tons of data to analyze the previous launch strategy to decide on factors such as when the drug should be launched, in which country, which healthcare providers to target, and so on. You can leverage GAN to augment the data and perform analysis to combat this issue. Though the results might not be 100% accurate, they gave the stakeholders a good starting point to develop their launch strategy. Other techniques that you can use include Synthetic Minority Oversampling Technique (SMOTE); here, instead of simply duplicating minority class samples, SMOTE generates synthetic examples by interpolating between existing minority samples and their nearest neighbors in the feature space. This helps the model learn a more general decision boundary and reduces the risk of overfitting.

Cautionary tale

Synthetic data is an excellent tool for simulating complex patterns and scenarios. However, it's important to note that challenges arise for high-risk use cases, such as predicting whether a patient is likely to contract COVID-19. Since COVID-19 was a unique event with no prior data, making accurate predictions is difficult. Synthetic data might fall short here, as there is no precise base dataset to apply synthetic data techniques effectively. The closest you can get here regarding data is to look at past pandemics to analyze the overall trends.

- **Buy third-party data**: Companies often want to diversify their target audience and explore new user bases. In such cases, procuring the data might be of interest.

  For example, consider a case where you are working on an AI prospecting strategy to target small business owners. Now, this might be a completely new target audience for the company, so there will be no prior data available to understand the small business ecosystem. Here, it might be best to procure data from vendors such as ZoomInfo to get the data and build a personalized AI prospecting strategy based on the industry, company size, revenue, and so on.

- **Diverse and representative data**: To build trustworthy and responsible AI solutions, it is essential to have data representing everyone in the population so that your algorithm can understand the patterns, even for minority populations. It is also necessary to de-bias data to ensure that no population group is favored more than the other based on race, gender, and so on.

  It is also important to avoid using **personally identifiable information** (**PII**) as much as possible, such as social security numbers. In some scenarios, such as cancer prediction problems, PII data such as gender and age are inevitable, as those features determine the course of treatment.

  For example, suppose you are building a prediction problem on whether the person is eligible for a high credit line. In this case, the historical data might show that men receive higher credit lines than women, as they have been in the workforce for longer or might have a higher net worth and salary than women. Here, it's a societal issue that cripples the data in some form or another. If you don't use gender as a training feature, the model will predict the high credit line based on other features such as current net worth, spending patterns, and so on, and wouldn't differentiate based on gender. So, it is essential to perform a detailed analysis to determine such attributes that might introduce bias to the model and take a step back to consider whether they impact the model results.

Considering the preceding points, the next question is, how much data is too much data? Though there is no one-size-fits-all here, there are some general guidelines that can be followed:

- Supervised ML problems need more labeled training data.
- The more complex the model is, the more data it will require.
- A general rule is that you need 10 times as many data points as there are features in your dataset. If there are 10 columns, you should have at least 100 rows.

- For LLMs, if you are fine-tuning, then it is essential to have a robust dataset that covers all scenarios, including edge cases.

Data should be a critical component of your AI strategy. Ensuring that adequate and high-quality data is available for use will lead you toward a successful outcome. This step might require some time and effort, but it can save you from the misery of building sub-optimal AI solutions. Once you have the data, the next factor is to look at your tech stack for building these AI solutions.

Tech stack

Most AI solutions in production require a robust technology stack. The local computers might not suffice to handle large amounts of data and provide a seamless user experience. On top of that, it is not easy for every company to build its own cloud infrastructure. This is an expensive undertaking and not required in most cases. Hence, they prefer existing cloud providers.

In some cases, such as if you are building a rules-based engine or a simple statistical analysis, you might want to opt for local deployment. But as even that solution scales and your user base grows, you will have to switch to a cloud provider.

If the goal is to build Gen AI solutions, we all know there is a huge environment constraint when leveraging the LLMs for your solutions. There is limited capacity. Even if you get access to the capacity, there is a chance that if multiple users are using your solution at the same time, they might face rate limit errors (which is basically a message to tell them that there is no capacity, so please try again later). This can cause disruption in user experience, and people might lose interest in your Gen AI solution. To mitigate this problem, you should ensure that you can provide constant throughput for your solution so that users don't face this error. This can be done by analyzing your existing traffic and ensuring that enough resources are available within your cloud platform during the busy time of the day. You should also consider the latency of the response. For example, reasoning models, such as o-series, will take a bit longer to respond, which might increase customer bounce rate or lead to an unsatisfactory experience for the customer.

Pro tip

Another thing to note is that if you choose a cloud platform, one key advantage is access to its cloud solutions architects and specialists, who can provide best practices for your use case, help optimize your solutions, and guide you through implementation. Make sure to leverage these valuable resources for expert advice.

Talent

While data and tech stack are important, you also need people who can leverage the required data and technology to create an impactful AI solution. Building AI solutions is complex; hence, having people with specialized skills is important.

AI applications require a specialized talent pool. Based on the use case, skills might vary, but knowing the basics of data science, ML, and statistics goes a long way. Another key factor to note is that your data scientists might know the data science stack well but may not be experts in MLops, which is the skill of managing and deploying AI solutions in production. For that, you might need talent that has the operations skill set – that is, they know how to write code in production in the most efficient way, as well as monitor and evaluate the AI solution continuously.

With the plethora of roles, it can be difficult to decide which folks are most relevant to the team. The general rule of thumb is to have a data scientist, as these are folks with deep expertise in crunching data and even building a proof of concept (PoC) or minimum viable product (MVP) with ML algorithms. Next, you might want **machine learning engineers** (**MLEs**) who have deep expertise in deploying viable POCs to production. In the end, it is also important to have AI product managers or product managers who can develop a go-to-market strategy for the AI product and also help to keep the project on track.

Given the pace at which AI is evolving, it is difficult to get "experts" in the field. Instead of chasing experts, it is important to hire folks with a growth mindset and a willingness to learn.

> Pro tip
>
> If you are considering deploying AI as a user interface application, you might also need a .NET developer, so ensure you have one on your team.
>
> Within a large organization, you might also need project or product managers to define milestones, keep everyone accountable, and ensure the smooth delivery of the AI solution.

In this section, we covered that in an enterprise setting, conducting a comprehensive feasibility analysis is crucial before implementing AI solutions. This involves evaluating technical and business viability to ensure the solution delivers measurable business value. Key variables to consider include data, tech stack, and talent. High-quality data is essential for AI success, and companies may need to augment or procure data. A robust tech stack, often involving cloud providers, is necessary for handling large data and ensuring a seamless user experience. Specialized talent with a growth mindset and willingness to learn is vital for leveraging data and technology effectively.

In the next section, we will explore opportunity sizing, which is important for understanding the potential impact and scalability of the AI solution. This helps in identifying the right opportunities to pursue and ensures that resources are allocated effectively for maximum business value.

Opportunity sizing

Opportunity sizing is a method that data scientists can use to quantify the potential impact of an initiative before deciding to invest in it. Although businesses attempt to prioritize initiatives, they rarely do the math to assess the opportunity, relying instead on intuition-driven decision-making. While this type of decision-making does have its place, it also runs the risk of being easily swayed by several subtle biases, such as information available, confirmation bias, and so on.

Opportunity sizing can be approached in various ways. In this section, we will cover two methods: directional T-shirt sizing and bottom-up using comparable methods.

Directional T-shirt sizing is a qualitative method where opportunities are categorized into sizes such as small, medium, large, and extra large based on their potential impact and feasibility. This helps in quickly assessing and prioritizing opportunities without detailed analysis. On the other hand, **bottom-up using comparable methods** involves a more quantitative approach where opportunities are sized by analyzing similar projects or initiatives.

Let's start the discussion with directional T-shirt sizing.

Directional T-shirt sizing

Directional T-shirt sizing is a qualitative method used to estimate the time and effort required for different phases of a project. It categorizes tasks into sizes such as **extra small (XS)**, **small (S)**, **medium (M)**, **large (L)**, and **extra large (XL)** based on their complexity and scope. This method helps in quickly assessing and prioritizing tasks without the need for detailed analysis.

The importance of directional T-shirt sizing lies in its ability to provide a quick and intuitive way to estimate project requirements. It facilitates consistency and standardization across teams, making it easier to communicate and align on project expectations. Additionally, it helps in identifying potential bottlenecks and resource needs early in the project planning phase, ensuring that projects are scoped realistically and managed effectively.

Let's say you're working on a recommendation engine for an e-commerce platform. Here's how you might categorize the tasks:

- **XS**: Setting up the initial project environment, including basic configurations and dependencies. This task is straightforward and requires minimal effort.

- **S**: Implementing basic recommendation algorithms using existing libraries. This involves some coding and testing, but is relatively simple.

- **M**: Integrating the recommendation engine with the e-commerce platform's user interface. This requires more effort as it involves ensuring seamless interaction between the recommendation engine and the platform.

- **L**: Enhancing the recommendation engine with advanced features such as personalized recommendations based on user behavior and preferences. This task is complex and requires significant development and testing.

- **XL**: Scaling the recommendation engine to handle large volumes of data and users. This involves optimizing the algorithms, ensuring high availability, and possibly migrating to a cloud infrastructure.

Using directional T-shirt sizing helps in quickly assessing and prioritizing tasks without detailed analysis. It provides a quick and intuitive way to estimate project requirements, facilitating consistency and standardization across teams.

Bottom-up using comparable methods

The bottom-up comparable methods sizing approach estimates the potential value of a business or product by leveraging comparable products, services, or markets. This method is beneficial when you have limited direct data but can draw parallels with existing businesses or market segments. The focus is on identifying similar entities and extrapolating their metrics to estimate your opportunity.

Here's how to apply the bottom-up comparable methods sizing approach step by step:

- **Identify relevant comparable products, services, or markets**: Look for products, services, or companies similar to what you're trying to size in terms of target audience, functionality, industry, or pricing model.

  For example, if you're launching a new cloud-based **customer relationship management (CRM)**, look at other SaaS companies that offer CRM solutions, such as Salesforce or HubSpot. For a new electric vehicle, you might look at Tesla or Rivian.

- **Gather data from comparable methods**: Research publicly available information and collect key metrics such as revenue, customer base, pricing, growth rate, and market share from comparable companies. Sources can include the following:

  - Annual reports or investor presentations
  - Industry benchmarks and reports

- Press releases and news articles
- Market research databases or market research
- Conduct surveys for the target user base

For example, for a new streaming platform, gather data on subscribers, **average revenue per user (ARPU)**, and market share from companies such as Netflix, Hulu, or Disney+.

- **Adjust for scale and market dynamics:** Adjust the data of different products to reflect key differences such as geography, target audience size, or pricing.

    For example, if you compare your product to that of a company operating in North America, but your product will launch globally, adjust the figures accordingly.

- **Use qualitative adjustments:** Consider qualitative differences, such as differences in brand strength, customer loyalty, or technology features.

    For example, if a brand already has a strong user base, the adaptation of any new product or service would be easier and users are more likely to engage with it compared to a new brand in the market. For startups, it is easier to build the brand by open sourcing their code or part of technology for a while, so users can trust them. These adjustments can be a bit tricky to implement but should be considered as a factor in your calculations.

- **Apply comparable metrics:** Once you've adjusted for differences, apply the comparable metrics (such as revenue per user or market penetration rate) to your business scenario.

    For example, if a comparable product in the same industry has an ARPU of $100 and a customer base of 1 million, estimate the ARPU and potential customer base for your product based on similarities in product offerings and market conditions.

In conclusion, both directional T-shirt sizing and bottom-up using comparable methods are methods for opportunity sizing. Directional T-shirt sizing provides a quick and intuitive way to estimate project requirements, while bottom-up using comparable methods offers a more precise and data-driven assessment. By leveraging these methods, you can effectively prioritize opportunities and allocate resources to maximize business value.

Another critical component of opportunity sizing is cost versus benefit analysis. In the next section, we will cover that in detail.

Performance cost versus benefit analysis

Cost versus benefit analysis is a critical step in justifying the assumed ROI and getting confidence from stakeholders. It involves evaluating the potential costs associated with an opportunity against the expected benefits to determine its overall value and feasibility. This analysis helps in making informed decisions by quantifying the financial impact and ensuring that the resources invested will yield significant returns.

Integrating cost versus benefit analysis with opportunity sizing allows organizations to prioritize opportunities based on their potential value. By comparing the costs and benefits, companies can identify which opportunities offer the highest ROI and allocate resources accordingly. This ensures that efforts are focused on initiatives that provide the most significant business value, leading to more effective and strategic decision-making.

Here is a framework for data scientists while determining it:

1. First, identify and estimate costs:

   - **Development costs:**

     - **Data collection and preparation**: AI models require large datasets. Estimating the cost of gathering, cleaning, and annotating data is critical. Acquiring quality data can be expensive for some projects, and generating high-quality data can be costly.

     - **Infrastructure**: AI projects often need significant computing power, especially training models. Consider cloud infrastructure costs (e.g., AWS, Azure, GCP, etc.), server hardware, and ongoing maintenance.

     - **Resources**: AI projects require skilled teams, including data scientists, AI/ML engineers, and domain experts, to estimate salaries, training, and consulting fees. If you hire consultants instead of full-time talent, the cost should be adjusted accordingly.

   - **Operational costs:**

     - **Deployment**: These are the costs associated with implementing the AI system in production, including integration with existing systems and automation pipelines.

     - **Monitoring and maintenance**: AI models degrade over time and need regular monitoring, updating, and retraining, which requires dedicated resources.

- **Regulation and compliance**: Depending on the industry (e.g., healthcare, finance, etc.), ensure compliance with legal and ethical standards, which can increase costs.

2. Next, estimate the benefits:

- **Increased efficiency**:

  - **Process automation**: AI can automate repetitive tasks, freeing up human resources for higher-value work. Quantify labor savings by reducing manual work hours (e.g., AI automating customer support or repetitive administrative tasks).

  - **Operational efficiency**: AI can optimize processes, such as supply chain management or predictive maintenance, reducing downtime and operating costs.

- **Revenue growth**:

  - **New revenue streams**: AI can create new products, services, or business models (e.g., personalized recommendations driving more sales, AI-enabled services such as virtual assistants, etc.).

  - **Customer experience**: AI-driven personalization can lead to higher customer retention, increased satisfaction, and higher average order value (e.g., tailored recommendations in e-commerce).

- **Improved decision-making**:

  - **Data-driven insights**: AI models help make faster and more accurate decisions by identifying patterns and trends that humans might miss. These insights can lead to better strategic planning, pricing, or product development.

  - **Risk mitigation**: AI models can identify potential risks, such as fraud detection, loan approvals, or cybersecurity. Quantify the value of reduced risks and avoided losses.

3. Next, develop market competitiveness to gain a competitive advantage. Being an early adopter of AI can give your business an edge in the market, improving customer loyalty, operational efficiency, and market share.

4. Perform ROI analysis:

    - **Total cost**: Add all identified costs (development, operations, talent, etc.)
    - **Total benefits**: Sum up the benefits of cost savings, increased revenue, or risk reduction

    $$ROI = \frac{\text{Total Benefits} - \text{Total Costs}}{\text{Total Costs}} \times 100$$

5. Conduct a sensitivity analysis:

    - **Best, expected, and worst-case scenarios**: Vary your assumptions about cost and benefit estimates to understand how sensitive your ROI is to changes in key variables
    - **Uncertainty factors**: Assess data quality, model accuracy, regulatory changes, or potential delays, and adjust the analysis accordingly
    - **Long-term versus short-term value**:
        - **Short-term value**: Quantify immediate benefits, such as cost savings or improved customer service, and compare them to upfront development and deployment costs.
        - **Long-term value**: Consider the value of scalability and learning over time. AI models can improve and provide increasing benefits as they get exposed to more data.
    - **Non-monetary benefits**:
        - **Strategic positioning**: AI projects often align with long-term innovation strategies, even if they don't provide immediate returns
        - **Customer and employee satisfaction**: Automating mundane tasks can lead to happier employees, and personalized AI-driven experiences can delight customers
        - **Brand perception**: AI might enhance your brand image, positioning you as a forward-thinking and tech-savvy organization

Now, let's look at an example. Let's say you are implementing an AI chatbot for customer service. The **cost** might include $100,000 in development and deployment, $50,000 annually for infrastructure and updates, and $100,000 annually in human resources to manage and monitor it. The **benefits** could include reducing customer service costs by $400,000 annually due to fewer human agents, faster response times, and improved customer satisfaction. This would result in an ROI as follows:

ROI = 400,00 − (100,000 + 50,000 + 100,000)/250,000 × 100 = 60%

This shows a strong positive return, but it should be taken with a grain of salt. All these investments assume everything will go as expected, which is rarely the case in real-world implementation.

Cost versus benefit analysis is essential for evaluating the overall value and feasibility of an opportunity. By comparing the costs and expected benefits, organizations can prioritize initiatives that offer the highest ROI, ensuring that resources are allocated effectively for maximum business value.

All the methods discussed previously are quantitative analyses. There are a few other factors that you should consider before prioritizing the AI use cases within an enterprise.

Analyze the risk level of the use case

Another important step is assessing whether the use case presents a high or low risk for the organization. If your company has low-risk tolerance, it's wise to start with low- to medium-risk AI use cases, such as the following:

- **Automated reporting**: Streamlining repetitive tasks and improving reporting accuracy
- **Internal chatbots**: Enhancing internal communications or customer service
- **Recommendation engines**: Personalizing product or service recommendations for users

Starting with manageable, lower-risk projects helps build confidence in AI capabilities and creates a foundation for scaling more complex, high-impact solutions.

If you work in a regulated organization (healthcare, finance, insurance, etc.), implementing low-risk use cases will help you gain confidence in the legal and compliance team and become comfortable with documentation. This will come in handy when implementing complicated use cases.

Analyze the scale of the use case

We all know AI thrives at scaling. It is possible that the problem was solved with existing tools or data analysis and was sufficient, but now the company's situation has changed.

For example, a company uses a simple rules-based marketing engine to send email campaigns to customers. However, after acquiring another company, the number of users has increased tenfold, leading to an influx of new data. In this case, AI might be a suitable solution. Therefore, it might be more effective to leverage AI to build recommendation engines for customers.

Analyze the historical solutions

When building an AI solution, it is essential to peek inside the organization and determine whether the problem has already been solved. This could have been achieved via a legacy tool or a simple statistical analysis. This is important for the following two reasons:

- Speaking with owners/stakeholders to check whether the problem has already been solved is a great way to know what didn't work in the past and whether AI can solve it

- This will also help you decide whether AI is the solution or whether there might be underlying issues that cannot be solved using AI

Let's understand this in detail with an example:

Example: Customer churn prediction in a subscription-based service

Background: A subscription-based video streaming company is facing a high churn rate. The product team suggests developing an AI model to predict which customers will likely churn and offer promotions to retain them proactively. Before that, the company should follow these steps to understand whether AI is needed to solve the problem:

1. **Speak with stakeholders**: Before jumping into developing an AI solution, the data science team meets with key stakeholders, including customer support. The data science team learns that the company has already tried manual churn analysis, analyzing customer feedback and usage data, but has failed. The marketing team mentions that retention campaigns have been launched in the past based on simple segmentation (e.g., customers who last logged in a week ago), but have yet to see significant improvement in retention rates. The operations team reveals frequent service disruptions in certain regions, which could drive customer dissatisfaction and churn.

2. **Insights from stakeholders**: The discussions reveal that AI alone might not fully address the churn problem. Service disruptions in certain regions likely drive customer dissatisfaction, but this is an operational issue that must be fixed before introducing an AI model.

3. **Determine whether AI is appropriate**: The team concludes that more than AI alone will be needed to solve the problem. While AI could help predict which customers will likely churn, it won't address the root cause (service disruptions).

4. **Solution**: They address the service issues and improve the overall customer experience. Once operational issues are resolved, an AI-based churn prediction model could add value by allowing the company to proactively engage at-risk customers before they decide to leave. Historical solutions are a great way to perform benchmarking as well.

5.   **Example**: Suppose you want to build an AI-based demand forecasting system to replace the existing platform. This could be that the demand planners are observing a decline in accuracy, hence a decrease in revenue. Now, let's say the legacy system provides the forecast using statistical methods such as Auto-ARIMA, but your new AI-based solution can skip to the advanced ML and neural network techniques. This way, you are building something that adds value to a demand planner's life. In addition, both systems can run in parallel for a few months to compare the accuracy, giving business users more confidence.

All these different kinds of analysis will help you uncover the potential of your use case and determine whether AI is needed for your solution. Conducting a detailed analysis will enable you to make informed decisions and gain confidence in your choices.

Case study — choosing the right battle

In this chapter, we have explored potential techniques to decide the best AI use case for your enterprise, including performing feasibility analysis, opportunity sizing, and looking at other factors such as risk and scale of the use case. Now, let's explore how this will play out in the real world.

Apex Bank, a fictitious leading mid-sized financial institution, has been investing heavily in digital transformation. As part of its 5-year innovation roadmap, the bank's leadership formed an AI task force to explore high-impact use cases that align with strategic priorities and offer measurable returns.

The task force shortlisted two potential AI projects:

- Customer churn prediction model
- Fraud detection system

Both projects were data-rich and technically feasible, but choosing the right one to prioritize was crucial given the limited budget and resource constraints.

- **Project 1: AI-driven customer churn prediction:**

    - **Overview**: This project proposed building an ML model to predict which customers were likely to close their accounts or stop using key products. The goal was to allow proactive engagement through targeted retention campaigns.

    - **Potential benefits of this project:**

        - Reduce customer attrition (estimated at 12% annually)
        - Improve customer lifetime value

- Enhance personalized marketing
- Increase in brand loyalty

- **Challenges associated with the project:**

- It required significant data integration from various systems (CRM, transaction logs, and call center data)
- Actions from predictions required coordinated changes in marketing and customer service departments
- Retention incentives risked eroding margins

- **Project 2: AI-powered fraud detection model:**

- **Overview:** This project involved building a real-time fraud detection engine using supervised ML techniques. It would analyze transactional behavior to flag anomalies for review.

- **Potential benefits of the project:**

- Reduce financial losses due to fraud (estimated at $8 million/year)
- Enhance customer trust and security perception
- Improve compliance with financial regulations

- **Challenges associated with the project:**

- It needed a robust real-time infrastructure
- False positives could impact user experience
- Model retraining requires continuous data quality monitoring

Evaluation criteria

The task force evaluated the two projects based on the following:

Criteria	Churn model	Fraud detection model
Strategic alignment	Medium (customer growth)	High (risk mitigation priority)
Business impact	Medium	High
Data availability	Low-moderate	High

Criteria	Churn model	Fraud detection model
Technical feasibility	Moderate	High
Stakeholder buy-in	Moderate	High
Risk	Moderate	High
Scale	High	High

Table 3.1: Criteria for evaluating projects

Based on the preceding parameters, a decision was made. We will discuss the viewpoint in the next section.

Decision: prioritizing fraud detection

Apex Bank selected the AI-powered fraud detection model for immediate development. Key reasons included the following:

- **Strategic fit**: Fraud mitigation was a board-level priority due to recent high-profile incidents
- **High ROI**: Preventing fraud had immediate, tangible financial benefits
- **Faster implementation**: Data was more centralized, and real-time capabilities were eventually introduced as part of the broader data strategy
- **Customer trust**: Strengthening fraud controls supported brand reputation and regulatory compliance

The churn prediction model was deprioritized but earmarked for future development once the data infrastructure matured.

Results and impact

Six months after implementation, the fraud detection system achieved the following:

- Significant reduction in fraud-related losses.
- Improvement in fraud detection accuracy versus previous rule-based systems.
- Real-time alerts with <1 second latency.
- Improved regulatory audit scores.
- Robust data monitoring frameworks. These were built to track changes in data and flag potential data drifts. This was not only helpful in this project but also in future AI solutions.

In this case study, since it involves a bank, fraud detection was its top priority. The primary reason people use a bank is to ensure that their money is safe, making fraud prevention the bank's main responsibility. On the other hand, if you work for an e-commerce company, your priority would be to provide personalized recommendations to users, as this would increase the company's cash flow. In summary, the frameworks we discussed, such as feasibility analysis and opportunity sizing, are excellent quantitative tools. However, it is also crucial to align everything with your business goals to make informed decisions.

Summary

In this chapter, we learned the importance of selecting an impactful AI project and the key factors to consider in doing so. We discussed methods such as feasibility analysis to determine whether the AI project is viable, based on factors such as the availability of high-quality data, the tech stack, and talent. We also explored opportunity sizing methods, primarily directional t-shirt sizing and bottom-up using comparables, to estimate the potential dollar impact of the project and effectively size different workstreams within an AI solution. Next, we examined how to perform a cost versus benefit analysis, which is another excellent way to determine whether you will achieve the required ROI compared to the resources invested in the project. Other factors to consider for making an informed choice include the scale and risk of the use case. Finally, we discussed a case study to bring everything together and see how it all plays out in action within an enterprise.

In the next chapter, we will learn how technical teams can secure sponsorship from senior leadership for AI-driven projects.

4

Beyond the Build: Gaining Leadership Support for AI Initiatives

Imagine this: you have identified the use case, the right technology, and talent, all the analysis is done, and you know your metrics, **return on investment (ROI)**, and so on, and it seems like the perfect time to start building your solution. Not so fast! You still need the resources to build the solution, so you must present all that analysis to someone who can provide that to you, a.k.a. your senior leadership. This is the most critical yet undermined step in the overall AI strategy. Most technical folks think crunching data and building models is their primary role, but this is far from the truth. Even as a data scientist, you must learn to sell your proposed AI solution to the senior leadership and end users.

To put this in context, let me give you an example: a company wants to expand its reach to an entirely new user base (this could be Gen Z or a small business). To support this goal, you propose to develop an AI-driven strategy to prospect and onboard the new user base into the ecosystem. If you think about it, this requires significant investment: purchasing external data, conducting text mining and analysis, building a predictive model, and integrating the solution with legacy systems. To build this, you need buy-in from senior leadership.

Throughout this chapter, you will discover practical tips on how technical teams can secure sponsorship from senior leadership. To better illustrate these concepts, we will conclude with a case study demonstrating how these strategies are applied in the real world.

We will cover the following key topics:

- Getting started with the discussion
- Crafting the AI narrative – from vision to buy-in
- How AI got the CXO support – a hypothetical scenario

Getting started with the discussion

To get the buy-in, you would probably start the discussion using a few slides that entail the following:

- **Primary and secondary research**: This might include the total number of new users in the US by specific parameters, such as state, net worth, and so on. This is to raise excitement among senior leadership about the market's potential. You might get these numbers from online reports (McKinsey, Bain, etc.), or you might perform back-of-the-napkin calculations to derive them. You might also be able to get this data by scouting within the company's internal database or speaking with someone who might have analyzed this population.

- **Data selection**: If it's a completely new user base, chances are you might have to buy the data, so you will include a list of vendors and the cost of procuring the data. This is where you should also call out any internal data you will use for the analysis or the final outreach product. One thing to note here is that it is not just about data collection but also about the transformations you would need to ingest it within your product. You don't have to call it out explicitly, but you should remember it while you are starting the build.

- **AI selection**: Depending on the audience, you might have to cover the AI techniques at a high level or go into the weeds of things. The AI strategy is a broader term, but here it refers to mentioning whether it is a **machine learning** (**ML**) solution or a Gen AI solution. This will determine the rest of the parameters that we discussed in the previous chapter, such as the required technology, talent, cost, and so on.

- **Roadmap**: Chances are that you wouldn't be launching an AI solution on day 1 and be done with it, so it's essential to define precise milestones and set expectations within the first few discussions. This is an evolving step, so it is important to be proactive about updating the milestones.

- **Setting expectations**: This is another critical step, as it clarifies that the AI solution will not solve all their problems but is rather a step in the right direction. For example, if you are building an internal chatbot, the expectations might be that suddenly the productivity will skyrocket, and all the people will just focus on innovation and creativity. While an internal chatbot will help with productivity, there could be a steep learning curve for individuals on how to prompt effectively and how to balance between their own judgment and responses by the chatbot. Such expectation settings and transparency should accelerate senior leadership support. During the expectation-setting phase, it is also important to highlight the iterative nature of AI/ML products; hence, the expectations for Phase 0 will be different from Phase 1.

Let's take an example. For any AI solution, the milestones might look like data preparation, testing your hypothesis, refining the hypothesis, evaluating your solution, deploying to production, and then continuous monitoring. This is not a one-size-fits-all, but general guidance on what your milestones might look like.

Throughout the AI development lifecycle, you need the support of your senior leadership. This chapter will serve as a guide on how to gain that buy-in and the steps to take proactively to achieve it successfully. Let's dive deeper!

Crafting the AI narrative — from vision to buy-in

Getting the buy-in and sponsorship involves multiple steps; here are a few best practices to consider when building the story:

1. Engage the right stakeholders early on and throughout the process:

    *   Bringing the right people into the decision-making process early, such as data scientists, AI specialists, and business leaders, is crucial. This is why **Chief Data Officers (CDOs)** and **Chief Data and Analytics Officers (CDAOs)** play an increasingly vital role. Having the right stakeholders on board ensures smoother project execution and increases the likelihood of securing necessary resources. When businesses are actively invested in AI solutions, the adoption process becomes a pull effect, where leaders are asking for these solutions, rather than a push effect, where you are forcing adoption.

    *   Involving the stakeholders is essential even after the solution has been built so that you can continue to get feedback and improve the AI solution. Business needs, user needs, and data inputs evolve over time, and so should the AI solution. Your stakeholders will play a pivotal role in communicating those evolving needs.

Pro tip

The best way to ensure that the business stakeholders are involved is to provide them with regular updates on the progress of your AI solution.

Also, please don't treat this relationship as transactional; instead, focus on building long-term relationships with stakeholders. This will help you build trust with them and also provide a pleasant working experience. Another important thing to keep in mind is to know the long-term and short-term goals of your stakeholders and leadership so you can fulfill those through your solution. This way, everyone has skin in the game, and it is a meaningful experience for everyone.

2. Include the "so-what" in your slides. The first question senior leadership will ask is, "*So what?*". This is your chance to justify the investment. Hence, it is essential to be proactive and include it in your initial slides. This will keep them engaged and interested in getting involved in the technical aspects of the presentation. The "so what" can be answered using the primary and secondary research you performed. Some examples of this are potential market size, revenue, and so on that the solution could bring once it is deployed.

Pro tip

It's always good to get a perspective on your slides (especially this one) from someone who directly reports to senior leadership or has known them for a year before the presentation. This will ensure that a fresh set of eyes reviews your presentation and provides you with candid feedback.

3. Perform due diligence on your data:

- The CXOs are usually well-versed with data such as market size, industry trends, and so on. If referring to numbers from public reports, refer to multiple sources before including them in your pitch deck. If the numbers are too far from the truth, it will set a negative tone for the presentation.
- For any internal aggregated data, ask the SMEs to review it before you put it in the deck. This will be your safety cushion when asked to justify the numbers.

Pro tip

Performing due diligence is usually time-consuming; it is recommended to include a week or two extra for these checks before you schedule your presentation.

4.   Present the roadmap of your product:

- Get comfortable with the fact that you wouldn't be able to achieve a perfect solution on day 1, and neither will anyone fund it just because you said it would work. You need to show incremental progress to get the right buy-in. Lay out what you plan to achieve and when (i.e., show your milestones along with the proposed outcome of each milestone).

    For example, the first phase of the roadmap could be building a solution for a limited user base. The milestones within that phase would be procuring data, ingesting data, building the first version of the model, sending the recommendations to that limited user base, getting feedback, and analyzing the results, just to name a few. This is just an example of a phase and milestone; it is best to modify these based on the framework followed in your organization.

- Depending on the type of solution and the organization, there is a possibility that you won't have all the answers on day 1. There is a strong possibility that the outcome from the first phase will determine whether you will proceed to the next phase. If that is the case, then keep the roadmap at a high level and plan for a limited time. There is no point in planning for the next 5 years if the solution might not see the light of day in the next 5 months.

Pro tip

The hardest part about building AI solutions is knowing when to stop or pivot. Having a phase-wise mindset and analyzing results after each phase will assist you in making an informed choice.

5. Schedule regular check-ins:

    - This one can be tricky, as senior leadership is often swamped and might not have the time to connect regularly. However, it is extremely important to keep them in the loop about the development of your solution and inform them about the progress.

    - This check-in should not only include the progress or the wins, but also the challenges you might be facing, and whether you need their help in mitigating any of those.

> **Pro tip**
>
> You can also send email updates instead of scheduling regular meetings.

6. Start with the basics first, such as the data and any prerequisites needed. When pitching the AI solution, it is tempting to boil the ocean and share the larger vision of the AI solution. While that is important, it is also essential to highlight the prerequisites first. This usually includes a comprehensive data strategy. This can entail the kind of data you need, the cost of procuring the data, any movement from on-premises to the cloud, and any access controls you might require. Presenting these aspects shows the clarity you have for the data and prepares the senior leadership for any kind of investment you might need from them.

> **Pro tip**
>
> It is a good idea to spend time with the infrastructure and data teams to get their input on the art of buying/curating the data, and the timelines to achieve the same. This will help you get a realistic timeline for data delivery, and you can adjust the other timelines accordingly.

7. Be upfront about the expectations. While it's tempting to think that an AI or ML-driven solution can solve all your problems, we know this is not 100% true. Hence, it is crucial to convey the expectations of the product realistically.

    For example, let's say that user engagement is declining for one of the products. You are tasked with analyzing and finding the reason for the decline. Once you perform the analysis, you find that most of your users have outgrown that product, so even though you might add a new user base, it will take a while for the engagement to grow, or worse, it might not grow at all.

Another example is that with the advent of ChatGPT, many companies are trying to transform their customer engagement bots to be more accurate. While the latest technology, such as GPT-4, might solve the issue, there could be underlying data challenges that no model could solve.

8. Lay out the challenges. Every AI solution comes with its own set of challenges. While it can block your product development, it also allows us to rethink our AI strategy. It is always good to highlight the challenges in building an AI solution for senior leadership.

9. Always have an elevator pitch:

   - Your senior leaders are limited in time and energy, so when they ask you what you have been up to, you should always have a minute of interesting pitch. This serves as a constant reminder of your product, and it also gets your product talked about in rooms where you are not present.

   - You can also use this elevator pitch in informal chats with senior leadership, maybe during meet-and-greets or internal events.

   Pro tip

   Instead of focusing on the algorithm, focus on the *what* and *why* of the workstream to have an impactful conversation.

Let's imagine a hypothetical scenario where a data scientist is building a recommendation engine for the firm, and the managing director meets them in the elevator and asks, "*How is it going?*". The pitch might be the following sample response:

> "We're building a recommendation engine that's already boosting engagement by over 20%. One challenge we faced early on was bias in the training data; it was skewing results toward a narrow user segment. To fix it, we rebalanced the dataset and introduced a feedback loop that adapts recommendations in real time. Now, the system personalizes content more accurately across diverse user profiles. It's exciting to see how this is driving both customer satisfaction and conversion. Happy to share more if you're interested!"

10. Have a plan B. The speed of innovation, especially within AI, is unmatched right now. With the advent of new models, priorities and strategies are bound to change. Having a plan B helps you prepare for factors you could control and some you couldn't. Plan B will help you pivot or pause the project if an extreme situation arises. Consider that you

have been in touch with your compliance team from day 1 and are negotiating the terms and conditions of the cloud platform. On the other hand, you are also speaking with the cloud provider about the evidence you could present to your cloud team. Despite you being proactive about everything, the cloud platform has not yet met specific auditory requirements, and they need some time to launch those for you. This is a situation where, most likely, you wouldn't be able to migrate your project to production and would have to halt the development.

Pro tip

You do not have to present this to leadership on day 1. Rather, it is a plan for you to have in your back pocket when someone asks or when such a situation arises. This is the last resort. Best practice is to build the AI solution in a modular (loosely coupled) fashion. This way, you can try to replace the components that don't work rather than scrap the entire solution.

All the preceding pointers are for data scientists or the technical community, but there is also an inherent responsibility of the senior leadership to cultivate and embrace the AI culture. Change brings anxiety within an organization. With AI, we have seen people worried about their jobs, and the anxiety is justified. Building AI solutions not only requires technical expertise but also a culture where new ideas and innovations are welcomed.

Developers and technical leaders need to seek support from upper management to celebrate the AI-first mindset. Here are a couple of things CXOs can do to achieve the same:

- **Invest in AI upskilling**: It is vital to hold AI seminars to upskill everyone in the company. Learning about the topic alleviates fear and cultivates a growth mindset. Learning can also be promoted by celebrating folks who are continuously completing certifications and motivating others to do the same.

- **Focus on hands-on experience**: Hold hackathons within the company to foster innovation. Teams can develop a use case or pick up one that they wanted to work on for a long time but couldn't due to time constraints. This is also a great way to develop new use cases that might benefit the company in the long run. Another great way to foster this is to hold apprenticeship programs where focused groups and experts work on an existing project. Still, as a stretch assignment, selected apprentices can continue to work on their day-to-day tasks and take this as an opportunity to learn new skills within the company.

In this section, we explored the best practices that technical teams can utilize to secure sponsorship from senior leadership. While executing any AI project is a costly endeavor, obtaining this sponsorship is a crucial step for successful implementation. Additionally, we discussed proactive measures that CXOs can take, such as investing in employee upskilling to prepare their workforce for an AI-driven future.

In the next section, we will illustrate how these practices can be applied by examining a hypothetical case study of a regulated company that successfully gained CXO support.

How AI got the CXO support — a hypothetical scenario

This is the story of a highly regulated company that aimed to build internal copilots to boost employee productivity.

Here were the key challenges in this initiative and how they were mitigated:

1. At first, leadership was hesitant to approve the budget to try proof of concepts (PoCs) or MVPs, afraid of the compliance and regulatory officers. What helped to solve this was involving compliance teams in the beginning to get the required paperwork done, so the developers could focus on building. Boundaries were set, such as not rolling out any PoC to external customers for the first few months.

2. Once the teams started building, there was cannibalization within the firm. Multiple teams were working on similar use cases with competing priorities. Having one common **center of excellence** (**CoE**) helped mitigate the issue. The CoE was a central place that knew about all the AI initiatives and would flag if multiple teams were working on the same use case. So either the teams would combine their efforts or pivot into something different.

3. Not everyone welcomes change; few leaders were ready to take the risks, but some were extremely apprehensive. So the ones who led the charge became an example for others. They were celebrated within the firm, which led to inspiring more people to come up with new ideas.

Gen AI was a black box for them. To bridge this gap, they invited experts to educate their employees on Gen AI and organized hackathons to help teams get comfortable with the technology. At the end of these hackathons/PoCs, teams presented their working demos to senior leadership, who were amazed by the potential of the technology. The company leveraged the CoE to vet these MVPs and eventually migrate the most impactful ones to production. The small working demo from the hackathon was supported by the right talent, resources, and legal buy-in.

Within eight months, one of the projects was rolled out to thousands of users. This project was a digital co-worker that helped analysts quickly pull data, write code, and documentation, so the developers could be more efficient. Feedback indicated that analysts who previously spent over five hours writing queries and answering business stakeholders' questions could now do so within an hour. They used the extra time to focus on strategic projects and found greater job satisfaction as they were no longer bogged down by mundane tasks. Some analysts even upskilled themselves on Gen AI to think of more use cases that could empower their peers.

The product's success was so significant that it received industry accolades and inspired competitors.

Here are the key lessons/takeaways from this case study:

- Educating your organization's people and empowering them to innovate not only elevates the organization but also sparks a domino effect, fostering a culture of continuous forward-thinking.

- Slides alone often fall short in showcasing the true impact of AI; you need a working demo to make the value tangible. Hackathons serve as an excellent way to achieve this, allowing teams to experiment, build, and experience AI's potential firsthand.

- Clearly demonstrating value through measurable success is crucial; time saved is often a key metric in these cases.

- Done is better than perfect, so it is always a good idea to celebrate progress rather than chasing perfection.

- Hackathons are a great way to kick-start PoCs development, and developers often thrive in a competitive environment.

- At the start of the AI journey, establishing a CoE with dedicated resources is essential to drive adoption and long-term success.

The case study serves as a mirror for enterprises that are skeptical about the impact of Gen AI within their teams or organizations. The first step to overcoming this skepticism is education, making upskilling a valuable starting point. While the benefits are not guaranteed, it is crucial to embrace the AI wave by beginning small but meaningful initiatives. This approach allows you to assess whether the impact is substantial enough to warrant scaling up or pivoting to another use case.

Summary

This chapter emphasized the importance of securing sponsorship from senior leadership for AI projects. It provided practical tips for technical teams on how to gain this support and concluded with a case study that demonstrates the real-world application of these strategies.

In the next chapter, we will focus on the steps following the securing of sponsorship, which involve starting the building process through a successful PoC.

Subscribe for a free eBook

New frameworks, evolving architectures, research drops, production breakdowns—AI_Distilled filters the noise into a weekly briefing for engineers and researchers working hands-on with LLMs and GenAI systems. Subscribe now and receive a free eBook, along with weekly insights that help you stay focused and informed.

Subscribe at `https://packt.link/80z6Y` or scan the QR code below.

5

Building an AI Proof of Concept and Measuring Your Solution

Proof of Concept, a.k.a, **PoC**, is perceived differently in organizations depending on their size, goals, end users, leadership strategy, and so on. We have all been in organizations of multiple sizes and have experienced this firsthand. To put this in context, in regulated industries, PoC might not even start until you have gained the required sponsorship and compliance approvals. But for start-ups or technology companies, PoC is a way to prove the idea, and they might operate in a "fail fast, innovate faster" mindset. Whatever organization you might be in, PoC is still the first step towards deploying the AI solution to production; hence, it is extremely important to spend time and resources on building it.

Each factor discussed in the previous chapters, such as framing the right AI problem, selecting the appropriate AI technology, and bringing the right stakeholders on board, is critical for building a compelling PoC. This chapter will explore how a well-executed PoC demonstrates the inner workings of your solution and helps gain the traction and buy-in needed for further development.

We will cover the following key topics in this chapter:

- PoC playbook – a guide to building effective PoCs
- Best practices for building a successful AI PoC
- Measuring the performance of a PoC
- Pilot to proof – a success story
- Putting it all together

PoC playbook — a guide to building effective PoCs

PoC is the first step to bringing your idea to life and showcasing the feasibility of your idea to investors or senior leadership within an organization. PoC can range from a simple model showcased in Excel to a sophisticated UI, depending on the use case, budget, resources, and time. It is possible to build the same use case with both Excel and a machine learning model. Let's say you are trying to perform forecasting. That can be achieved in Excel using simple statistical techniques such as ARIMA, and you could use a Python library for it. However, you cannot build a neural network model in Excel, which can be easily coded in Python using standard libraries. Such scenarios highlight the importance of using a code-first approach, rather than tools such as Excel.

In simple words, it is a small-scale, low-risk experiment designed to test the feasibility and potential impact of an AI solution for a specific use case. Consider your PoC as a rehearsal before the grand performance.

Let's dive further into the benefits of building a PoC:

- **Cost-effective**: Building a full-fledged AI solution requires time and resources, but building a PoC requires significantly fewer resources and saves time.

- **Fail fast and improve faster**: A PoC helps you prove whether the idea is suitable for the enterprise. You can quickly pivot to a new idea if the results are unfavorable.

- **Rapid deployment**: A PoC is a great way to test new features within a product and assess its advantages. This way, you can learn about the features that will work in the real world and include them in the roadmap. The ideal duration of building a PoC should be 4 to 6 weeks, but can vary depending on the complexity of the use case, data availability, team skill set, and so on.

- **Early issue detection**: A PoC allows you to detect potential issues in the product that might have been a roadblock in the later stages of development.

- **Valuable data and knowledge**: The PoC process provides insights into data needs, AI tools, and required skill sets for future projects.

Creating a PoC

Though we have covered a few of these steps in earlier chapters, we are reiterating them here to contextualize everything. Creating a PoC usually involves well-defined documentation outlining the project's requirements and objectives, as well as the responsibilities assigned to each stakeholder. Another outcome of a successful PoC is a roadmap of deployment to production.

Here is the five-step process that generally works for an enterprise:

1. **Define the need**: If you have reached this stage of creating a PoC and read the previous chapters, you have figured this out. This will include framing the problem, identifying the end users, analyzing historical solutions, defining the unique proposition, and estimating the resources needed to build the solution.

2. **Pick the technical approach**: When creating an AI solution, more often than not, you have a choice between multiple models. You could be choosing between a simple statistical model (e.g., ARIMA) and a deep learning model (e.g., LSTM), let's say, for a forecasting task. It is important to pen down all the approaches and ensure that you pick an approach for PoC that can be executed using limited resources. After a successful PoC, you can pick up a resource-intensive approach. Another thing to note is that data availability will also determine the approach.

   Sometimes, it is not about choosing just one model; it could be about using an array of different models to make an informed decision on what can be used for production. For example, in the case of forecasting tasks, depending on your data, deep learning might be a more effective approach, but you can only know that if you have compared the performance with statistical techniques such as ARIMA.

3. **Creating a working PoC**: Tons of people confuse this step with boiling the ocean, but that's not the purpose of the PoC. An ideal PoC should be a scaled-down yet working version of the solution. It should have the most crucial functionality and a basic UI for your end users to test the product. Avoid the nice-to-have features here and stick with a basic working model.

4. **Iterate and improve**: The PoC is not the final product, which means that during its testing, you will discover issues that should be mitigated in the next phase of the project, which is usually building an MVP. It is important to document all the feedback from your end users or any individuals who are testing your product.

5. **Create a roadmap**: Based on the PoC results, you will have a few action items. These could include refining the PoC, halting the project at PoC but documenting the learnings that could be applied to other projects, pivoting to another version of the solution, or migrating to production. It is important to socialize the next steps and milestones for your project so that everyone is informed.

In the next section, we will double-click on some possibilities that could arise after the PoC has been built and shipped.

Critical tactical decisions post-PoC for AI adoption

After building the PoC, it is essential to analyze the performance and make critical decisions to determine the next steps in your AI journey. Here are the three basic paths to consider:

1. **Refine the PoC:** Once the PoC is built, the next step is to analyze the results in detail to identify areas for improvement. This can include the following:

    a. **Improving model performance:** If the AI solution is underperforming or delivering results that aren't meeting expectations, a different approach may be required to improve accuracy.

    b. **Enhancing data quality:** During the PoC, you might realize that specific data is missing or of low quality. Refining the PoC could involve cleaning and strengthening the dataset or adding new, more relevant data.

    c. **Improving user experience:** Gathering feedback from end users and stakeholders is essential to understanding how the solution performs in real-world scenarios. Refining the PoC might include adjustments to make the solution more user-friendly or aligned with the business's needs.

    d. **Changing the success metric:** It is also possible that the metric you thought was relevant for the use case is no longer impactful, so it might be a good idea to take a step back and consider the success metrics.

    End result: You would gather the feedback on the refined PoC and create a **minimal viable product (MVP)**. The details for building the MVP are mentioned in Step 3.

2. **Pivot:** Sometimes, the results of a PoC show that the initial approach is not delivering the expected value or that business goals changed while you were building the PoC. In such cases, you might need to pivot:

    a. **Rethink the approach:** If the PoC proves that the original AI approach is not viable (e.g., due to high complexity, lack of data, or poor performance), it may be necessary to explore alternative AI models, algorithms, or even business problems to solve.

    b. **Revisit problem framing:** It's possible that the problem you set out to solve wasn't framed correctly for an AI solution. You may need to redefine the business challenge or explore other use cases that are a better fit for AI.

    c. **Change the technology stack:** Sometimes, a pivot might involve switching to a different technology, AI model, or toolset better suited to achieving the desired business outcomes.

End result: You would do thorough testing and evaluation again, gather feedback from your end users, and make a determination on whether the project should be deployed to production.

3. **Build an MVP:** If the PoC delivers promising results, the next logical step is to build an MVP. This involves the following:

    a. **Scaling the solution**: The MVP is a more robust version of the PoC that can be deployed to a larger audience. It will likely need additional features, security measures, and scalability improvements to handle more complex use cases or larger datasets.

    b. **Integrating with existing systems**: Building an MVP requires integrating the solution with other systems and workflows in the organization. This ensures that the AI solution can operate within the business ecosystem.

    c. **Testing real-world performance**: The MVP phase includes extensive testing to ensure the AI solution works well in a real-world environment. You'll need to monitor **Key Performance Indicators (KPIs)** and make adjustments as necessary.

    d. **Gathering user feedback**: As with the PoC, it's important to continue gathering feedback from stakeholders and end users to refine the solution during the MVP stage.

    e. **Leverage cloud platforms**: A practical approach to scale the AI solution is to leverage cloud infrastructure. Managed AI services, such as AI/ML platforms offered by cloud hyperscalers can streamline the process of training, deploying, and maintaining AI models at scale while delivering high availability and resilience.

    f. **Change management**: Change management is critical to successfully adopting AI within your organization, as it often requires significant shifts in roles, responsibilities, and processes. Without a proper change management process in place, you could meet resistance from teams accustomed to legacy workflows, which can delay AI deployment or, worse, cause the initiative to fail.

    g. **Communicate clearly:** To combat resistance, you must communicate how AI will enhance rather than replace existing roles. Align your AI projects with overarching business goals to show how AI adoption supports broader organizational success. Leadership should foster a culture that encourages experimentation and values data-driven decision-making.

End result: By now, all stakeholders and senior leadership should be convinced of the solution. This is the point after which you start creating deployment plans for production and gathering the required resources.

We discussed the three critical decisions you would have to make post the PoC creation. But to lead to a successful outcome, there are certain best practices you can follow. In the next section, we will discuss the best practices in detail.

Best practices for building a successful AI PoC

We understand there is no blueprint for best practices around the AI PoC, but this is what we have learned from our combined experience of shipping multiple PoCs across different domains:

- Opt-in for agile methodology to have more flexibility in your AI project.
- Define success for your AI project in the beginning. Then, set incremental goals and milestones to track progress throughout the PoC.
- Secure sponsorship from senior leadership before beginning the development.
- Ensure that you have high-quality data before the development. This will set you up for success. This includes detailed data quality checks, robust data cleaning measures, and a plan to augment data through synthetic data generation techniques, if necessary.
- Partner with experienced AI consultants and solutions architects to guide the PoC.
- Invest in training and development to upskill your team in AI. The training and development can be in terms of inviting experts, giving the opportunity for folks to attend conferences, or providing free subscriptions to e-learning platforms.
- If integrating with a legacy solution, document a detailed plan highlighting how the integration will work. This plan should also include decommissioning any components to make the solution more effective.
- Meet your stakeholders regularly to update them on PoC progress and seek their input to address concerns and incorporate suggestions.
- To avoid last-minute hassle, focus on data governance during the PoC stage. This should include data anonymization, access controls, compliance requirements, and encryption to protect sensitive data.
- You should have a plan to deploy to production, as that is the goal. Include the next steps, resources, and timeline for deployment to keep everyone informed. Here, it is also important to define what success will look like in production.

- Meet with the model review committee from the get-go to seek their input and ask your data scientists to start the documentation during the PoC development phase to avoid missing out on any details.

- Start with simple models for PoC so you can manage them with limited resources.

- Develop a framework for testing and evaluating your AI solutions with clearly defined metrics. We will explore this in the upcoming section.

- Plan the scalability of your AI solution from the start. This means developing PoC AI that can grow and adapt as your business needs evolve. It also means allocating cloud resources to scale faster.

- Define KPIs to track the PoC's success against its objectives.

- Regularly analyze performance data to identify areas for improvement and optimize AI models accordingly.

- Normalize failing so your team members are continuously innovating and evolving to a better AI-driven solution.

- Create a detailed report summarizing the PoC process, including successes, failures, and key takeaways to inform future development.

- Every AI initiative should be part of a broader strategic vision that aligns with enterprise-wide goals. Establish clear KPIs from the outset to measure the success of your AI projects, then ensure that cross-functional teams support AI initiatives to foster collaboration.

- Your organization should implement ethical AI frameworks to ensure the responsible use of AI. You should also establish a dedicated AI ethics board and stay updated with evolving regulations to address compliance needs and maintain public trust in your AI deployments. It is also important to comply with the regulations of the country of residence, such as if you are an EU resident, the laws are more stringent than those in the US (please refer to the *EU AI Act*: https://artificialintelligenceact.eu/).

At the end of the day, remember the PoC is the first step towards deploying to production, so ensure that the overall strategy includes that, so you and your organization are prepared for deployment.

Though building a PoC might seem like an obvious choice for most use cases, there are also scenarios when building a PoC is unnecessary. Let's uncover some of those here:

- If the use case is time-sensitive, such as forecasting drug supply during a pandemic, since this is a life-and-death kind of use case, you might want to jump straight to the final product

- If the task just involves simple statistical methods and there is no plan for leveraging complex ML or deep learning algorithms, here the PoC investment cannot be justified

Building an AI solution is one part of the equation, but measuring its success is equally important to prove its worth. Measuring the AI solution is one of the biggest challenges practitioners face, so we propose a framework to reduce the burden. In the next section, let's dig deep into what metrics matter for AI success.

Measuring the performance of a PoC

There is a famous saying, "You can't improve what you can't measure." This is the case for enterprise AI solutions as well. Once you have built the PoC, you need to justify the investment; hence, it becomes vital to have a robust framework to help you track your AI solutions. As the AI solutions evolve and move from PoC to MVP, relying on the technical model performance gives you an incomplete picture of your AI solution. The technical metrics provide us with the relative performance of the predictive model compared to the baseline, such as random guessing, but offer no direct derivation of the business value of the model. Along with that, we also have to consider that models are not launched in silos; they are usually part of a system where the model is either integrated into a legacy system or launched as an application. You need to be able to track the performance of the AI system as well.

To cover all these aspects, we propose the following guidelines, which provide a 360-degree view of how the AI solution is performing so that you can make appropriate remediation. Measuring the PoC is the same as measuring the performance of the AI system, which we cover in detail in future chapters. Following is a quick snapshot of the metrics that you might want to consider.

Model metrics

These metrics evaluate the technical performance of the AI/ML model and ensure that it meets the expected level of accuracy, efficiency, and reliability. We will discuss this in more detail in *Chapter 6*.

System metrics

With the advent of GenAI systems, it has become critical to measure how your overall system is performing. GenAI systems are complicated and often consist of multiple components, such as data, prompts, and foundation models, all presented as a UI or integration within a tool.

Here are some metrics to consider while tracking system quality:

- **Data relevance**: The degree to which all data is necessary for the current model and project. Outdated or irrelevant data can introduce biases and inefficiencies, leading to harmful outputs.

- **Data and AI assets and reusability**: The percentage of your data and AI assets that are discoverable and usable. It is crucial to maintain a system where you can measure data drift and update the data as soon as performance is below the threshold.

- **Throughput**: This is the volume of information a generative AI system can handle in a specific period. Calculating this metric involves understanding the model's processing speed, efficiency at scale, parallelization, and optimized resource utilization.

- **System latency**: This is the time it takes the system to respond with an answer. This includes any networking delays, data latency, model latency, and so on. Compromised system latency can hamper user experience and significantly reduce adoption within an organization or brand royalty. Speaking with your cloud provider to provide constant throughput is crucial, so you don't have to worry about significant traffic hitting your application simultaneously.

- **Integration and backward compatibility**: The upstream and downstream systems APIs can integrate directly with GenAI models. You should also consider whether the next version of models will impact the system built on top of existing models (not just limited to prompt engineering).

Business metrics

These are some of the most difficult to define. But we like to think of them as follows: What do you define as a "success" for the AI/ML system?

Align this with the KPI for the use case example: for a recommendation, it could be retention or an increase in net new customers; in that case, success might look like a 5% increase in net new customers.

Some examples of business value improvement metrics include the following:

- Customer service

  - Reduction in average handling time and cost per interaction

  - Lift in customer satisfaction (NPS)

- Marketing

  - Time saved (e.g., hours) from streamlined processes: brief writing, editing, collaboration, and so on.

  - Higher **Return on Ad Spend (ROAS)** due to increased personalization

  - Augmented creativity and idea generation

- Healthcare

    - Increased time with patients by reducing administrative burdens

    - Better patient outcomes from clear, consistent care plans

    - Improved efficiency, reduced wait times, and higher care capacity

- Retail

    - Lift in revenue per visit

    - Increases in sales through AI-driven product suggestions

    - Improvements in customer satisfaction/experience

- Product development

    - Percentage of content influenced by generative AI tools

    - Employee hours saved from automating processes

    - Accelerated time-to-value from product launches

Safety metrics

According to KPMG, 61% of people aren't sure they can trust AI systems. Trusting AI means being confident about its decisions and feeling okay sharing data to help it improve. But many people worry about three risks: AI compromising our privacy, harming society, or not being tested enough to be reliable.

1. **Bias assessment**: It is critical to measure the representativeness of data. Bias gets crippled through data. Hence, ensuring the dataset is diverse and represents all classes is important. Bias can cripple your data in the following three ways:

    1. **Selection bias**: This occurs when data is selected that isn't representative of the population as a whole and, therefore, presents a bias.

    2. **Systematic bias**: A consistent error that repeats itself throughout the model.

    3. **Response bias**: Data participants respond to questions in a way deemed false or inaccurate.

    To combat the bias, here are a few data pre-processing steps that can be done proactively:

    - Be mindful of outliers, as removing them might not be the best solution. It is crucial to analyze the outliers as they might be an indication of a population that is missing from your data.

- Handling missing variables can also be a key indicator in introducing bias. If missing values are ignored or replaced with the "average" of the data, you are effectively altering the results. Your data collection would then be more biased to results than reflecting the general "average."

- Over-filtering data can often result in the absence of representation of the original data target.

- Masking PII is also a great practice unless you are building a healthcare solution in which age or gender is an essential parameter in determining the outcome.

  Along with bias in data, it is also important to track bias in your AI system. This could look like men receiving better offers or richer credit lines than women. Within GenAI solutions, it is important to have robust safety systems in place that block any kind of harmful attack. Even if the user tries to jailbreak the solution, the LLM will be able to block it by responding, "I am sorry, I can't answer this," or something similar.

2. **Prompt injections**: Prompt injection attacks happen when users subvert a language model's programming by providing alternate instructions in natural language. For example, the model would execute code instead of translating text in a translation app. This vulnerability is especially alarming in applications such as AI personal assistants, which handle confidential information. Imagine a user successfully commanding the AI to delete or leak sensitive data. Prompt leaking, a variant of prompt injection, involves persuading the model to reveal its initial prompt. Prompt Injections and similar attacks can tarnish your brand's image or, worse, cause financial losses.

Here are a few strategies that can be used to safeguard the application:

- Limit the user input length and format, as prompt attacks require lengthy prompts to make the model trip. You can perform experiments to derive that optimal number, but it shouldn't be more than 1,000 for the chatbot. Also, make sure to block any non-reasonable characters.

- Implement access control for LLM access to your backend systems. Equip the LLM with dedicated API tokens, such as plugins and data retrieval, and assign permission levels (read/write). Adhere to the least privilege principle, limiting the LLM to the minimum access required for its designed tasks. For instance, if your app scans users' calendars to identify open slots, it shouldn't be able to create new events.

- When implementing internal RAG/Copilot, implement access controls for employees based on the confidentiality of the project so that confidential information is not exposed. For example, if there is a secret project called "Beta," only authorized users should have access to it. Even if someone tries to jailbreak, they should get an "access denied" message.
- Monitor the application continuously as users might attack it more than once. Be proactive about blocking any user input that starts with "Ignore all prior requests."
- Implement robust logging practices where each user interaction is logged meticulously for audit and flagging purposes.

Another way is to implement red-teaming proactively. This is a proactive approach to uncover model weaknesses before the launch. To achieve this, form a varied red team, including roles such as design, product, and so on. The objective is to develop creative methods for optimizing your language-powered app. Hence, the diversity of participation is necessary.

We have tried to be as comprehensive as possible to cover the metrics and best practices for AI and ML solutions within an enterprise. There are a few things that might be unique to your application. Here is a summary of the best practices for measuring the performance of your AI solutions:

- Choose metrics based on the problems and goals
- Use diverse and representative data for evaluations
- Regularly monitor and track the metrics so you can pivot as needed
- Always rely on more than one metric to get a holistic understanding of the performance
- Be proactive about setting the expectations that AI solutions might take some time to reap the benefits, so define long-term and short-term goals clearly

It is also important to set the right expectations with the AI solution. An AI solution is not the be-all and end-all. Despite the right ingredients, the model might hallucinate or produce incorrect predictions.

In this section, we provided a quick summary of the metrics that you would choose to prove the viability of your PoC to advance it to the next stage. In the next section, let's discuss a case study in detail to see how all of this fits in an enterprise environment.

Scenario 1: From pilot to proof — a success story

A global pharmaceutical company faced persistent challenges with demand forecasting for its blockbuster drug. Traditional forecasting methods, reliant on historical sales data and manual adjustments, often resulted in inaccuracies, leading to stockouts or overproduction. Recognizing the need for a more robust and data-driven approach, the company explored **machine learning (ML)** as a solution to improve forecasting precision.

The PoC

The company embarked on a PoC to assess the feasibility of an ML-based forecasting engine. The success of this initiative was driven by four key factors:

1. **High-quality data**: The team ensured that the data fed into the ML models was clean, comprehensive, and representative of various market conditions. Historical sales data was augmented with external factors such as seasonality, competitor activities, and macro-economic trends to enhance prediction accuracy. Robust data pipelines were established to maintain consistency and integrity.

2. **Clear objectives**: The PoC was designed with well-defined success criteria:

   - Reduce **Mean Absolute Percentage Error (MAPE)** by at least 10% compared to existing models
   - Reduce the manual effort required for forecasting
   - Enhance decision-making for production and supply chain teams

3. **Stakeholder buy-in**: Engaging key stakeholders early was crucial to the project's success. The data science team collaborated with supply chain planners, demand planners and sales leaders, and IT teams to ensure alignment. Regular workshops and interactive sessions helped address concerns, set expectations, and secure executive sponsorship.

4. **Rapid prototyping and iteration**: Instead of a lengthy development cycle, the team built a working prototype within a few weeks using cloud-based ML platforms. They iterated quickly based on feedback, refining model features and incorporating domain expertise to improve performance.

Moving to production

After the PoC demonstrated a 10% improvement in forecasting accuracy, leadership approved the full-scale deployment. Key steps in transitioning to production included the following:

- **Automation and integration**: The ML model was integrated into the company's existing demand planning tools, enabling seamless data ingestion and automated updates

- **User training and adoption**: Supply chain and sales teams were trained on how to interpret and act on ML-generated forecasts, ensuring smooth adoption
- **Continuous monitoring and refinement**: A governance framework was established to monitor performance, retrain models with new data, and adapt to evolving market conditions

Results and impact

Within six months of deployment, the company saw the following:

- A 10% reduction in MAPE, reducing instances of stockouts and excess inventory
- Improved operational efficiency, with less manual intervention required in the forecasting process
- Greater business agility, allowing the company to respond faster to market shifts

Key takeaways

Here are the key takeaways from this scenario:

- High-quality data is the foundation of any successful ML initiative.
- Clear objectives ensure alignment and measurable success.
- Securing stakeholder buy-in early accelerates adoption and smooths the transition to production.
- Rapid prototyping and iterative development enable quick wins and continuous improvement.
- Education is the key to success. It is important to decode technical concepts for the business stakeholders so that they feel confident about the PoC.

This scenario illustrates how a successful PoC can evolve into a scalable enterprise AI solution that delivers measurable ROI and business impact. By grounding your approach in solid data fundamentals and a clearly defined objective, you can confidently move toward a production-ready AI deployment.

Scenario 2: Failed AI PoC — predictive maintenance for industrial equipment

A mid-sized manufacturing firm specializing in industrial HVAC systems wanted to reduce downtime and maintenance costs by implementing an AI-based predictive maintenance solution.

PoC objective: Build a machine learning model that could predict equipment failures at least 48 hours in advance, using sensor data from compressors, motors, and temperature regulators.

PoC setup

- **Data sources**: Historical sensor logs, maintenance records, and technician notes
- **Model used**: Random Forest classifier trained on labeled failure events
- **Timeline**: Six-week sprint with a cross-functional team of data scientists, IT engineers, and operations managers

Outcome

- The PoC was shelved after 8 weeks
- The team concluded that more groundwork was needed in data engineering, stakeholder alignment, and change management
- The company reverted to scheduled maintenance and postponed AI adoption

Here's what went wrong with the PoC:

- **Unclear problem definition**:

  - The team didn't align on what constituted a "failure". Some considered any downtime a failure, while others only counted catastrophic breakdowns.
  - KPIs were vague. "Reduce downtime" was not quantified, and no baseline was established.

- **Poor data quality**:

  - Sensor data was inconsistent. Some machines had missing logs; others had different sampling rates.
  - Maintenance records were handwritten and poorly digitized, making them unusable for training.

- **Technical limitations**:

  - The model showed promising results in Jupyter notebooks but failed in real-time deployment.
  - It couldn't handle streaming data and crashed frequently due to memory overload.

- **No business buy-in**:

  - Operations managers didn't trust the predictions and continued using manual checks.

- The model flagged false positives, leading to unnecessary maintenance and frustration.
- No ROI analysis was done, and stakeholders saw it as a "science experiment".

So, here are the lessons learned:

- Define success metrics upfront and align them across teams
- Invest in data readiness before modeling
- Engage business stakeholders early and often
- Validate technical feasibility in real-world conditions

In this section, we explored two case studies, which are basically two sides of a coin: one was a successful PoC with great results, stakeholder buy-in, and a clear path to production, while the other was a failed PoC, which did provide invaluable insights to the organization but did not make it to production. These case studies should provide clear guidelines on what to do and what not to do while creating PoCs within your organization. Let's wrap up this chapter by reviewing a PoC checklist.

Putting it all together

Here is a quick and actionable checklist that you could refer to for successful PoCs:

1. Met clearly defined objectives:

    - Did it solve the defined problem?
    - Did it meet the KPIs or success thresholds you established upfront?
    - Were these results validated using real or representative data?

    If it does not meet all the objectives, reflect to see what might be missing and fix that before proceeding to the next step.

2. Demonstrated technical viability:

    - Are the model performance metrics (accuracy, precision, recall, etc.) strong?
    - Can it handle real-world data without breaking or misfiring?
    - Does it scale or integrate with existing systems?

    If it fails here, consider more iterations before production.

3. Showed business value:

   - Did it improve speed, efficiency, revenue, or customer experience?

   - Do business stakeholders see its potential?

   - Is the ROI promising if scaled?

   If the business value is unclear, the PoC may not be ready to move forward.

4. Gained stakeholder confidence:

   - Are non-technical decision-makers excited about it?

   - Was it explained clearly, with a compelling demo or result summary?

   - Is there momentum to proceed with a pilot or full deployment?

   If there is still resistance from senior leadership, this is where you would like advocates within the organization to vouch for you; these could be your business stakeholders, who push for the change.

5. Final success indicators:

   - Proved your hypothesis

   - Delivered measurable business or process value

   - Earned stakeholder support

   The end goal is to have a clear path to production.

Summary

In this chapter, we explored how to build a successful **Proof of Concept (PoC)** that lays the foundation for deploying an enterprise-ready AI solution. A PoC often serves as the first glimpse into what the final solution might look like, making it essential to focus on the fundamentals: defining a clear objective, securing the right data, and establishing success criteria. These elements are critical to ensuring your PoC is not just a technical exercise, but a strategic step toward production.

In the next chapter, we'll dive into best practices for machine learning development.

References

- BairesDev. (n.d.). *How to Build Trust in AI: Key Metrics to Measure User Confidence*. BairesDev Blog. https://www.bairesdev.com/blog/trust-in-ai-key-metrics-user-confidence/

- Built In. (n.d.). *Performing Opportunity Sizing. Built In.* https://builtin.com/articles/opportunity-sizing

- Codefinity. (n.d.). *How to Choose the Right Metric for Your Model.* Codefinity Blog. https://codefinity.com/blog/How-to-Choose-the-Right-Metric-for-Your-Model

- Devansh. (n.d.). *7 methods to secure LLM apps from prompt injections and jailbreaks.* Medium. https://machine-learning-made-simple.medium.com/7-methods-to-secure-llm-apps-from-prompt-injections-and-jailbreaks-11987b274012

- Django Stars. (n.d.). *How to Create an Effective AI Proof of Concept (AI PoC).* Django Stars Blog. https://djangostars.com/blog/how-ai-proof-of-concept-can-save-you-money/

- GlobalNodes. (n.d.). *Overcoming Challenges in Generative AI POCs: Strategies for Success.* DEV Community. https://dev.to/globalnodes/overcoming-challenges-in-generative-ai-pocs-strategies-for-success-3nhb

- Google Cloud. (n.d.). *KPIs for Gen AI: Why measuring your new AI is essential to its success.* Google Cloud Blog. https://cloud.google.com/transform/kpis-for-gen-ai-why-measuring-your-new-ai-is-essential-to-its-success

- Google Developers. (n.d.). *Understanding and framing an ML problem.* Google. https://developers.google.com/machine-learning/problem-framing/problem

- Graphite Note. (n.d.). *How Much Data Do You Need for Machine Learning?* Graphite Note. https://graphite-note.com/how-much-data-is-needed-for-machine-learning/

- Harvard Business Review. (2023, October). *How AI Can Help Leaders Make Better Decisions Under Pressure.* Harvard Business Review. https://hbr.org/2023/10/how-ai-can-help-leaders-make-better-decisions-under-pressure

- Rackspace Technology. (n.d.). *Eight Common Blockers When Transitioning AI from PoC to Production.* Fair by Rackspace. https://fair.rackspace.com/insights/eight-blockers-transitioning-ai-production/

- Scalable AI. (n.d.). *AI Metrics That Matter: Navigate Your Project to Success.* Scalable AI Insights. https://insights.scalableai.com/index.php/ai-metrics-that-matter-navigate-your-project-to-success/

- Stratoflow. (n.d.). *What Is a POC and How to Create a Proof of Concept?* Stratoflow. https://stratoflow.com/proof-of-concept-definition/

- Twine. (n.d.). *Bias in Data Collection: How to Identify and Correct Data Bias.* Twine Blog. https://www.twine.net/blog/bias-in-data-collection/

Get This Book's PDF Version and Exclusive Extras

UNLOCK NOW

Scan the QR code (or go to `packtpub.com/unlock`). Search for this book by name, confirm the edition, and then follow the steps on the page.

Note: Keep your invoice handy. Purchase made directly from packt don't require one.

Part 3

Deploying and Proving ML Value

In *Part 3* of this book, we will provide a comprehensive guide to the complete, end-to-end life cycle of a **machine learning** (**ML**) system, moving from defining its purpose to proving its causal impact on the business. We will start with the foundational framework for success, moving beyond simple accuracy to define multi-dimensional, business-aligned goals, essential guardrail metrics to prevent unintended harm, and surrogate metrics to track long-term objectives. Next, we will dive into "productization," which is the critical process of operationalizing models from experimental notebooks into robust, production-grade systems. We will discuss MLOps best practices, the importance of reproducible pipelines for code and data, and the architectural choices for model serving. Finally, we will explore the science of causal inference to answer the critical question, "Did the system do what it was intended to do?", covering the "gold standard" of randomized control trials (A/B testing) as well as advanced observational techniques and optimization methods such as multi-arm bandits.

This part contains the following chapters:

- *Chapter 6, Beyond Accuracy: A Guide to Defining Metrics for Adoption*
- *Chapter 7, From Model to Market: Operationalizing ML Systems*
- *Chapter 8, From Metrics to Measurement: Experimentation and Causal Inference*

6

Beyond Accuracy: A Guide to Defining Metrics for Adoption

As we discussed in *Chapter 1*, the idea for any successful ML application is to have a measurable metric. ML generally is an iterative process, and the idea is to improve experiments or enhancements.

Defining success for AI/ML models is far more nuanced than selecting a single metric. It requires a structured, multi-dimensional approach. This chapter begins by establishing the importance of clear success metrics and the foundational principles that make them effective. It then explores the role of guardrail metrics to prevent unintended side effects, followed by a discussion on operational latency and the evolving nature of model performance. The narrative continues by highlighting the misalignment between technical loss functions and business metrics and introducing surrogate metrics as a practical solution for bridging short- and long-term goals. We also delve into multi-objective optimization through the Pareto frontier, cost considerations in scaling AI solutions, and finally, the critical role of responsible AI in ensuring fairness, transparency, and societal alignment. Through these interconnected themes, the chapter provides a holistic framework for defining, measuring, and sustaining success in AI/ML systems.

The following key topics will be covered in the chapter:

- The need to define success metrics
- Fundamental principles of a success metric

The need to define success metrics

A crucial first step when operationalizing AI/ML models is clearly defining what "success" looks like. Without an established success criterion, there is no structured way to assess the effectiveness of a model. A well-defined success metric serves as a feedback loop, enabling teams to track the progress and performance of a model in real time. It ensures alignment between business goals and model behavior, helping stakeholders make informed decisions. Moreover, it provides a foundation for setting thresholds, triggering alerts, and guiding model improvements over time.

When success metrics are missing or poorly defined, teams may deploy underperforming models, misallocate resources, or optimize for the wrong objectives, which ultimately lead to financial losses, degraded user experience, and loss of stakeholder trust.

Fundamental principles of a success metric

For a success metric to be meaningful, it must adhere to the following key principles:

- **Specific**: The metric must directly align with the business objective and should not be ambiguous. This ensures that the AI/ML model is solving the right problem.
- **Measurable**: A metric is only useful if it can be quantified. Measurability is essential for tracking progress and for drawing insights from the model's performance.
- **Actionable**: The chosen metric should provide meaningful insights that lead to specific actions. If a metric signals poor performance, it should be clear what steps need to be taken to improve it.
- **Realistic**: Success metrics should be attainable, given the available resources and constraints.
- **Time-bound**: The performance of the AI/ML model should be evaluated within a defined time frame to monitor its effectiveness over short-term and long-term periods.

Take, for example, a recommendation engine used in an e-commerce platform. A specific success metric could be the **conversion rate** (**CR**), which measures the percentage of users who made a purchase after interacting with product recommendations. The CR is specific (it measures purchases), measurable (the ratio of conversions to interactions), actionable (changes can be made to improve it), realistic (based on past performance), and time-bound (evaluated daily, weekly, or monthly). Is defining a success criterion good enough to ensure success? Maybe not. Another example is improving customer experience with chatbots, which can answer initial queries and provide relevant responses. In such cases, success metrics could include a reduction of customer service calls or an increase in the **net promoter score** (**NPS**) based on surveys.

Another example is responding with visualizations for business reports when the user asks in their language of choice. If we take a lot of time to come up with the business report and visualization, it's a bad user experience, and we will miss out on the market. AI models without a well-defined success metric often struggle to drive adoption. This is evident with text generation models, where comparing generated messages or aligning them with ground truth can be challenging. Various evaluation techniques have been proposed, each with its own assumptions. For instance, if the focus is on high-quality messages, BLEU scores are commonly used; for diversity, ROUGE scores are more appropriate. In cases where both quality and diversity need to be optimized, MS-Jaccard may be a better choice. While these are quantitative methods for evaluating generated text, they come with specific assumptions, and understanding these can help mitigate potential issues. With the recent advancement in leveraging another LLM for evaluation, as suggested in *Reference-Guided Verdict: LLMs-as-Judges in Automatic Evaluation of Free-Form Text* by Sher Badshah, the sky is the limit. Next, let's look at guardrail metrics, which ensure that while models optimize for success, they don't unintentionally harm other critical business objectives. In the following section, we'll explore how to define, monitor, and enforce these guardrails effectively in production systems.

Guardrail metrics — balancing short-term success with long-term objectives

Sometimes optimizing one metric can have unintended consequences on other important aspects of the business. Guardrail metrics help maintain a balance between the primary success criterion and other essential business objectives. While optimizing for success, businesses must ensure that they don't compromise other key performance indicators.

Let's take that e-commerce recommendation engine as an example again. Say you've got a system recommending products to users. You could define your success metric as **CR**, which tracks the percentage of users who make a purchase after clicking on a recommendation. CR ticks all the boxes. It's specific (measuring purchases from recommendations), it's measurable (it's just a ratio), it's actionable (if the CR drops, you know you need to tweak something), it's realistic (you know based on historical data what's achievable), and it's time-bound (you could measure it daily, weekly, or monthly).

But is that enough? Just having a success metric in place, does that guarantee the model's success? Not quite. There's more to it, guardrail metrics. These are the metrics that help us avoid unintended consequences. Think about it: if all you're focused on is boosting the CR, what happens if the AI model starts pushing aggressive recommendations that users find annoying or overwhelming? Sure, the CR might go up in the short term, but you could damage the long-term relationship with your customers. Not a great idea, right?

Another example in finance would be predicting churn from a subscription program where various reward offers are given to retain valuable customers. However, if the cost sensitivity is not taken into consideration as a guardrail, the reward program may cost a large sum of money to run and may not justify the **return on investment** (**ROI**) from the model.

This paves the way for us to not only measure CR in product recommendations or churn rate in subscription programs, but also to determine whether guardrails are maintained in terms of annoyance, which can be measured as daily active users or app deletion every week, or costs to justify ROI.

Operational latency

Another essential consideration is operational latency, which refers to whether the system can provide timely predictions under realistic conditions. Meeting **service-level agreements** (**SLAs**) for response times often depends on architectural choices, such as whether models are served in real time or in batches. While **large language models** (**LLMs**) offer impressive capabilities, they can be slow without specialized infrastructure. Balancing speed, cost, and performance becomes critical here, especially as real-time systems may require significant infrastructure investments. Usually, it's a great idea to monitor the 95th percentile or 99th percentile latency for most ML applications, especially customer-facing solutions.

Evolving metrics – monitoring model performance over time

Here's another thing to consider, metrics *change*. Yes, ML/AI solutions live in a world of assumptions and assumptions change, so do metrics. What worked for you when you first deployed the model might not work six months down the line. At the start, you might focus on something such as user engagement or click-through rates to make sure the model is doing its basic job of getting recommendations in front of people. But as the model matures, you'll shift your focus to more business-oriented metrics such as lifetime value or long-term customer retention. AI models aren't static, and neither should your metrics be. *You've got to adapt* as the model grows, as the market shifts, and as business priorities change.

Performance can evolve in three ways:

- **Deteriorating performance**: Over time, an AI/ML model might suffer from performance degradation. For example, the quality of predictions may drop due to changes in user behavior, market conditions, or shifts in data distribution. This phenomenon, known as data drift, requires businesses to regularly retrain and update the model. For instance, a recommendation model that once had a high conversion rate might see a dip due to evolving customer preferences, necessitating updates in feature engineering and retraining.

- **Improving performance**: Sometimes, a model may start performing better over time, either due to improved data quality, larger datasets, or model refinement. It's crucial to continuously measure success metrics even when performance improves. However, businesses should also be cautious when a metric shows sustained improvements without corresponding external factors. This could point to overfitting or model gaming, where the model starts to exploit shortcuts in the data instead of learning generalizable patterns. Another example for improvement in performance over time can become evident with reinforcement approaches, where online learning updates the environment parameters to reach the optimal goal.

- **Stagnant performance**: If the performance of the model remains static over an extended period, it's time to explore new techniques or conduct feature engineering. Even if the metric doesn't deteriorate, it could indicate that the model is no longer adapting to changing environments or is not sufficiently optimized.

By regularly monitoring and revising models, businesses can ensure that their AI/ML solutions stay relevant and impactful over time.

Linking model metrics to business wins

What's the point of building a super-accurate AI model if it doesn't actually help a company make more money or work better? A model can get a perfect score on paper, but if it has no impact on real-world business goals such as keeping customers happy or cutting down on waste, then it's really just a waste of time and money.

The key is to pick the right way to measure success, and that really depends on what kind of problem you're trying to solve with your AI. We'll look at a few ways to measure success.

- **Supervised learning (did the model learn the right answers?)**: This is the most familiar type of AI, where we give the model a bunch of examples with the correct answers and ask it to learn the pattern.

- **For classification models (is it this or that?)**: When a model has to sort things into buckets, such as flagging an email as "spam" or "not spam," just looking at overall accuracy can be a trap, especially if one bucket is way bigger than the other. It's better to use a few specific tools:

  - **Precision and recall**: You have to think about these two together. Imagine you're a bouncer at a club. You want to let in all the cool people (recall), but if you're not careful, you might let in some trouble-makers. On the other hand, you could be super strict and only let in people you're 100% sure are cool (precision), but you might turn away a lot of great people. The F1-score helps you find the right balance between these two goals.

- **ROC curve and AUC**: This is basically a report card for how good the model is at telling two groups apart. The final score, **area under the curve** (AUC), tells you how confidently it can separate one from the other. An AUC of 1.0 is a perfect score, while 0.5 means the model is just flipping a coin.

- **Calibration**: This is all about trust. If your weather app says there's a 70% chance of rain, you expect it to rain about 7 out of 10 times. A well-calibrated model is one whose confidence you can actually believe.

- **For regression models (guess a prediction/number)**: When the model is trying to predict a specific number, such as a house price or company sales, we measure success by how close its guesses are:

  - **Mean absolute error (MAE)**: This is the most straightforward measurement. It tells you, on average, how far off your model's guess was. If the MAE for a sales forecast is $500, it means your predictions are off by about $500 on average. It's simple and easy to understand.

  - **Root mean squared error (RMSE)**: This one is a bit different because it gets really upset about big mistakes. It penalizes a single, wildly wrong guess much more than a bunch of small errors. You'd use RMSE when being way off is a business disaster, like not ordering nearly enough of your most popular product.

- **Unsupervised learning (did we find any useful patterns?)**: With unsupervised learning, we don't give the model any answers. We just give it a pile of data and ask it to find interesting structures or groups on its own.

- **For clustering (grouping things)**:

  - **Silhouette score**: After the model has grouped your data, this score tells you whether those groups actually make sense. A high score means the clusters are dense and well-separated, like distinct friend groups at a party. A low score means all the data points are just mixed together in one big, messy blob.

  - **Davies-Bouldin index**: Think of this as the "anti-social" score for clusters. A low score is good—it means each cluster remains distinct and doesn't overlap with others, indicating clean separation.

- **For dimensionality reduction (simplifying things):**

  - **Explained variance**: Imagine summarizing a 500-page book into a 10-page summary. "Explained variance" tells you what percentage of the original plot you kept. A 95% score means your short summary is excellent and captures almost everything important, proving your simplified data is still highly useful.

- **Knowledge-based AI (is our digital expert actually an expert?)**: This type of AI doesn't learn from data patterns but operates on a pre-programmed "brain" of facts and rules, like a digital encyclopedia or an expert system for diagnosing machine failures. Success isn't about statistical error; it's about correctness and utility.

  - **Coverage**: How comprehensive is our digital librarian's library? If it's a medical diagnostic tool, does it cover 50 diseases or 1,000? This measures the breadth of its knowledge.

  - **Query accuracy**: When you ask a question, does it give the right answer? If the AI is designed to help technicians fix engines, its advice must be correct. The business metric is simple: a higher "first-time fix rate" for the technicians using it.

  - **User satisfaction**: This is the ultimate test. Do the doctors, lawyers, or engineers using the system actually trust its advice and find it helpful? A high satisfaction score means the AI isn't just smart, it's useful.

- **Generative AI (did we create something good?)**: Generative AI is all about creating new content: text, images, code, or music. The metrics here are often more subjective, blending technical scores with human judgment.

  - **For text generation (LLMs):**

    - **BLEU/ROUGE scores**: For tasks such as summarization or translation, these scores compare the AI's output to a human-written "gold standard." It's like a teacher grading a summary by checking how many key phrases from the original text were included.

    - **Perplexity**: This technical metric measures how "confused" a model is by a sentence. A low score means the model finds the text predictable and natural-sounding, which is a good sign of fluency.

    - **Human evaluation**: This is the gold standard. Real people rate the output on a scale for fluency (does it sound natural?), coherence (does it make sense?), and helpfulness (did it answer the question well?).

- **For image generation:**

  - **Fréchet Inception Distance (FID):** This is like an AI art critic. It asks two questions: 1) "Are these images sharp and realistic?" (quality) and 2) "Are you showing me a wide variety of creative images, or just the same cat picture over and over?" (diversity). A low FID score is better.

  - **Aesthetic score and human preference:** Ultimately, art is subjective. Models are often trained on human ratings to learn what people find visually appealing. The key business metric is often user engagement. Do people download, share, or upvote the images the AI creates?

- **Reinforcement learning (is our bot learning to win?):** This is where an AI agent learns by doing things and getting feedback, like a pet learning a new trick through treats.

  - **Cumulative reward:** This is basically the AI's total score. In a video game, the reward is points. For AI managing an ad campaign, the reward could be the total profit earned. The goal is always the same: make the cumulative reward as high as possible.

In the end, all these technical stats are just clues. They help us understand whether the model is working correctly under the hood. But the true test of success is whether it actually solves the real-world problem it was designed for. The metrics are just the tools; the business impact is the real prize.

Linking model optimization to business metrics

In the ML world, a loss function is a mathematical function used to measure the difference between the predicted output of a model and the actual outcome. It is central to the training process, guiding the optimization of the model through a step update gradient descent. However, the loss function is typically not directly aligned with business metrics, which makes metric selection more nuanced.

For example, in fraud detection, the model's objective is to classify transactions as "fraudulent" or "not fraudulent." The loss function for this classification task might be cross-entropy, which measures the divergence between the predicted probabilities and the true outcomes. However, from a business perspective, the relevant success metrics could be precision (the ratio of correctly predicted frauds to total fraud predictions) or recall (the ratio of correctly identified frauds to actual fraud cases). Precision might be critical for minimizing false positives, while recall could be essential for detecting as many fraudulent cases as possible.

A common example of misalignment is if the objective is to improve F1 score (consider both precision and recall as a harmonic mean) for an imbalanced class problem, cross-entropy wouldn't be a great choice since minimizing cross-entropy loss could result in a model that performs well on the majority class but poorly on the minority class, which is not desirable.

Often, loss functions are designed to be differentiable for gradient descent to work efficiently, while business metrics, such as precision or recall, are often non-differentiable. This misalignment presents a challenge in direct AI/ML model optimization. Techniques such as focal loss have been developed to address imbalances in classification tasks, particularly in scenarios where the model is required to focus more on challenging examples rather than easy ones.

When the business metric is non-differentiable or sequential decision-making, techniques such as **reinforcement learning** (**RL**) may be employed, which focus on learning from feedback rather than direct optimization through a loss function. RL can optimize for a non-differentiable metric by using rewards and penalties to guide model training, making it particularly useful in scenarios where traditional loss functions fall short.

Navigating long-term metrics – the surrogate metric problem

Many business strategies aim to optimize long-term success. However, long-term metrics are often hard to measure in real time, creating a challenge for model development teams. Businesses often rely on short-term metrics as proxies for long-term goals, with the assumption that improving these short-term metrics will eventually lead to long-term success. Big leap of faith, right?

For instance, a social media platform may use **daily active users** (**DAU**) as a short-term metric if increasing DAU will also lead to improved long-term user retention. However, this leap of faith can be problematic, as optimizing for a short-term metric might not always lead to the intended long-term result. Surrogate metrics are often employed in such situations, acting as a stand-in for long-term objectives. Surrogates are needed as proxies for long-term metrics with the idea of providing more real-time feedback, which is often needed for building a more robust ML/AI solution.

To operationalize AI/ML models effectively, businesses must identify surrogate metrics that are temporally stable, highly correlated with the long-term goal, and minimally sensitive to short-term fluctuations. The goal is to ensure that short-term optimization leads to sustainable, long-term success. This process is still an open field of research, and businesses need to continuously evaluate and validate whether their surrogate metrics are indeed leading to the desired long-term outcomes.

In the banking sector, predicting customer churn presents unique challenges. Unlike many industries, banking customers often hold multiple products simultaneously—such as savings accounts, checking accounts, credit cards, loans, and investment portfolios. Here, churn doesn't always mean a complete exit from the bank; instead, it can involve a gradual reduction in product usage or a shift of key services to competitors. Like subscription-based businesses, churn may occur much later in the customer journey, making it difficult to detect and address in time. To proactively manage this, banks often rely on surrogate metrics that signal early signs of disengagement, allowing them to intervene before the customer fully disengages.

These surrogate metrics should be thoughtfully aligned with specific business goals. For instance, if the goal is to increase product usage and engagement, a meaningful metric could be a noticeable reduction in transactional activities, logins, or other forms of customer interaction within a defined timeframe. When the objective is to retain high-value customers and balances, banks might track a significant drop in account balances, say, by a certain percentage, as an early warning signal. Similarly, for reducing overall attrition, the closure of key accounts can serve as a clear indicator of churn. Finally, to boost cross-selling or upselling efforts, banks may monitor reductions in the number of active products held by customers, as such declines often precede broader disengagement. By carefully selecting and monitoring these surrogate metrics, banks can gain actionable insights into customer behavior, enabling timely interventions to prevent churn.

Dealing with multiple objectives — the Pareto frontier and optimization techniques

In most real-world applications, businesses often have multiple objectives, each of which plays a critical role in overall success. The challenge lies in optimizing multiple objectives simultaneously without compromising one for the other. This is where the concept of the Pareto frontier comes into play.

The Pareto frontier is a boundary that represents the optimal trade-offs between competing objectives. Any point on the frontier represents a solution where improving one objective will degrade another. For example, an e-commerce platform might want to optimize both user engagement and profit margins. However, increasing engagement by offering excessive discounts could negatively impact profit margins.

To navigate such trade-offs, businesses can employ techniques such as **reinforcement learning** or **Bayesian optimization**, which help in learning a scalarization of the objectives by combining them using linear weights or deploying heuristic search. These weights can be adjusted to prioritize different objectives based on business priorities. For instance, at one point in time, maximizing user engagement may be the primary goal, while at another time, profitability may take precedence.

By leveraging RL or Bayesian optimization, businesses can explore the Pareto frontier and make informed decisions about how to balance their competing objectives. Would balancing the goals of business be enough to reach adoption, or do we need to be more responsible while doing so?

Cost/ROI considerations

Operationalizing AI also raises questions about cost. Maintaining systems, especially those requiring real-time inference or continual training, can be expensive. The cost of infrastructure, including specialized hardware for LLMs, must be weighed against the model's expected ROI. Organizations face tough decisions about whether to invest in high-performance systems or consider more efficient alternatives, such as smaller models, which may trade off some accuracy for lower costs.

Need for responsible AI

In an AI era where machines try to outthink humans, the ethical deployment of AI has never been more critical. AI impacts various societal aspects, including mental health, spreading misinformation, job displacement, and socio-economic challenges. **Responsible AI (RAI)**, therefore, is necessary to mitigate these adverse effects and ensure fairer AI solutions are built and are accountable and transparent.

With increasing AI regulations worldwide, such as in the EU and China, and regulatory initiatives across the United States, organizations need to adopt RAI practices to comply with legal requirements. Ensuring RAI means avoiding biases and inaccurate decisions, which is paramount for public services, the private sector, and regulated institutions. Shifting towards a human-centered approach in AI practices is essential. This means practitioners should aim to focus not just on compliance but also on understanding the socio-technical impacts of AI systems on stakeholders.

Every organization should aim to adopt RAI as a culture and not to think of it as a checklist. It is imperative to develop explainable and trustworthy AI systems that can provide comprehensible explanations needed for decision-making, fostering trust, and enabling users to make informed decisions.

So, at the end of the day, *defining success* for AI/ML models isn't just about picking up a metric and running with it. You need a well-thought-out approach that considers business goals, the model's evolution over time, and the broader impact on customers. And don't forget those guardrail metrics. They'll save you from making short-term gains at the cost of long-term sustainability.

> **Note**
>
> Defining success for AI models isn't merely a technical exercise. It requires a thoughtful, holistic approach. Success metrics must align with business goals, adapt over time, and account for trade-offs, costs, and societal impacts. Getting this right is arguably the most critical step in operationalizing AI, ensuring models deliver sustained, meaningful value to businesses and society alike.

Summary

This chapter outlined a holistic playbook for measuring ML success. It started with defining specific, measurable, and actionable metrics aligned with business goals, then adding guardrails to avoid harmful side effects. Next, we discovered how to link technical performance to business value, manage evolving metrics, and ensure responsible, cost-effective AI adoption. This foundation is vital for building trustworthy systems. In the next chapter, we'll explore how to operationalize these models and bring them from experimentation to scalable, production-ready solutions.

Subscribe for a free eBook

New frameworks, evolving architectures, research drops, production breakdowns—*AI_Distilled* filters the noise into a weekly briefing for engineers and researchers working hands-on with LLMs and GenAI systems. Subscribe now and receive a free eBook, along with weekly insights that help you stay focused and informed.

Subscribe at `https://packt.link/80z6Y` or scan the QR code below.

7

From Model to Market: Operationalizing ML Systems

In the previous chapter, we established the foundational framework for success in **machine learning (ML)**. We learned that to deliver real-world value, we must define what success looks like, moving beyond simple model scores to a multi-dimensional view that includes SMART metrics aligned with business goals, guardrail metrics to prevent unintended harm, and surrogate metrics to track long-term objectives. With this critical understanding of what to measure, we now confront the second half of the battle: operationalization.

A model with perfect metrics that remains in a research project is a missed opportunity. For companies to truly benefit from ML, we must bridge the gap from an experimental model to a production-grade system. This means not just deploying the model, but getting people to adopt it, weaving it into the daily workings of the business, and ensuring that it aligns with the company's strategy. For companies to benefit, we need to make sure it's operationalized. What do we mean by that? It's not just about deploying the model. It's about getting people to adopt it, showing its impact, and weaving it into the daily workings of the business. Plus, it needs to line up with the company's short-term and long-term strategy. You can have the most sophisticated ML model in the world, but if no one's using it or it's expensive to run or, worse, it's misaligned with the company's goals, you're missing out.

In this chapter, we shift focus to what it truly takes to operationalize these models, ensuring that they can move beyond notebooks and proof-of-concept environments into production systems that are scalable and maintainable. This includes a deep dive into the technical and organizational considerations for model productization: the infrastructure needed to support continuous deployment, the role of monitoring and observability, and how feedback loops help models evolve in real-time contexts.

A core enabler of this transformation is code modularization, whether through procedural scripts, object-oriented design, or high-level frameworks. We will examine how these different approaches impact the maintainability and flexibility of ML pipelines. Frameworks offer powerful abstractions that simplify the design of distributed systems, handle hardware acceleration, and enable reproducibility at scale.

Finally, we'll look at how recent advancements, such as those in **large language models (LLMs)** and agent-based orchestration, are reshaping the way ML systems are built and deployed. With application frameworks such as LangChain and Langraph, deep learning-based frameworks such as PyTorch and TensorFlow, and emerging protocols such as **Model Context Protocol (MCP)**, developers now have an unprecedented toolkit to build intelligent, context-aware, and continuously learning systems.

This chapter aims to equip you with both the practical tooling and the architectural mindset needed to move from experimental models to robust, enterprise-ready ML systems. Whether you're building your first pipeline or scaling a fleet of production models, the concepts discussed here are essential to doing it right and doing it sustainably.

The following key topics are covered in this chapter:

- Understanding the foundations for sustainable operationalization
- Bridging SDLC and ML development cycles
- Infrastructure and architecture choices for AI/ML deployments
- What's next in ML systems?

By the end of the chapter, you will understand how to productize models for real-world impact, modularize ML code effectively, and leverage modern frameworks to build scalable, maintainable AI systems.

Understanding the foundations for sustainable operationalization

Once the right metrics are defined and aligned with business goals, the next essential step in operationalizing ML solutions is productization. While building high-performing models is a critical milestone, it represents only the beginning of the journey. The true value of ML emerges when experimental prototypes are transformed into robust, maintainable, and scalable products that integrate seamlessly into business workflows. Productization provides the foundation for this transformation, emphasizing reproducible code, iterative feedback loops, and disciplined engineering practices. These practices ensure that ML systems remain adaptable, transparent, and cost-effective over time, minimizing technical debt while balancing rapid experimentation with long-term maintainability. In this section, we will explore the principles of ML productization, showing how they accelerate deployment and enable continuous learning and business impact. By tying these practices back to the earlier discussion on metrics, we position productization as the bridge between model development and real-world adoption.

From sandbox to real-world success: the need for productization

Moving ML models from experimentation to production requires far more than high accuracy scores on a test dataset. Success in the real world hinges on whether models can reliably deliver business value, adapt to changing conditions, and scale effectively. ML models are inherently expensive—not just in terms of initial development but also in ongoing maintenance, infrastructure, and monitoring costs. This complexity grows dramatically with deep learning and LLMs. Therefore, it becomes critical to evaluate the trade-off between model complexity and incremental business value.

The following table highlights the critical trade-offs between model performance, training time, and memory usage:

Algorithm	Training time complexity	Prediction time complexity	Auxiliary space complexity	Remarks
Linear regression	$O(n*m^2 + m^3)$	$O(m)$	$O(m)$	Low runtime and space complexity.
Logistic regression	$O(nm)$	$O(m)$	$O(m)$	Low runtime and space complexity.
Naive Bayesian	$O(n*m)$	$O(c*m)$	$O(c*m)$	Works well with high-dimensional data.

Algorithm	Training time complexity	Prediction time complexity	Auxiliary space complexity	Remarks
Decision trees	O(nlog(n)d)	O(d)	O(p)	Efficient for handling both numerical and categorical data, but can be prone to overfitting.
Gradient boosting	O(nlog(n)dr)	O(dr)	O(pr + br)	br << dr; br is the number of boosting rounds, and dr is the depth of each tree in the boosting process.
Random forest	O(nlog(n)*dntree)	O(dntree)	O(pntree)	dntree is the depth of an individual tree in the random forest, and pntree is the number of parameters or features used in each tree. Provides better generalization than a single decision tree.
Support vector machine (SVM)	O(n²m + n³)	O(mnsv)	O(nsv)	High training time but low space complexity. Suitable for low-latency problems and small datasets.
K-means	O(nmki)	O(mk)	O(nm + km)	Fast and scalable for large datasets, but sensitive to initialization and requires choosing k.
K-nearest neighbors (KNN)	O(1)	O(nm)	O(nm)	No training time, but high prediction time. Requires storing the entire dataset.

Algorithm	Training time complexity	Prediction time complexity	Auxiliary space complexity	Remarks
Hierarchical clustering	$O(n^3) = O(n^2\log(n))$	$O(mn)$	$O(n^2)$	High training time, high runtime, and high space complexity. Not suitable for low-latency applications.
DBSCAN	$O(n^2) / O(n\log(n))$	$O(mn)$	$O(n)$	Better than hierarchical clustering in terms of time and space complexity. Handles noise and clusters of arbitrary shapes.
Principal component analysis (PCA)	$O(nm*\min(n, m) + m^3)$	$O(Im)$	$O(Im)$	The complexity of covariance matrix computation is $O(nm \times \min(n, m))$. Eigenvalue decomposition is $O(m^3)$. $O(Im)$ is for the transformation matrix. Reduces dimensionality effectively but can be computationally expensive.
t-distributed stochastic neighbor embedding (t-SNE)	$O(n^2)$	$O(nq)$	$O(n^2)$	t-SNE requires significant computation and memory. Has a quadratic time and space complexity in the number of data points. It requires $O(3n^2)$ of memory, making it impractical for large datasets.

Table 7.1: Time and space complexities of popular ML models

Supervised learning algorithms

Generally speaking, supervised learning algorithms vary greatly in their speed and resource needs. At one end, you have the efficient workhorses: linear and logistic regression and naive Bayes. These models are incredibly fast to train, typically scaling linearly with your data size ($O(n)$). This makes them perfect for creating quick baselines or for situations where you have massive datasets and need a simple, interpretable model.

In the middle are tree-based models. A single decision tree is quite fast to train and extremely fast for making predictions. However, its tendency to overfit is often addressed by using ensembles. Random forest and gradient boosting are far more powerful and accurate because they combine hundreds of trees, but this comes at a cost as their training time is significantly longer, and they require more memory.

Then there are the specialists. SVMs are a tale of two models: with a linear kernel, they are as fast as logistic regression. But for complex, non-linear problems, they use kernels that make training time explode ($O(n^2)$), rendering them impractical for large datasets. Finally, KNN is the "lazy learner." It does zero work during training; it just memorizes the entire dataset. This makes prediction extremely slow ($O(n*m)$) and memory-intensive, as it has to compare every new point to all the old ones.

Unsupervised learning algorithms

For unsupervised tasks such as clustering, K-means is the sprinter. It's very fast and scales well, making it a go-to for partitioning large datasets into a predefined number (k) of clusters. In contrast, DBSCAN is a bit slower but much more flexible; it can find oddly shaped clusters and automatically identify noise without you needing to specify the number of clusters. At the far end is hierarchical clustering, which is extremely slow ($O(n^2)$ to $O(n^3)$) and memory-hungry, making it suitable only for small datasets where you need to explore nested cluster structures.

For dimensionality reduction, PCA is the standard, efficient choice. It's generally fast at transforming your data into a lower-dimensional space, though its speed can suffer if you have a massive number of features (m). On the other hand, t-SNE is a powerful tool designed specifically for visualization. It excels at creating meaningful 2D or 3D maps of high-dimensional data but is notoriously slow ($O(n^2)$) and memory-intensive, limiting its use to smaller datasets where visual exploration is the primary goal.

So, you've built a great ML model that shows a lot of promise. What's next? The hardest part isn't just creating a smart algorithm; it's turning that algorithm into a reliable product that people can use. This crucial step is called **productization**.

Think of it like this: a brilliant chef can create a stunning new dish in their kitchen. Productization is the process of designing a restaurant and a system that can perfectly recreate that dish for hundreds of customers every single night.

To do this successfully, the process needs to be engineered for the real world. This means the following:

- **Modular design**: Building the model in interchangeable pieces, so it's easy to update or fix one part without breaking the whole system
- **Robust versioning**: Keeping a strict record of all changes, like a detailed cookbook that tracks every tweak to a recipe
- **Automated pipelines**: Creating an "assembly line" that automatically tests and deploys new versions of the model, ensuring quality and speed
- **Thoughtful infrastructure**: Choosing the right hardware and cloud services to ensure that the model can handle heavy demand without crashing

In short, productization is the bridge between a cool experiment and a valuable business tool. It's the engineering foundation that ensures an ML model delivers consistent, reliable results, and it's what we'll be diving into next.

Before that, let's discuss why feedback loops matter.

It's common to celebrate a model that achieves high accuracy in an offline test. However, this often fails to translate into production success. Real-world environments are dynamic and unpredictable, and models trained solely on historical data may underperform once deployed. Feedback loops are essential to close this gap. They enable continuous learning and model refinement after deployment. Several challenges may surface in production:

- Missing behavioral patterns in training data
- Key influencing factors excluded from feature sets
- Sampling biases that cause a model to overfit certain subgroups

The feedback loop allows organizations to address these challenges systematically:

- **User feedback**: End users can reveal gaps in model predictions that internal testing missed. For example, an e-commerce recommendation system might ignore seasonality, leading to poor product suggestions.

- **Data drift monitoring**: Over time, shifts in user behavior or market conditions can degrade model performance. Monitoring drift enables timely model retraining.

- **Data augmentation**: New edge cases encountered in production can enrich the training dataset, improving model robustness.

Ultimately, the journey from prototype to production is iterative. Deployed models must be continuously monitored, refined, and retrained to remain useful. Productization, supported by active feedback loops, transforms static models into adaptive, high-performing systems.

Beyond feedback: why productization accelerates ML value creation

Feedback loops are only part of the equation. Productization unlocks additional benefits critical to long-term ML success:

- **Scalability**: Experimental models often falter under real-world data volumes or user loads. Productization ensures that systems can scale effectively.

- **Maintainability**: Production systems require rigorous monitoring and maintenance. Productization encourages practices such as version control, automated testing, and modular design to simplify upkeep.

- **Innovation**: Productized systems enable faster innovation. By modularizing components, teams can easily experiment with new models or data sources without disrupting the entire pipeline.

- **Technical debt management**: Rapid experimentation often leads to shortcuts that accumulate technical debt. Productization provides a chance to reduce this debt, clean up code bases, and build more stable systems.

Consider an e-commerce recommendation engine. Without productization, adding new categories or scaling to a larger user base would be cumbersome. A productized system, however, is designed to handle evolving business needs through modular architecture and clear handoffs between data science and engineering teams.

Code reproducibility: the bedrock of reliable systems

Reproducibility is fundamental for scaling and maintaining ML solutions. Without it, collaboration, debugging, and deployment become fraught with risk. Key reproducibility practices include the following:

- **Version control**: Tools such as Git and **data version control (DVC)** help track changes to code, datasets, and models
- **Containerization**: Docker and Kubernetes create consistent runtime environments across development and production
- **Automated pipelines**: CI/CD tools automate testing and deployment, reducing human error

These practices ensure that models can be reliably reproduced, audited, and transferred across teams and systems. Reproducibility is a non-negotiable prerequisite for robust AI productization. Applying first principles of thinking to ML code encourages clarity, efficiency, and maintainability. Effective code design focuses on simplicity, modularity, and separation of concerns:

- **Readable and modular code**: Clean, well-structured code improves collaboration and speeds up debugging
- **Comprehensive documentation**: Clear explanations help teams understand model behavior and maintain code over time
- **Separation of data, models, and logic**: Decoupling data pipelines, model training, and inference layers increases flexibility and reduces system fragility

In modern ML architectures, this often involves integrating feature stores or data APIs to decouple feature engineering from modeling. Such designs improve both scalability and speed of deployment.

Minimizing technical debt

Unchecked technical debt can cripple M initiatives. It often arises from rushed experiments, undocumented workflows, and ad-hoc pipeline extensions. To reduce technical debt, consider the following:

- **Standardize practices**: Establish shared coding, data, and model governance standards
- **Refactor regularly**: Schedule time for code base cleanup and optimization
- **Modularize pipelines**: Design pipelines so that individual components can evolve independently

Proactive technical debt management ensures that ML systems remain adaptable and sustainable over time.

Balancing experimentation with refactoring

ML development requires a delicate balance between fast experimentation and disciplined engineering. Both are necessary for sustainable success.

Effective strategies include the following:

- **Isolated experimentation**: Rapid prototyping in sandboxed environments minimizes production risks
- **Scheduled refactoring**: Allocate time for cleaning and optimizing code bases regularly
- **Controlled releases**: Only integrate thoroughly validated changes into production systems

This balance enables innovation without sacrificing long-term maintainability, leading to stable and adaptable AI solutions.

AI/ML productization is not merely a technical exercise; it is a strategic enabler of long-term business value. By embedding recurrent feedback loops, ensuring code reproducibility, applying sound engineering principles, and managing technical debt, organizations can turn promising AI experiments into durable, scalable solutions.

Productization ensures that models are not just accurate in the lab but impactful in the real world. It transforms ML from a research effort into a reliable, repeatable, and continuously improving business capability. By adopting these foundational practices, organizations can unlock the full potential of AI and build systems that deliver measurable impact for years to come.

As organizations move from experimentation to production, the next critical step is aligning AI/ML workflows with established software engineering practices. This requires bridging the gap between traditional **software development life cycles (SDLCs)** and the unique demands of ML systems.

Note

We emphasize that successful AI deployment goes beyond building accurate models—it requires productization to transform prototypes into scalable, maintainable solutions integrated within business workflows. Key practices include establishing feedback loops, ensuring reproducible and modular code, managing technical debt, and balancing rapid experimentation with systematic refactoring. These foundations enable AI systems to adapt and evolve with changing data and business needs, ensuring sustained value. Ultimately, productization bridges the gap between development and real-world impact.

Bridging SDLC and ML development cycles

The development of ML systems shares similarities with traditional software development but introduces unique complexities due to its dynamic nature. Unlike conventional software, where code is the primary artifact, ML systems depend equally on data, model configurations, and infrastructure, all of which continuously evolve. This necessitates robust life cycle management practices that encompass versioning of code, data, and infrastructure to ensure reproducibility and maintainability. Furthermore, ML is not just about delivering a static model file but about managing an entire pipeline that automates data processing, model training, evaluation, and deployment. Modular design, through procedural programming, object-oriented principles, and modern frameworks, is essential to handle this complexity by making ML systems scalable, maintainable, and adaptable to change. This section explores these foundational concepts, drawing parallels to **software development life cycle (SDLC)** while emphasizing the dynamic, evolving nature of ML systems and best practices for modularizing code bases to support sustainable AI/ML operations.

Code and data versioning in ML

In SDLC, code versioning is a standard practice that allows developers to track changes, revert to previous versions, and collaborate on code. In the ML development cycle, however, data versioning is equally important. In traditional software development, the behavior of the software remains relatively stable as long as the code remains unchanged. However, in ML systems, even if the code remains the same, changes in the underlying data can drastically affect the model's behavior.

Without proper versioning of both data and code, AI/ML teams might find it difficult to reproduce results or explain model behavior after deployment. A model might have been trained on a particular dataset, and when new data becomes available, its performance might change significantly. Thus, to ensure reproducibility and maintain consistency in deployments, both code and data should be versioned.

Additionally, versioning is not limited to data and code but also extends to the infrastructure. Infrastructure versioning ensures that the environment in which the model was trained (such as specific hardware configurations, dependencies, and libraries) is reproducible. This becomes crucial when deploying the model across different environments, whether on-premises, in the cloud, or on edge devices.

Just as code versioning allows for rollback in a traditional SDLC, model versioning ensures that teams can roll back to previous models when new deployments cause unexpected results.

Is ML a model file package or a pipeline?

One of the most critical and often misunderstood aspects of ML is whether it is merely a model file package or a complete pipeline. The short answer is that ML is a dynamic and evolving component that requires three levels of versioning: data, code, and infrastructure. Without proper versioning and tracking across these dimensions, reproducing results and maintaining ML systems becomes extremely challenging.

A common misconception is that sharing a pickle file (`.pkl` or `.h5`) or any other serialized model file (e.g., TensorFlow Saved Model, ONNX, or PMML) is enough to reproduce an ML model's output. However, this is far from sufficient. A model file is essentially a frozen state of learned parameters without context about the data used to train it, the preprocessing pipeline, hyperparameters, or even the specific hardware or software stack used during training. Without this metadata and supporting infrastructure, simply sharing a model file is like handing someone a locked safe without providing the key or the combination to open it.

Why persisting the entire ML pipeline matters

To ensure that ML systems are reproducible and maintainable, we need to store and version not only the trained model but the entire pipeline, which includes the following:

- **Data processing steps**: The exact transformations applied to raw data before feeding it into the model. This includes handling missing values, feature engineering, scaling, and encoding categorical variables.

- **Feature selection and engineering**: Specific steps used to generate the features that the model relies on. If these are not versioned, even the best-trained model will not work correctly when new data arrives.

- **Model training configuration**: Hyperparameters, training epochs, optimizer settings, and validation criteria used in training the model.

- **Code base versioning**: The specific version of the code, libraries, and dependencies used to train and deploy the model.

- **Infrastructure dependencies**: The runtime environment, GPU availability, cloud-based services, or containerized deployment strategies used in the ML pipeline.

For example, consider a recommendation system for an e-commerce platform. If a data scientist merely shares the trained model file but does not document the feature extraction logic (e.g., how user behavior data was transformed into input vectors), a different engineer trying to replicate the model later may generate different results due to slight variations in preprocessing.

A more robust approach is to use tools such as MLflow, DVC, or Kubeflow Pipelines to track and manage the full life cycle of ML models. These tools help with versioning, experiment tracking, and deployment consistency, ensuring that the ML pipeline remains reproducible and scalable across different environments.

The following diagram illustrates the various components that make up a complete and reproducible ML pipeline, extending beyond model training to include data handling, deployment, and monitoring. It emphasizes why persisting through every stage is essential for long-term reliability and scalability:

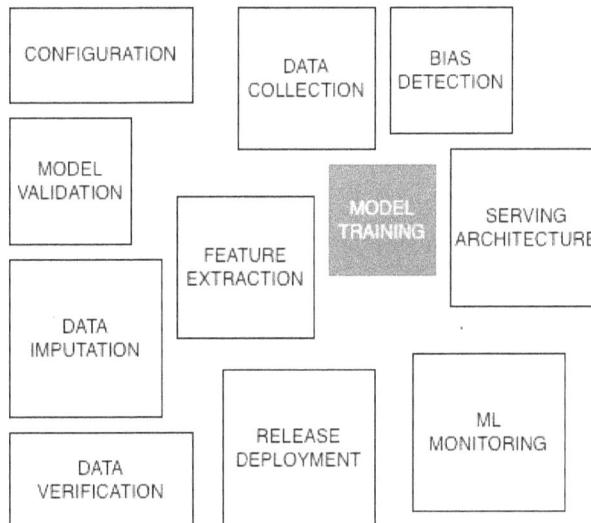

Figure 7.1: ML pipeline components beyond model training, including data, deployment, and monitoring

As we have components established for production workflows, the next critical step is discussing best practices for building pipelines. Since ML is different from a typical SDLC pipeline, frameworks are discussed extensively with their associated benefits in the following sections.

Pipelines: ensuring scalability and stability

One of the most critical components of deploying ML models at scale is the concept of pipelines. A pipeline automates the end-to-end process of data ingestion, preprocessing, model training, evaluation, and deployment, ensuring that the system is stable, scalable, and repeatable.

In traditional ML workflows, models are often treated as static files. Once trained, they are saved and deployed. However, this approach leads to several challenges, such as ensuring that the model is retrained on updated data, handling model versioning, and integrating new features.

Google's influential paper, *Hidden Technical Debt in Machine Learning Systems*, highlights how building pipelines rather than relying on static model files helps manage technical debt. The paper argues that the complexity in ML systems arises not just from the models themselves but from the surrounding systems that handle data, feature engineering, monitoring, and more.

A well-designed pipeline ensures the following:

- **Data is continuously refreshed**: New data is automatically ingested, processed, and passed through the model
- **Model retraining is automated**: Whenever new data or features are introduced, the model can be retrained, evaluated, and redeployed without manual intervention
- **End-to-end traceability is maintained**: Pipelines track every stage of the process, ensuring that every model version is reproducible

By building pipelines, ML teams can automate the deployment process and reduce the risk of manual errors. They also make it easier to scale models across multiple environments, integrate new data sources, and experiment with new models.

Modularization in ML code: procedural programming, OOP, and frameworks

Code modularization plays a critical role in ensuring maintainability, scalability, and adaptability of AI/ML solutions. Various approaches to modularization, including procedural programming, **object-oriented programming** (**OOP**), and frameworks, offer different benefits and trade-offs. Choosing the right approach is crucial for building robust and extensible ML systems.

Procedural programming focuses on writing sequences of instructions that the computer follows step by step. While procedural code is easy to write and understand in small projects, it quickly becomes unwieldy in larger systems. As the size of the codebase grows, the lack of modularity leads to code duplication, difficulties in debugging, and increased technical debt.

For AI/ML systems, procedural programming can be effective when the code base is small, but as more data sources, models, and features are added, it becomes more challenging to manage. This is where OOP or frameworks become important. Here is a representational example of OOP:

```
# Procedural approach for data preprocessing
import pandas as pd
from sklearn.preprocessing import StandardScaler

def load_data(filepath):
    return pd.read_csv(filepath)

def preprocess_data(df):
    scaler = StandardScaler()
    df[['feature1', 'feature2']] = scaler.fit_transform(
        df[['feature1', 'feature2']]
    )
    return df

data = load_data('data.csv')
data = preprocess_data(data)
```

While this approach works for small projects, as the number of steps grows (e.g., handling missing values, feature selection, and model training), procedural code becomes harder to manage and debug.

OOP offers a way to modularize code by organizing it into reusable objects that encapsulate both data and methods. While OOP is more difficult to set up initially compared to procedural programming, it offers significant long-term benefits, especially for ML systems. In OOP, models, datasets, and preprocessing steps can be represented as objects, each with its own methods and attributes. This structure makes it easier to maintain, extend, and debug the code base, as changes to one part of the system are less likely to affect others.

The major challenge with OOP is that it requires a more disciplined design approach up front. However, once set up, it can significantly improve code maintainability and scalability, particularly for large, complex systems. The following code shows OOP style. Code is structured as reusable classes rather than independent function calls:

```
class DataPreprocessor:
    def __init__(self):
        self.scaler = StandardScaler()

    def fit_transform(self, df):
        df[['feature1', 'feature2']] = self.scaler.fit_transform(
            df[['feature1', 'feature2']]
        )
        return df

# Usage
preprocessor = DataPreprocessor()
data = preprocessor.fit_transform(data)
```

Using OOP, different components such as data preprocessing, model training, and evaluation can be modularized, making it easier to maintain and scale ML projects.

Frameworks: scalable solution for complex workflows

While structured code, whether procedural or object-oriented, brings a great deal of clarity and maintainability, there are deeper challenges in ML that require more than just good code organization. As projects grow, they face complexities that cannot be solved by design patterns alone. Issues such as scalability, distributed computation, hardware acceleration, and reproducibility become central concerns, especially in production-grade systems where large datasets and intensive models are the norm. Frameworks step in here as indispensable tools.

To appreciate why frameworks are essential, it's helpful to think through a simple but fundamental scenario: training a model on data distributed across multiple machines. Suppose you have a dataset that spans 10 machines. In such a setting, model training isn't about fitting 10 separate models independently. Instead, you still want to produce a single unified model that benefits from all the available data.

But how does this happen? It's not simply a matter of sending all the data to one machine, that would defeat the entire purpose of distributed processing. Instead, distributed training methods are employed, where each machine works on its slice of the data, computes partial updates to the model, and then synchronizes those updates with others. These machines communicate, either through a centralized parameter server that coordinates updates or by sharing gradients directly in a peer-to-peer fashion using collective communication protocols, such as those provided by libraries, such as Horovod or **NVIDIA Collective Communication Library (NCCL)**.

The following figure shows how a data-parallel approach to distributed training involves splitting up the data and training on multiple nodes in parallel:

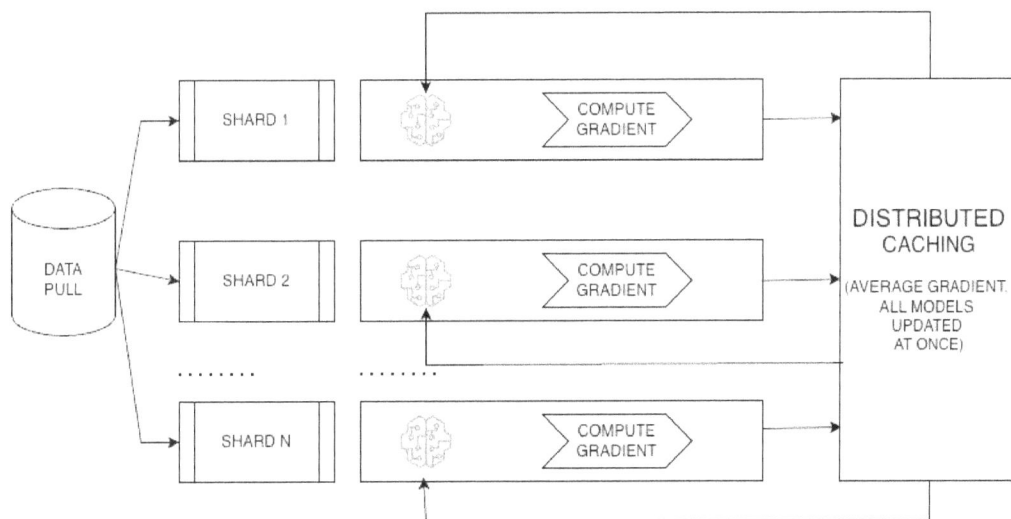

Figure 7.2: A data-parallel approach to distributed training

In synchronous cases, the gradients for different batches of data are calculated separately on each node but averaged across nodes to apply consistent updates to the model copy in each node.

Designing and building these kinds of distributed systems manually would be an enormous engineering effort, requiring expertise in networking, parallel computing, optimization, and more. However, modern ML frameworks abstract most of these details. Frameworks such as TensorFlow, PyTorch, and Horovod enable developers to train models at scale without having to worry about the low-level mechanics of distributed computing.

But the value of frameworks doesn't stop distributed training. They also offer capabilities that are crucial for every stage of the ML pipeline. They handle hardware acceleration, automatically taking advantage of GPUs or TPUs where available. They provide tools for model checkpointing, enabling training jobs to recover interruptions without starting over. They support automatic logging and experiment tracking, which are essential for reproducibility in research and production. They also integrate easily with cloud platforms and orchestration tools, allowing models to move seamlessly from experimentation to deployment.

Similarly, a TensorFlow Extended pipeline is a sequence of components that implement an ML pipeline, which is specifically designed for scalable, high-performance ML tasks. That includes modeling, training, serving inference, and managing deployments to online, native mobile, and JavaScript targets.

Each framework tends to have its own area of strength. Scikit-learn, for instance, remains a go-to solution for classical ML tasks involving structured or tabular data. It's particularly well-suited for smaller-scale problems and rapid prototyping. TensorFlow and PyTorch, by contrast, dominate in deep learning applications, especially for unstructured data such as images, audio, and text. When it comes to graph neural networks, PyTorch Geometric provides specialized tools that make it easier to build models designed to learn from graph-structured data. In the domain of probabilistic modeling and Bayesian inference, frameworks such as PyMC3 and TensorFlow Probability offer powerful abstractions for building complex probabilistic models.

The following diagram illustrates a modular developer platform for building and managing ML applications:

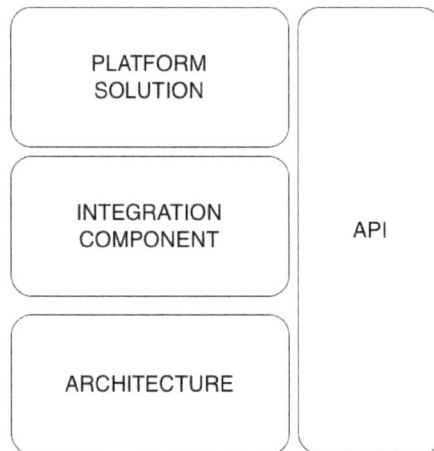

Figure 7.3: A modular developer platform

The platform solution layer offers tools for debugging, testing, and monitoring model workflows. The integration component connects external systems, data sources, and model providers. The architecture layer defines the system's core runtime and execution framework. An API runs alongside all layers, enabling programmatic access and seamless integration.

The ecosystem of frameworks has expanded significantly with the rise of LLMs. In this space, new frameworks have emerged to manage the specific challenges that LLMs present challenges such as chaining together multiple prompts, integrating external data sources, and orchestrating reasoning across several agents. LangChain and LangGraph are two prominent examples that simplify the development of applications powered by LLMs. These frameworks make it easier to build complex workflows where models interact with tools, databases, and APIs, while retaining memory across interactions. This concept of memory retention, where a system can carry forward context from one step to another, is foundational for enabling systems that exhibit generalized intelligence.

More recently, advances such as the MCP have taken this a step further, providing infrastructure for sharing context and memory between different LLM agents, enhancing their collaborative capabilities. These mechanisms allow LLM-powered systems to remember previous interactions, making them far more capable of solving multi-step problems, reasoning over long conversations, or coordinating actions among multiple agents.

Frameworks are, in many ways, the unsung heroes of modern ML. Without them, much of what is now considered routine, from training models on massive datasets to deploying them at scale, would be out of reach for all but the most specialized teams. They don't just structure code; they also offer ready-made solutions to problems that arise at the intersection of ML, software engineering, and distributed systems.

In essence, frameworks allow ML practitioners to focus on modeling and experimentation, rather than the plumbing of distributed computing, hardware optimization, or workflow orchestration. They provide an invisible scaffolding that holds up the entire ML life cycle, from research to production, while promoting reproducibility, efficiency, and scalability.

By offering these high levels of abstractions or APIs from these frameworks, it has enabled key innovation in AI. Whether it's training a model on a petabyte-scale dataset or building a conversational AI agent capable of long-term memory, frameworks make it possible to realize these ideas with far less effort than would otherwise be required. As the field continues to evolve, frameworks will likely remain at the core of this progress, enabling the next wave of scalable, intelligent systems.

Here's an overview of the scikit learn framework as a **minimal** example optimized for simplicity, readability, and reusability:

```python
from sklearn.pipeline import Pipeline
from sklearn.preprocessing import StandardScaler
from sklearn.linear_model import LogisticRegression
```

```
pipeline = Pipeline([
    ('scaler', StandardScaler()),
    ('model', LogisticRegression()) ])
pipeline.fit(X_train, y_train)
```

This approach ensures that data preprocessing and model training are part of the same workflow, improving maintainability and reducing the risk of mismatched transformations.

Here are the advantages of frameworks:

- Built-in best practices for reproducibility and efficiency
- Pre-optimized functions that reduce development time
- Integration with cloud platforms and distributed computing

However, frameworks can also be limiting when dealing with edge-case scenarios not supported out of the box. In such cases, a hybrid approach that combines OOP principles with framework utilities is often the best solution.

ML systems are fundamentally different from traditional software in that they must manage dynamic components such as data, models, and infrastructure in addition to code, and also memory in the case of LLMs. As such, reproducibility, versioning, and pipeline persistence are essential. Modular design, whether through procedural programming, OOP, or frameworks, is foundational for building scalable, maintainable, and robust ML solutions. These practices not only streamline development but also enable systems to evolve smoothly in production environments.

Note

ML development requires managing dynamic components beyond just code, including data and infrastructure, to ensure reproducibility. Unlike traditional software, ML demands comprehensive versioning and pipeline persistence rather than static model files. Modular design via procedural, object-oriented, or framework-based approaches enhances scalability and maintainability. These principles enable robust, scalable ML systems that evolve efficiently in production environments.

With an understanding of how both structured coding paradigms and third-party frameworks support the development and scaling of ML systems, the next step is to explore the underlying infrastructure and architectural choices that enable these solutions to operate reliably in production environments.

Infrastructure and architecture choices for AI/ML deployments

When deploying AI/ML models in real-world scenarios, selecting the appropriate infrastructure is paramount. Different cloud service models offer varying levels of abstraction, from complete control over the underlying infrastructure to fully managed services. The primary models considered are **Infrastructure as a Service (IaaS)**, **Platform as a Service (PaaS)**, **Software as a Service (SaaS)**, and **Container as a Service (CaaS)**. Each of these models presents a unique set of trade-offs in terms of operational effort, flexibility, and cost.

Understanding IaaS, PaaS, SaaS, and CaaS in AI/ML deployments

When deploying AI/ML models in real-world environments, choosing the right infrastructure is crucial for balancing control, flexibility, and ease of use. Different cloud service models offer varying levels of abstraction, from complete control over infrastructure to fully managed services. The four primary models to consider are IaaS, PaaS, SaaS, and CaaS. Each of these offers trade-offs between operational effort, flexibility, and cost:

- **IaaS** provides the most control and flexibility by offering virtualized computing resources over the cloud, such as virtual machines, storage, and networking. With IaaS, organizations have complete control over their environment, which allows for customized configuration and setup, but this also means they are responsible for managing and maintaining the underlying infrastructure.

  - **Key features of IaaS:**

    - **Complete control:** Users control the operating system, storage, and networking configurations, which provides significant flexibility.

    - **Customization:** IaaS is highly customizable, allowing for specific hardware and software configurations.

    - **Scalability:** Users can scale resources up or down based on demand.

  - **Pros:**

    - **Flexibility:** IaaS provides the highest level of flexibility for AI/ML workloads. Data scientists and engineers can choose the exact hardware specifications, including GPUs or TPUs, for large-scale training or inference tasks.

- **Cost efficiency for large operations**: IaaS can be more cost-effective for large, continuous AI/ML operations that require intensive compute resources, as users pay only for what they use.

- **Cons**:

  - **Operational overhead**: Managing the underlying infrastructure requires significant technical expertise and resources, increasing operational complexity.

  - **Maintenance**: Users are responsible for maintaining the infrastructure, such as updating the operating system, managing security, and handling failures.

- **Use case**: IaaS is ideal for businesses with significant technical expertise, large-scale AI/ML workloads, and specific requirements for compute resources. For example, companies performing deep learning with complex models that require extensive GPU processing often opt for IaaS.

- **PaaS** abstracts much of the infrastructure complexity by providing a platform that includes the operating system, middleware, and runtime environment. Users focus on developing, deploying, and managing applications without worrying about infrastructure management.

  - **Key features of PaaS**:

    - **Preconfigured environment**: The platform comes with pre-configured development tools, databases, and servers.

    - **Simplified deployment**: PaaS allows developers to deploy applications quickly without worrying about the underlying hardware or operating system.

    - **Built-in scalability**: PaaS solutions offer easy scaling options as demand grows.

  - **Pros**:

    - **Faster time to market**: Developers can focus on building and deploying AI/ML models without the complexity of managing infrastructure. This leads to faster development cycles.

    - **Reduced operational work**: PaaS reduces the need for system administration, security management, and hardware maintenance.

- **Integrated tooling**: Many PaaS solutions come with built-in tools for ML, such as model deployment, monitoring, and versioning systems, making it easier to integrate AI/ML workflows.

- **Cons**:

    - **Less flexibility**: PaaS environments are more constrained than IaaS. If the platform does not support specific configurations or tools required for advanced AI/ML models, users may face limitations.

    - **Cost**: While PaaS reduces operational overhead, it can be more expensive for continuous, high-volume AI/ML workloads due to premium charges for built-in services and scalability.

- **Use case**: PaaS is suitable for organizations that want to speed up the development and deployment process without the complexity of managing infrastructure. For example, AI start-ups looking to prototype and deploy machine learning models quickly may prefer PaaS.

- **SaaS** provides fully managed software solutions over the cloud, with minimal involvement required from the user. The service provider handles everything from infrastructure to application management. In the AI/ML context, SaaS platforms offer pre-built AI tools, APIs, and services that businesses can directly integrate into their workflows.

    - **Key features of SaaS**:

        - **Pre-built solutions**: SaaS platforms offer ready-to-use AI/ML services such as natural language processing, image recognition, and recommendation engines.

        - **Zero infrastructure management**: All infrastructure, software updates, and security are managed by the provider.

        - **Easy integration**: SaaS solutions are designed to be easily integrated into existing workflows with minimal customization required.

    - **Pros**:

        - **Minimal technical overhead**: SaaS eliminates the need for infrastructure or platform management, allowing teams to focus entirely on business use cases.

        - **Quick deployment**: SaaS solutions can be deployed quickly without the need for development or deep technical expertise in AI/ML.

- **Predictable costs**: SaaS models are typically subscription-based, making budgeting predictable.

- **Cons:**

  - **Limited customization**: SaaS solutions offer limited flexibility. Users must rely on the features and capabilities provided by the platform.

  - **Dependency on vendor**: Businesses become reliant on the SaaS vendor for updates, scalability, and performance improvements.

  - **Data privacy**: With SaaS, sensitive data may need to be transferred and stored with third-party vendors, raising potential privacy concerns.

- **Use case**: SaaS is ideal for businesses looking for fast and easy-to-use AI solutions without investing heavily in infrastructure or AI expertise. For example, a marketing firm might use a SaaS-based AI tool for customer segmentation and targeting without needing to build custom models.

- **CaaS** offers a middle ground between IaaS and PaaS by providing container-based virtualization. Containers allow for packaging an application and its dependencies together, ensuring that it runs consistently across different environments. In AI/ML deployments, containers can be used to encapsulate models, making them portable and easy to deploy across various infrastructure setups.

  - **Key features of CaaS:**

    - **Container orchestration**: CaaS solutions often include tools such as Kubernetes for orchestrating, scaling, and managing containerized applications.

    - **Portability**: Containers can be easily moved across environments, from on-premises to cloud to hybrid, without requiring changes to the application or its dependencies.

    - **Automated management**: Many CaaS platforms provide automated management of container clusters, reducing the operational burden on users.

  - **Pros:**

    - **Flexibility and portability**: Containers provide flexibility by allowing models to be deployed on any infrastructure that supports containers, ensuring consistency across environments.

- **Scalability**: With CaaS, scaling containerized AI/ML models becomes more straightforward. Orchestration platforms such as Kubernetes make it easier to manage large-scale deployments.

- **Reduced infrastructure management**: While not as hands-off as PaaS or SaaS, CaaS reduces the infrastructure management workload by abstracting container orchestration.

- **Cons**:

  - **Complexity in setup**: Setting up and managing containers, especially in large-scale production systems, can require specialized knowledge in containerization technologies.

  - **Operational overhead**: While less than IaaS, CaaS still requires some degree of infrastructure management, especially when scaling up containerized AI/ML applications.

- **Use case**: CaaS is ideal for organizations that want flexibility and portability while reducing the complexity of managing infrastructure. For instance, a company deploying AI models across multiple environments, whether on-premises or cloud, can benefit from the portability and consistency offered by CaaS.

Comparing the economies of IaaS, PaaS, SaaS, and CaaS

When choosing between these cloud service models, it is important to consider the trade-offs between control, complexity, and cost:

- IaaS offers the most control but requires significant operational effort. It is cost-effective for large-scale, resource-intensive operations but may lead to higher costs in terms of maintenance and management.

- PaaS abstracts much of the infrastructure complexity, making it faster and easier to develop and deploy applications. While PaaS reduces operational overhead, it can be more expensive for continuous, large-scale operations due to the premium on managed services.

- SaaS provides the least amount of operational work, as everything is managed by the vendor. However, it offers the least flexibility and is often suitable for businesses that need quick solutions without needing extensive customization.

- CaaS strikes a balance between flexibility and ease of use, offering a more portable and scalable option for deploying AI/ML models. CaaS is more complex than PaaS but provides better control over the infrastructure while reducing some operational overhead compared to IaaS.

Note

Organizations must carefully evaluate their specific needs, technical capabilities, and budget to choose the appropriate model. For businesses with highly specialized AI/ML workloads requiring control over infrastructure, IaaS or CaaS may be more suitable. For businesses prioritizing speed, flexibility, and low operational burden, PaaS or SaaS would be ideal choices. In deploying AI/ML use cases to the real world, organizations face a range of challenges from productization to modularization, data and code versioning, pipeline automation, and infrastructure choices. By selecting the right service model (IaaS, PaaS, SaaS, or CaaS) based on their specific needs, businesses can optimize operational efficiency, reduce costs, and ensure scalable and maintainable AI solutions.

As we move from architectural foundations to the realities of deploying ML models in production, it's essential to consider the surrounding tooling, such as logging, versioning, monitoring, and artifact management, that support operational excellence and long-term sustainability.

Other MLOPs design considerations required to support model deployment

The process of operationalizing AI/ML models extends far beyond building and deploying the model. It encompasses defining the right success metrics, ensuring continuous monitoring and improvement, handling long-term and multi-objective optimization, and integrating the models into applications where they can provide real business value. The integration of models into diverse environments, from cloud-based systems to edge devices in remote locations, requires a thoughtful approach to model size, data privacy, and resource constraints.

As businesses continue to adopt AI/ML models, focusing on operational efficiency and model scalability will be key to unlocking their full potential. Emerging technologies such as federated learning and model diffusion techniques offer promising avenues for ensuring that AI solutions are not only high-performing but also adaptable to real-world constraints. By addressing these challenges, organizations can drive the adoption of AI/ML technologies, improve their business processes, and achieve long-term success.

Planning and tools for deploying an ML model in production

Deploying an ML model into production involves several critical steps and planning aspects to ensure smooth operation, maintainability, and scalability. Various tools and best practices are required to handle different stages of the ML life cycle. Here, we outline key areas to focus on before deploying an ML model and discuss the tools available for each:

- **Code versioning**: This ensures that different versions of the ML pipeline, including pre-processing scripts, training code, and inference logic, are well managed. It helps track changes, collaborate with teams, and roll back to previous states if necessary.

  - **Popular tools:**

    - **GitHub**: A widely used platform for source code management and version control
    - **GitLab**: Similar to GitHub but with built-in CI/CD capabilities
    - **AWS Code Commit**: A managed source control service integrated with AWS services
    - **Bitbucket**: Supports both Git and Mercurial, often used for enterprise applications

  - **Best practices:**

    - Use branching strategies (e.g., GitFlow) to manage development, testing, and production releases
    - Implement code reviews and pull requests to ensure quality control
    - Automate code deployment using CI/CD pipelines

- **Artifact management**: Once an ML model is trained, it should be stored securely for versioning, retrieval, and deployment. This ensures that the same model version is used consistently across different environments.

  - **Popular tools:**

    - **JFrog Artifactory**: A universal artifact repository manager supporting multiple package formats
    - **Azure Artifacts**: Integrated into Azure DevOps for storing dependencies and build artifacts
    - **Nexus Repository**: Supports binaries, Docker images, and ML models

- **Best practices:**

    - Store trained models with metadata, including hyperparameters and dataset versions

    - Maintain version control over model artifacts using semantic versioning

- **Build and deployment tool**: Automating the build and deployment process is crucial to maintaining efficiency in production environments.

    - **Popular tools:**

        - **Jenkins**: A widely used CI/CD tool for automating builds and deployments

        - **GitHub Actions**: Provides workflow automation directly within GitHub

        - **Poetry**: A dependency management tool for Python that simplifies packaging and versioning

        - **AWS CodeBuild**: A fully managed build service in AWS

    - **Best practices:**

        - Use containerization (Docker) for consistent deployment environments

        - Automate testing and deployment using CI/CD pipelines

- **Logging and monitoring**: These are essential for detecting issues in production, tracking model performance, and troubleshooting failures.

    - **Popular tools:**

        - **Elasticsearch**: A distributed search and analytics engine for logging and search-based analytics

        - **Prometheus**: Used for monitoring applications and infrastructure with real-time alerting

        - **Fluentd and Logstash**: Tools for log collection, transformation, and storage

    - **Best practices:**

        - Store logs centrally and index logs for efficient retrieval

        - Implement real-time alerts for failures and performance anomalies

- **Visualization and dashboarding**: Visualizing logs, performance metrics, and business KPIs is crucial for maintaining operational insights.

- **Popular tools:**

    - **Grafana**: A powerful dashboarding tool integrated with Prometheus for visualizing performance metrics

    - **Kibana**: Works with Elasticsearch to analyze and visualize logs and search queries

    - **Tableau and Power BI**: Used for creating business intelligence dashboards

- **Best practices:**

    - Set up **role-based access control (RBAC)** for visualization tools

    - Create custom dashboards for monitoring ML performance and infrastructure metrics

- **Model monitoring and logging**: Tracking model performance over time is essential to detect drift, bias, and degradation in accuracy.

    - **Popular tools:**

        - **MLflow**: Tracks experiments, manages models, and facilitates deployment

        - **Kubeflow**: A Kubernetes-native ML platform for training, serving, and monitoring models

        - **AWS SageMaker model monitor**: Monitors models in production for drift detection

    - **Best practices:**

        - Automate retraining triggers based on model performance decay

        - Store model predictions along with input features for auditing and analysis

- **Containerization and orchestration**: Deploying ML models in production often requires scalable, portable, and efficient infrastructure solutions.

    - **Popular tools:**

        - **Docker**: Packages ML models with their dependencies into lightweight containers

        - **Kubernetes**: An orchestration tool for deploying and managing containerized applications

        - **Amazon EMR**: A managed cluster platform for big data processing

- **Best practices:**

  - Use containerized inference servers (e.g., TensorFlow Serving or Torch-Serve) for scalable deployments

  - Optimize resource allocation using auto-scaling policies in Kubernetes

- **Data versioning and management:** Versioning datasets ensures reproducibility and traceability of ML experiments.

  - **Popular tools:**

    - **DVC:** Manages datasets and ML pipelines

    - **Google BigQuery:** A serverless data warehouse supporting large-scale analytics

    - **Delta Lake:** An open source storage layer for managing structured and semi-structured data

  - **Best practices:**

    - Store datasets in immutable formats (e.g., Parquet or ORC) for efficiency

    - Implement access control to regulate data modifications

- **Managed cloud services for ML deployment:** Cloud providers offer managed services that simplify ML deployment and scaling.

  - **Popular tools:**

    - **Azure Functions:** A serverless compute service for executing code in response to events

    - **AWS Lambda:** Serverless function execution without managing infrastructure

    - **Google Cloud Run:** Deploys containerized applications with automatic scaling

  - **Best practices:**

    - Use serverless architectures for lightweight, event-driven ML applications

    - Integrate with API gateways (e.g., Amazon API Gateway) for exposing ML models as services

Note

Deploying an ML model into production requires careful planning across multiple dimensions, including code versioning, artifact management, monitoring, and infrastructure. Leveraging the right tools helps ensure reproducibility, scalability, and maintainability. Organizations should adopt best practices such as versioning code and data, automate CI/CD pipelines, and implement robust monitoring solutions to streamline ML operations. By carefully selecting and integrating these tools, ML models can be efficiently deployed, monitored, and maintained for long-term success.

Model serving practices

Deploying an ML model into production is an essential step in transforming AI research into practical applications. However, choosing the right deployment strategy is critical to ensuring efficiency, scalability, and responsiveness. Various deployment approaches, including REST APIs, shared databases, streaming model deployment, graph model architecture, vector embedding architecture, and reinforcement learning, cater to different operational needs.

This section explores these approaches and provides a decision-making framework to help select the appropriate model-serving method based on performance, latency, and use case requirements:

- **REST API-based model deployment: Representational state transfer application programming interfaces (REST APIs)** are one of the most widely used approaches for serving ML models. In this method, models are wrapped within an API and exposed as a service, allowing external applications to send requests and receive predictions.

    - **Advantages:**

        - Easy integration with web applications and microservices
        - Scalable using load balancers
        - Can be containerized using Docker and orchestrated using Kubernetes

    - **Challenges:**

        - High latency when handling large-scale real-time inference requests
        - Requires additional infrastructure to manage authentication and rate-limiting

    - **Example use case:** A fraud detection system where a financial application sends transaction details to an API, which returns a fraud probability score

- **Shared database for model serving**: In this approach, the ML model generates predictions that are stored in a database, which is then accessed by various applications.

    - **Advantages**:

        - Ensures consistency as all users access the same prediction results
        - Reduces computational overhead for models that do not require real-time inference

    - **Challenges**:

        - Prediction updates are batch-based, limiting real-time adaptability
        - Storage overhead increases as the number of predictions grows

    - **Example use case**: A recommendation system that precomputes personalized content suggestions and stores them in a database for retrieval by users

- **Streaming model deployment**: Streaming model deployment involves integrating models with real-time data pipelines using technologies such as Apache Kafka, Apache Flink, or Spark Streaming.

    - **Advantages**:

        - Supports continuous learning by dynamically updating models with incoming data
        - Ideal for applications requiring low-latency and real-time decision-making

    - **Challenges**:

        - Requires robust infrastructure and monitoring to handle large-scale data streams
        - Increased complexity in debugging and maintaining streaming pipelines

    - **Example use case**: Real-time sentiment analysis of social media posts where incoming text is processed instantly to detect sentiment shifts

- **Graph model architecture**: Graph-based model serving is used when relationships between entities need to be captured dynamically, such as in social networks or knowledge graphs.

    - **Advantages**:

        - Effective for applications requiring deep relational analysis
        - Enables efficient querying and traversing of interconnected data

- **Challenges:**

  - Requires specialized databases such as Neo4j or Amazon Neptune
  - Computationally intensive for large-scale graphs

- **Example use case:** Fraud detection in financial transactions where relationships between entities (users, accounts, and transactions) are modeled as a graph

- **Vector embedding architecture:** Vector embedding-based serving stores high-dimensional representations of data, enabling fast similarity searches and recommendations.

  - **Advantages:**

    - Optimized for applications requiring nearest-neighbor searches, such as image retrieval and recommendation systems
    - Efficient storage and querying using **approximate nearest neighbors (ANN)** techniques

  - **Challenges:**

    - Requires specialized libraries such as FAISS or Annoy for optimized indexing
    - High memory consumption when handling large embedding spaces

  - **Example use case:** Personalized movie recommendations where user preferences are stored as vector embeddings and matched against movie embeddings

- **Reinforcement learning-based serving: Reinforcement learning** (RL) models dynamically update their policy based on feedback from the environment.

  - **Advantages:**

    - Adaptive learning mechanism that improves over time
    - Effective for decision-making applications requiring real-time adjustments

  - **Challenges:**

    - Computationally expensive, as continuous training and inference are needed
    - Requires substantial historical data to bootstrap the learning process

  - **Example use case:** Dynamic pricing models for e-commerce that adjust product prices in real time based on demand and competitor actions

Decision criteria for selecting the appropriate model-serving method

When selecting a deployment strategy, various factors need to be considered, including performance requirements, latency constraints, and use case specifics. The following decision criteria can help guide the selection process:

- **Performance requirements:**

  - If the model needs to handle high-throughput requests, a REST API or streaming deployment with load balancing is recommended

  - For applications that rely on precomputed outputs, a shared database approach is more efficient

- **Latency considerations:**

  - For applications requiring real-time decision-making (e.g., fraud detection, autonomous vehicles, etc.), a streaming model or vector embedding architecture is ideal

  - In contrast, batch processing workloads (e.g., predictive maintenance) can leverage database-based deployment

- **Scalability needs:**

  - If the model must scale dynamically based on demand, Kubernetes-based REST API deployments or streaming frameworks are the best choices

  - For use cases with large volumes of interconnected data, graph model architectures provide scalability advantages

- **Complexity and maintainability:**

  - REST APIs offer the easiest integration for standard applications

  - Streaming deployments and RL require more complex infrastructure and monitoring

  - Graph architectures necessitate specialized databases and query optimizations

- **Use case alignment:**

  - **Web applications:** REST API deployment

  - **Recommendation systems:** Vector embedding architecture

  - **Financial fraud detection:** Graph model deployment

  - **Autonomous systems:** RL-based serving

Note

Efficiently serving ML models requires a well-thought-out deployment strategy that aligns with an application's requirements. The choice of deployment approach, whether REST API, shared database, streaming model, graph model, vector embeddings, or RL, depends on performance needs, scalability, latency constraints, and complexity considerations. By leveraging the right model-serving methodology, organizations can enhance their AI-driven applications, ensuring high efficiency and reliability in production environments.

While deploying models is a significant milestone, sustaining their effectiveness in real-world environments requires continuous learning and adaptation. Integrating feedback loops into ML systems enables models to evolve with user behavior, environmental changes, and business goals, driving long-term performance and relevance.

Integrate feedback loops for continuous improvement

ML models do not exist in isolation; they operate in dynamic environments where user preferences, external conditions, and business objectives evolve over time. To ensure continuous improvement and long-term effectiveness, integrating feedback loops into ML pipelines is crucial. Feedback mechanisms allow models to adapt, refine predictions, and optimize outcomes based on real-world observations.

This section explores different types of feedback, based on user, environment, domain-specific, and metric, while outlining strategies for seamless feedback integration into ML pipelines.

Here are the types of feedback for model refinement:

- **User feedback**: User feedback is one of the most valuable sources for improving ML models, particularly for recommendation systems, search engines, and personalization algorithms.

  - **Examples**:

    - **E-commerce recommendation systems**: Customer clicks, purchases, and dwell time provide implicit signals of product interest

    - **Search engines**: Query reformulations, click-through rates, and bounce rates help refine search ranking models

    - **Chatbots and virtual assistants**: User sentiment analysis and repeated questions highlight areas requiring model adjustments

- **Integration strategies:**

    - Implement real-time monitoring of user interactions and collect explicit (ratings, reviews) and implicit (clicks, hovers, and session duration) feedback

    - Utilize bandit algorithms to dynamically adjust recommendations based on new feedback

    - Employ A/B testing to measure the impact of incorporating user feedback into model refinements

- **Environmental feedback for RL and adaptive systems**: In dynamic settings where actions influence future states, RL provides a structured way to integrate feedback from the environment.

    - **Examples:**

        - **Autonomous vehicles:** Adjusting driving policies based on changing road conditions

        - **Trading algorithms:** Updating portfolio strategies based on market fluctuations

        - **Dynamic pricing:** Adjusting product prices in response to real-time demand and competitor actions

    - **Integration strategies:**

        - Use reward functions to evaluate model actions and determine optimal adjustments

        - Implement off-policy learning to learn from past interactions without retraining the entire model

        - Leverage multi-armed bandits for balancing exploration (new strategies) and exploitation (optimal strategies)

- **Domain-specific feedback for industry-specific adaptation**: Different industries require specialized feedback mechanisms tailored to unique constraints and objectives.

    - **Examples:** Marketing and media mix optimization professionals allocate budgets across various channels (TV, digital ads, and social media) and require feedback mechanisms to adjust spending dynamically:

        - **Short-term feedback: Click-through rates (CTRs)**, conversion rates, and engagement metrics provide immediate performance signals

- **Long-term feedback**: Brand awareness, customer **lifetime value** (**LTV**), and retention metrics indicate broader strategic success

- **Integration strategies**:

  - Use multi-touch attribution models to analyze customer journeys and adjust channel weights accordingly
  - Apply causal inference techniques (e.g., difference-in-differences and propensity score matching) to estimate the true impact of marketing interventions
  - Utilize Bayesian optimization to continuously fine-tune media mix allocation based on evolving feedback

- **Metric-based feedback (short-term vs. long-term optimization)**: Metrics serve as proxies for model success, but distinguishing between short-term and long-term objectives is critical.

  - **Examples**:

    - **Short-term metrics**: Accuracy, precision, recall, and CTR
    - **Long-term metrics**: Customer retention, profitability, and brand value

  - **Integration strategies**:

    - Define intermediate proxies (e.g., customer engagement score) that correlate with long-term objectives
    - Design reward functions in reinforcement learning that balance short-term gains with long-term stability
    - Simultaneously optimize for competing objectives using Pareto front analysis

Short-term metrics, such as accuracy, precision, recall, or CTR, are easier to measure but can lead to unintended consequences if over-optimized, such as overfitting user clicks while overlooking long-term engagement. Long-term metrics, such as customer retention, profitability, or brand value, offer deeper strategic insight but are harder to quantify and often require indirect methods of measurement.

Mechanisms for seamless feedback integration in ML pipelines

To operationalize feedback mechanisms, organizations must develop robust strategies for integrating feedback loops directly into ML pipelines:

- **Automating feedback collection and processing**: To streamline feedback integration, organizations should implement automated data collection and processing pipelines.

    - **Best practices**:

        - Establish event-driven architectures using tools such as Apache Kafka or AWS Kinesis to capture real-time feedback
        - Store structured feedback in feature stores (e.g., Feast or Tecton) to ensure consistent access across models
        - Use data versioning tools (e.g., DVC or MLflow) to track changes in feedback data

- **Continuous model retraining and deployment**: To keep models updated with the latest feedback, organizations should implement continuous retraining and deployment pipelines.

    - **Best practices**:

        - Adopt MLOps practices using CI/CD tools (e.g., Jenkins or GitHub Actions) to automate model retraining and deployment
        - Implement drift detection algorithms to monitor shifts in user behavior and trigger retraining when necessary
        - Leverage online learning frameworks to adapt models incrementally without full retraining

- **Human-in-the-loop (HITL) integration**: In scenarios where automated feedback is insufficient, integrating human feedback ensures higher-quality model updates.

    - **Best practices**:

        - Implement active learning techniques where the model queries humans for labels when uncertainty is high
        - Use crowdsourcing platforms (e.g., Amazon Mechanical Turk) to gather domain-expert feedback
        - Establish feedback dashboards to enable analysts and decision-makers to review and validate automated predictions

- **Balancing exploration and exploitation**: To ensure continuous improvement, models must balance between leveraging existing knowledge (exploitation) and trying new strategies (exploration).

  - **Best practices**:

    - Use epsilon-greedy strategies to occasionally test alternative recommendations

    - Implement Thompson sampling to dynamically allocate resources based on feedback

    - Apply contextual bandits to optimize decisions in real time based on user interactions

> **Note**
>
> Integrating feedback loops into ML pipelines is essential for maintaining model relevance, improving performance, and ensuring alignment with business goals. By leveraging user feedback, environmental feedback, domain-specific feedback, and metric-driven feedback, organizations can create adaptive, self-improving ML systems. A well-structured feedback integration strategy ensures that models continuously evolve to meet the changing needs of users, industries, and long-term objectives.

MLOps is a discipline that focuses on automating and streamlining the deployment, monitoring, and management of ML models in production. Borrowing principles from DevOps, MLOps ensures stability, scalability, and maintainability of ML systems while reducing technical debt.

First, we should understand the need for MLOps in production ML. Unlike traditional software development, ML introduces new complexities such as the following:

- **Data dependencies**: Models rely on constantly evolving datasets, making them susceptible to data drift

- **Model versioning**: Unlike code, ML models continuously change with retraining, requiring version control

- **Pipeline complexity**: End-to-end ML pipelines involve data preprocessing, feature engineering, training, validation, deployment, and monitoring

- **Operationalization**: Ensuring reproducibility, continuous integration, and deployment is non-trivial

MLOps bridges the gap between research and production by standardizing the life cycle of ML systems, leading to greater reliability and efficiency.

Key components of MLOps include the following:

- **Automated data ingestion and validation**: Ensuring data quality before training
- **Feature engineering pipelines**: Standardizing feature generation to avoid duplication
- **Model versioning and experiment tracking**: Using tools such as MLflow and DVC to track model changes
- **CI/CD for ML pipelines**: Automating training, testing, and deployment with Jenkins, GitHub Actions, or Kubeflow
- **Monitoring and logging**: Real-time tracking of data drift, model performance, and system health
- **Model retraining and rollback**: Automated retraining with fallback mechanisms for degraded models

Adopting MLOps best practices reduces ML technical debt by improving reproducibility, scalability, and maintainability.

Systematic feedback: continuous learning in ML systems

ML models are not static artifacts; they must continuously learn from real-world feedback to maintain accuracy and effectiveness. Systematic feedback loops help refine models through the following:

- **Online and offline feedback loops**:
  - **Offline feedback**: Periodic batch updates using new labeled data
  - **Online feedback**: Real-time learning from user interactions, such as RL updates in recommendation systems
- **Implementing feedback mechanisms**:
  - **User feedback**: Explicit ratings, engagement metrics, and CTRs
  - **Domain-specific feedback**: Expert annotations and manual reviews
  - **Performance metrics**: Monitoring precision, recall, AUC-ROC, and accuracy shifts

- **Challenges in feedback integration**:

    - **Feedback delay**: Offline models suffer from latency in updates

    - **Bias in feedback data**: User interactions may reinforce existing biases

    - **Automation risks**: Over-reliance on feedback without validation can lead to drift

A robust feedback mechanism ensures that ML systems evolve with changing user needs and business goals.

Data drift, model drift, and monitoring strategies

ML models degrade over time due to shifts in data distributions and evolving patterns in real-world data. Understanding and mitigating these drifts are critical to sustaining model performance:

- **Understanding data drift**: Data drift occurs when input features change over time, leading to discrepancies between training and production data:

    - **Types of data drift**:

        - **Feature drift**: Changes in individual feature distributions (e.g., average customer age increases over time)

        - **Concept drift**: Changes in the relationship between inputs and outputs (e.g., fraud detection models failing after a major policy change)

        - **Prior probability shift**: Class distributions evolving (e.g., an increase in fraudulent transactions during holidays)

- **Understanding model drift**: Model drift happens when a trained model's performance declines due to data drift or changing external conditions:

    - **Major causes of model drift**:

        - Changes in user behavior

        - New product features that alter interactions

        - Regulatory changes affecting data patterns

- **Detecting and mitigating drift**:

    - **Drift detection metrics**:

        - **Kolmogorov-Smirnov (KS)** test

        - **Population stability index (PSI)**

        - Jensen-Shannon divergence

- **Mitigation strategies:**
    - Continuous retraining on recent data
    - Dynamic weighting of older and newer data
    - Model ensemble methods to adjust for drifted features

Monitoring data and model drift ensures ML systems remain robust and relevant over time.

Architecture considerations in ML systems

Building a scalable ML architecture requires balancing flexibility, performance, and operational efficiency:

- **Microservices versus monolithic ML architecture:**
    - **Monolithic architecture:** Centralized ML pipeline, easier to develop but harder to scale
    - **Microservices architecture:** Modular approach enabling independent scaling of components such as data processing, model inference, and monitoring

- **Infrastructure choices:**
    - **Cloud versus on-premises:** Cloud platforms such as AWS Sagemaker and Google Vertex AI provide scalability, while on-premises solutions offer greater control
    - **Containerization and orchestration:** Docker and Kubernetes enable scalable deployment across multiple environments

- **Real-time versus batch processing:**
    - **Batch processing:** Suitable for periodic model retraining and scoring
    - **Real-time inference:** Low-latency inference for applications such as fraud detection and recommendation systems

Designing a scalable ML architecture ensures efficient productionization and long-term maintainability.

Bias identification and mitigation

Bias in ML models can lead to unfair outcomes, regulatory issues, and loss of trust. Identifying and mitigating bias is critical to responsible AI deployment:

- **Types of bias in ML models:**

    - **Sampling bias**: Underrepresentation of certain groups in training data
    - **Label bias**: Subjective labeling leading to skewed learning
    - **Automation bias**: Over-reliance on algorithmic decisions without human oversight
    - **Measurement bias**: Inaccurate feature collection affecting predictions

- **Techniques for bias detection:**

    - **Disparate impact analysis**: Examining how different demographic groups are affected
    - **Counterfactual fairness testing**: Checking whether model decisions change when sensitive attributes (e.g., race and gender) are altered
    - **Explainability tools**: SHAP and LIME help interpret model decisions

- **Bias mitigation strategies:**

    - **Rebalancing training data**: Ensuring diverse representation
    - **Fairness constraints**: Incorporating fairness-aware algorithms such as adversarial debiasing
    - **Post-processing adjustments**: Calibrating model outputs to reduce disparities

Mitigating bias is essential for ethical AI and compliance with fairness regulations.

> **Note**
>
> Establishing a robust operational backbone for ML systems requires implementing MLOps best practices, integrating systematic feedback, monitoring drift, designing scalable architectures, and mitigating bias. By following structured methodologies outlined in MLOps frameworks, organizations can build resilient, scalable, and trustworthy ML solutions. Addressing hidden technical debt through automation, continuous monitoring, and fairness measures ensures long-term sustainability and operational excellence in AI-driven applications.

As we round out our exploration of MLOps and deployment strategies, it's equally important to look ahead toward the evolving challenges and innovations shaping the next frontier of AI/ML systems, especially those designed for real-world, resource-constrained environments.

What's next in ML systems?

One of the key challenges in operationalizing AI/ML models for business success is ensuring that the models are well integrated into the application environments they are designed to support. It's not enough to have a high-performing model in a development or cloud environment. Models need to be efficiently deployed in real-world scenarios, where limitations such as computing resources, network availability, and privacy concerns must be addressed.

In many cases, businesses may not have access to the same infrastructure in production environments as they do during model development. For instance, organizations operating in remote areas, such as logistics or agricultural sectors, may not always have reliable cloud access or high-performance computing infrastructure. This requires AI/ML models to be lightweight and capable of running on edge devices with limited computational power. Similarly, models may need to operate without constant access to Wi-Fi or cloud services, which further complicates their deployment.

Reducing model size: diffusion techniques for smaller devices

AI/ML models, particularly deep learning models, are known for their large size and computational demands. Model diffusion techniques aim to reduce the size of these models while retaining their ability to make accurate predictions. Some of the most used techniques for this purpose include the following:

- **Model pruning**: This technique involves removing the less important parameters from the model, reducing its size while maintaining performance. Pruning can be done during training or after the model has been trained.

- **Quantization**: In quantization, the precision of the model's parameters is reduced. For example, instead of using 32-bit floating-point numbers to represent the weights, 8-bit integers could be used. This reduction in precision helps decrease the size and computational requirements of the model, allowing it to run on less powerful machines.

- **Knowledge distillation**: This technique involves training a smaller "student" model to mimic the behavior of a larger "teacher" model. The student model is lighter and more suitable for deployment on edge devices, but still captures the important patterns learned by the teacher model.

These approaches allow businesses to deploy AI/ML models on devices with limited memory, processing power, and network connectivity, ensuring that the operationalization process is not hindered by hardware constraints.

Federated learning: ensuring data privacy and efficient learning

Another key consideration in operationalizing AI/ML models is data privacy and minimizing data transfer. Traditional ML methods typically rely on collecting data from various sources, centralizing it, and then training the model on this centralized dataset. However, this approach may not be feasible in scenarios where privacy regulations (e.g., GDPR) or network limitations prevent the large-scale transfer of data.

Federated learning (FL) offers a promising solution to this challenge. In FL, the model is trained across multiple devices or servers (referred to as "clients") that each hold local data samples. Rather than transferring the data to a centralized server, each client trains a local version of the model using its data and only shares the learned parameters (such as model weights) with a central server. The server aggregates these updates from all clients to create a global model. This allows learning to happen in a distributed manner, ensuring the following:

- **Data privacy**: Sensitive data remains on local devices and is not transferred, reducing the risk of privacy breaches. Only model updates (not raw data) are shared, which helps maintain privacy compliance.

- **Minimal data transfer**: Since only model parameters are communicated between clients and the server, this approach significantly reduces the amount of data that needs to be transferred, making FL more suitable for environments with limited network bandwidth or intermittent connectivity.

- **Efficient learning**: Despite the decentralized nature of FL, the aggregated model often performs as well as, or even better than, a model trained on centrally collected data. This is because FL benefits from leveraging a more diverse set of data sources, which can improve generalization across various contexts.

For example, in the healthcare industry, FL can be used to build predictive models for patient diagnosis without requiring hospitals to share sensitive patient data. Each hospital can locally train the model using its internal data, and the updates can be shared to improve the global model without violating privacy regulations.

Optimizing for resource-constrained environments

In scenarios where businesses operate in environments with low computational resources or limited connectivity (such as remote industries, rural healthcare, or IoT-driven supply chains), AI/ML models need to be optimized to run efficiently in such settings. This can be achieved through a combination of the following:

- **Edge computing**: Deploying models on edge devices (such as mobile phones, sensors, or IoT devices) ensures that inference can be made locally without needing to send data back to the cloud. This reduces latency and dependence on continuous connectivity.

- **On-device learning**: In some cases, models need to learn and adapt in real time on the device itself, especially in dynamic environments where data patterns shift rapidly. Edge learning algorithms can be employed to fine-tune models on-device without requiring access to centralized data or training resources.

- **Compression algorithms**: Techniques such as model compression, parameter sharing, and low-rank matrix factorization allow the model to fit within resource-constrained environments without significant loss in accuracy.

By ensuring that AI/ML models can operate effectively even in resource-limited settings, businesses can expand the reach of their AI solutions and ensure seamless adoption across diverse operational environments.

> **Note**
>
> This concluding chapter delved into the future of ML, focusing on addressing current challenges through emerging trends. It explored innovations for efficiency, such as diffusion techniques for smaller devices, model pruning, quantization, and knowledge distillation, alongside advancements in privacy-preserving collaborative learning, such as FL. To stay abreast with these rapidly evolving technologies, you should actively follow leading AI research conferences (e.g., NeurIPS, ICML, and ICLR), read reputable AI/ML journals and blogs, participate in online courses and communities, and engage with industry reports and open source projects.

Summary

This chapter explored the foundational elements necessary for the successful operationalization of AI/ML systems. It began by emphasizing the importance of clearly defined success metrics, distinguishing between short-term indicators such as accuracy or click-through rate and long-term objectives such as customer retention or business impact. From there, it examined how traditional SDLCs differ from ML workflows, and how aligning the two requires rethinking processes around data, experimentation, and deployment timelines. The discussion then turned to infrastructure and architecture choices, including cloud, on-premises, and edge environments, and the tooling required to support scalable model deployment. Key considerations included model serving strategies, integration into application environments, and leveraging MLOps to manage life cycle complexity. The chapter also delved into mechanisms for continuous learning and adaptation, introducing feedback loops (from user behavior, environment, and metrics) and techniques such as A/B testing, causal modeling, and reward shaping.

Finally, the chapter looked ahead to the evolving needs of ML systems operating in constrained or decentralized settings. It highlighted lightweight deployment through model compression, diffusion, and distillation, as well as privacy-preserving learning with federated approaches. Together, these insights offer a forward-looking view into building resilient, scalable, and adaptive ML systems that remain effective across diverse business contexts and infrastructure realities.

As we transition to the next chapter, we will build upon this foundation by exploring how organizations can rigorously evaluate AI-driven decisions and model interventions. This next discussion shifts focus from *operational readiness* to *empirical validation*, covering experimental design, causal inference, and metric-driven evaluation frameworks that not only ensure that models perform in production but also that they generate measurable, trustworthy impact.

8

From Metrics to Measurement: Experimentation and Causal Inference

In the previous two chapters, we established the foundational framework for *what to measure* and also explored *how* to build and operationalize the ML systems that deliver our products. Now, we should bridge the gap between deployment and value. This chapter addresses the most critical question in any business: "Did the ML system do what it was intended to do?"

Answering this question is the science of causal inference. It's the set of tools that allows us to move beyond simple correlation ("Our ecommerce sales went up after we launched the credit card feature") to causation ("Our ecommerce sales went up *because* we launched the credit card feature").

Without rigorous measurement, it is impossible to determine whether changes lead to meaningful improvements or are simply due to random chance or other external factors. This chapter explores the three families of measurement methods: the gold-standard randomized control trials, the clever observational methods used when experiments aren't possible, and the new, powerful advanced ML models that handle complex, high-dimensional data.

The following key topics will be covered:

- Randomized control trials – the gold standard with limitations
- Why can't we just use machine learning?
- Observational methods – statistical approaches
- Observational methods – advanced ML models for causal inference

Randomized control trials — the gold standard with limitations

Randomized control trials (RCTs), also known as A/B tests, are considered the gold standard for measuring the impact of interventions by randomly assigning users to control and treatment groups.

What is A/B testing?

An A/B test, or RCT, is an experiment where a population of customers is randomly split into two or more groups: a control group (group A) that receives the existing experience, and one or more treatment groups (group B, C, etc.) that receive a new version of that experience (e.g., a new feature, a different ML model, or a new UI).

Why is A/B testing important? It is the gold standard for measuring impact. By randomizing, we ensure that the *only* systematic difference between the groups is the change we introduced. This eliminates selection bias and other confounding factors, allowing us to confidently state that any observed difference in metrics is *caused* by our change.

Its key benefit includes a direct, unbiased measure of causal impact.

Here are some fundamentals to note:

- **Control versus treatment groups**: The control is the baseline; the treatment is the change. The comparison between these two groups is the core idea we want to measure.
- **Hypothesis-driven testing**: Every test must begin with a clear hypothesis. For example: "We believe that *bringing a Personalized ML Model in the journey of user cohort in Item Page (the change) will increase the add-to-cart rate* (the metric) for *new users on mobile* (the population) because *it improves purchase relevance with personalized targeting* (the rationale)."
- **Metrics and KPIs selection**: You must define your metrics *before* the test.
    - **Primary/goal metric**: The single metric that will determine whether the test is a success (e.g., *conversion rate*).
    - **Secondary/objective metrics**: Other metrics you expect to improve (e.g., *average order value*).
    - **Guardrail metrics**: Metrics you must not harm (e.g., *page load time, app uninstalls*).

- **Sample size and statistical significance**: We should decide the required sample size. This depends on your baseline metric, the **Minimum Detectable Effect** (**MDE**) you care about (e.g., "I only want to launch this if it improves conversion by at least 1%"), and your desired levels of statistical significance (p-value) and statistical power.

- **Randomization and bias reduction**: The random assignment (the "randomizer") is the most critical piece. It must ensure that every user has an equal chance of being in any group and that the assignment is independent and unbiased.

Here's how you should design an A/B test:

- **Defining the objective**: What business problem are you solving?

- **Choosing the right variant(s)**: Will this be an A/B test (one control, one treatment) or an A/B/n test (e.g., testing red, green, and blue buttons against the original)?

- **Determining the sample size and power analysis**: A test without enough power (sample size) may be inconclusive even if the feature *is* better. This is a common and wasteful mistake.

- **Determining the qualified/triggered population**: Who should be in this experiment? *Everyone*? Or, only users who *see* the feature (e.g., only users who scroll to the bottom of the page see the new footer)? Defining this "trigger" is critical for analysis.

- **Experiment duration**: How long must you run the test to get the required sample size? This is often a trade-off between speed and confidence. You must also run it long enough to capture natural weekly variance (e.g., user behavior is different on weekends).

Running an A/B test includes the following:

- **Implementation best practices**: Ensure the test runs cleanly. A bug in the code that only affects the treatment or control group will invalidate your results.

- **Ensuring data integrity**: Monitor data pipelines to ensure you are logging events correctly for all groups.

- **Contamination**: Be wary of users "contaminating" other groups. Examples include network effects (a feature in one group makes the product better for *all* users) or users on multiple devices (seeing the control on their phone and the treatment on their laptop).

- **Sample ratio mismatch (SRM)**: A critical health check. If you set your test to be 50/50, but your data shows a 52/48 split, it signals a bug in your randomization or logging, and your results cannot be trusted.

- **Common pitfalls**: Peeking at results early (invalidates frequentist tests), running too many variants at once, or ending a test the moment it becomes significant (p-hacking). Abide by the time you have dedicated to running the test to avoid common failures.

To choose the right statistical test, the specific mathematical test you use to calculate the p-value and confidence interval depends entirely on the type of metric you are measuring.

The following flowchart provides a decision-making framework:

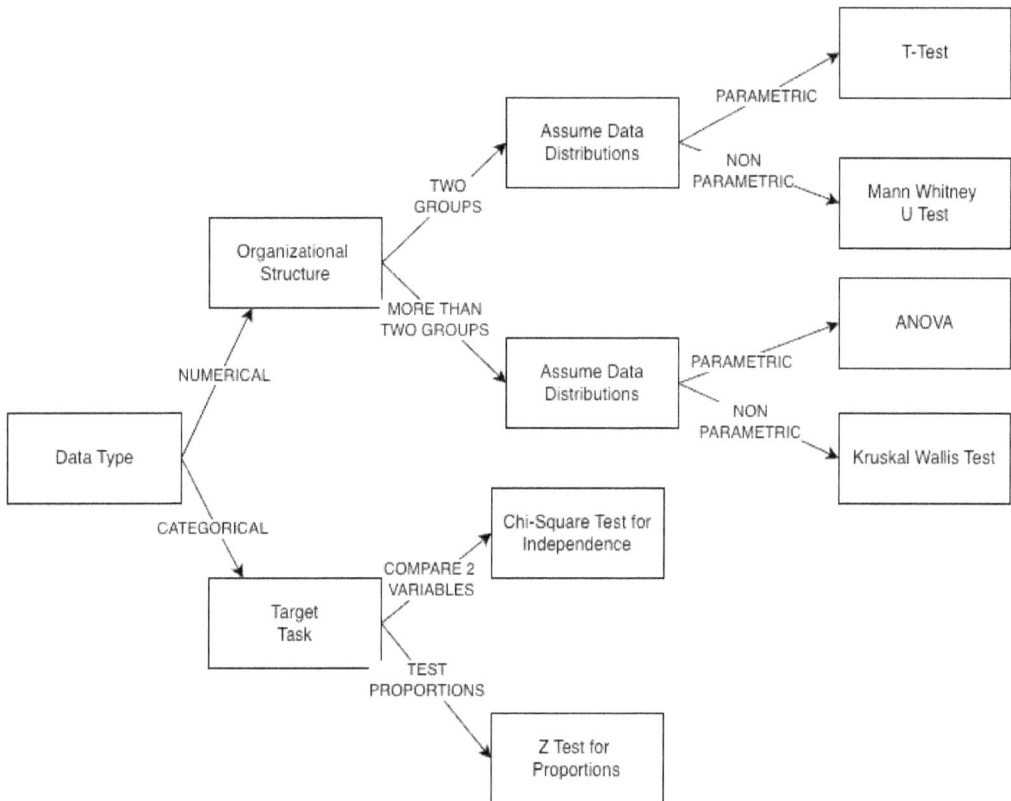

Figure 8.1: A flowchart to help in choosing the statistical test

Here is how to interpret this for A/B testing:

- **Identify your data type:**

  - **Categorical**: Is your metric a proportion or a rate (e.g., click-through rate, conversion rate, "did the user convert: yes/no")? If yes, you compare proportions. The common test for this is the Z-test for proportions or a chi-square test.

- **Numerical**: Is your metric a continuous or discrete number (e.g., average revenue per user, session duration, number of items purchased)? If yes, proceed to the next step.

- **Determine your organizational structure (groups):**

  - **Two groups**: This is the standard A/B test (control versus treatment).

  - **More than two groups**: This is an A/B/n test (e.g., control versus treatment A versus treatment B).

- **Assume data distributions:**

  - **Parametric (assumes normal distribution)**: If your numerical data is normally distributed (like a bell curve), you can use parametric tests. For two groups, this is the t-test. For more than two groups, this is **ANOVA (Analysis of Variance)**.

  - **Non-parametric (makes no assumption)**: Web and business data are often not normally distributed; they are usually skewed (e.g., a few "whale" users spend a lot, while most spend little). For this skewed data, non-parametric tests are safer and more robust. For two groups, use the Mann-Whitney U test. For more than two groups, use the Kruskal-Wallis test.

- **Uplift measurement:**

  - **Absolute lift**: (Treatment Metric - Control Metric). Example: 2.2% - 2.0% = 0.2%.

  - **Relative lift**: (Absolute Lift / Control Metric). Example: 0.2% / 2.0% = 10%.

- **When to call a test:** You should call a test when your pre-determined duration or sample size is met, not when it first becomes significant (unless you are running sequential testing or a multi-arm bandit).

Here's how you should interpret and act on results:

- **How to make data-driven decisions**: Firstly, all results are useful, especially the negative ones. Knowing what doesn't work is as useful as knowing what does. If the result is positive and significant, launch it. If negative, remember it.

- **What to do when results are inconclusive**: A "flat" or non-significant result is a learning opportunity. This is where segmentation or cohort analysis is crucial. Does the overall flat result hide that the feature *hurts* iOS users but *helps* Android users? Does it work for new users but not returning ones? Digging into cohorts can uncover these hidden insights and lead to a partial launch or a new iteration.

- **Documenting learnings**: Again, every test, win or lose, teaches you something. Document them in a central repository to build institutional knowledge.

Next are some advanced topics to note:

- **Bayesian versus frequentist approaches:**

  - **Frequentist (traditional)**: This method was described previously. It is rigid, requires a fixed sample size, and answers: "What is the probability of this data, given no effect?"

  - **Bayesian**: This is a more intuitive approach that answers the direct business question: "What is the probability that B is better than A?" It provides a "probability of betterment," is flexible (you can "peek" and stop the test at any time), and is often easier to communicate.

- **Personalization and segmentation**: In cohort analysis, there is an idea of moving beyond a "one-size-fits-all" launch to launch features for specific user segments who benefit most. This is often the case; not all models work well for all customer cohorts. Knowing where a model works and where it cannot provides insights to the Data Science team to augment features or models.

Multi-arm bandit approaches for optimization

A/B tests are great for finding a single "winner," but they come with a "regret" cost as half of your users are stuck in the (potentially worse) control group for the entire test. **Multi-arm bandit (MAB)** approaches solve this by balancing exploration (trying out all variants) with exploitation (sending more traffic to the current winner).

How it works:

MABs dynamically allocate more traffic to the "arm" (variant) that is performing best, reducing the cost of experimentation and maximizing the metric during the test.

Example:

Optimizing LLM-generated creatives: Imagine you use an LLM to generate 20 different ad headlines for a new campaign. Running a traditional A/B test with 20 variants would be incredibly slow and would expose users to many bad headlines. This is a perfect use case for an MAB. The MAB system would do the following:

- **Explore**: Initially, it shows all 20 headlines to a small, equal number of users.
- **Exploit**: As it gathers click-through data, it quickly identifies the top 3-4 performing headlines.

- **Optimize**: It automatically starts sending the majority of traffic to these "winners" while still allocating a tiny amount of traffic to the other variants, just in case one of them starts to perform better. This approach finds the best creative faster and with less lost revenue.

The question arises as to how the bandit is decided in MAB. The MAB system needs a way to decide how to balance exploration with exploiting known winners. This is where specific algorithms come in. Two of the most popular and effective strategies are **Upper Confidence Bound** (UCB) and Thompson sampling.

- **Upper Confidence Bound (UCB)**: This algorithm is "optimistic" and comes from the frequentist school of thought. For each variant (or "arm"), it calculates the current average performance plus an "uncertainty bonus."

  - This bonus is large for variants with very little data (high uncertainty).

  - This bonus is small for variants that have been tested heavily (low uncertainty).

  - The bandit then always picks the arm with the highest combined score (performance + bonus). This strategy effectively forces the system to try out less-tested headlines, just in case they are hidden gems, while still favoring proven winners.

- **Thompson sampling**: This comes from the Bayesian school of thought or "probabilistic" approach, which is often a top performer in practice. Instead of tracking just one number (such as average click-through rate), it maintains a full probability distribution (a range of likely values) for each arm's performance.

  - A new, untested headline has a very wide distribution (e.g., "Its true click-through rate could be anywhere from 1% to 10%").

  - A well-tested winner has a very narrow distribution (e.g., "I'm 99% sure its rate is between 4.9% and 5.1%").

  - To make a choice, the algorithm takes one random sample from each arm's distribution and simply picks the arm that produced the highest sample for that round. This naturally gives the proven winners more traffic while ensuring that uncertain (but potentially great) options still get a chance to be chosen and prove their worth.

So far, we've explored methods such as randomized control trials, a.k.a. A/B tests and MABs, which fall under the umbrella of active experimentation. Their power comes from one crucial capability: our ability to *control* assignments and randomize which users see which variant. This randomization is the "gold standard" because it ensures that, on average, the groups being compared are similar in every way except for the change we are testing.

But what happens when you can't run an experiment?

- What if the data is already collected?
- What if it's technically impossible or prohibitively expensive to randomize users into a control group?
- What if it's unethical or expensive to withhold a new feature (such as a critical security patch) from one group?

We are often left with a wealth of observational data. We can see what happened; for example, which users naturally decided to use a new feature, and which didn't, but we cannot say with certainty why their outcomes were different or whether the outcome is a true representation of users opting for the feature.

This is the fundamental challenge of observational causal inference: separating correlation from causation. In observational data, the groups we want to compare are almost never alike. Users who chose to adopt a new feature might be more engaged, iPhone users, more tech-savvy, or newer to the platform than those who didn't. Did the feature make them more engaged, or were they just more engaged to begin with?

This is where a new toolkit of quasi-experimental methods becomes essential. The following sections will introduce powerful techniques designed to mimic an experiment by intelligently accounting for these underlying differences and isolating the true causal impact of a feature. We will move from "what happened?" to "what *would have* happened?"

Why can't we just use machine learning?

Now we know we can't just use experiments to model historical interventions. We can't randomly assign some users to "get a loan" and others not. In such cases, we rely on quasi-experimental methods for measurement, which use statistical techniques to approximate an experiment using historical data.

But can we use function approximation machine learning here? Unfortunately, the answer is no, and the explanation is a bit involved. Let's understand, through the following figure, what a predictive model, at the most fundamental level, does:

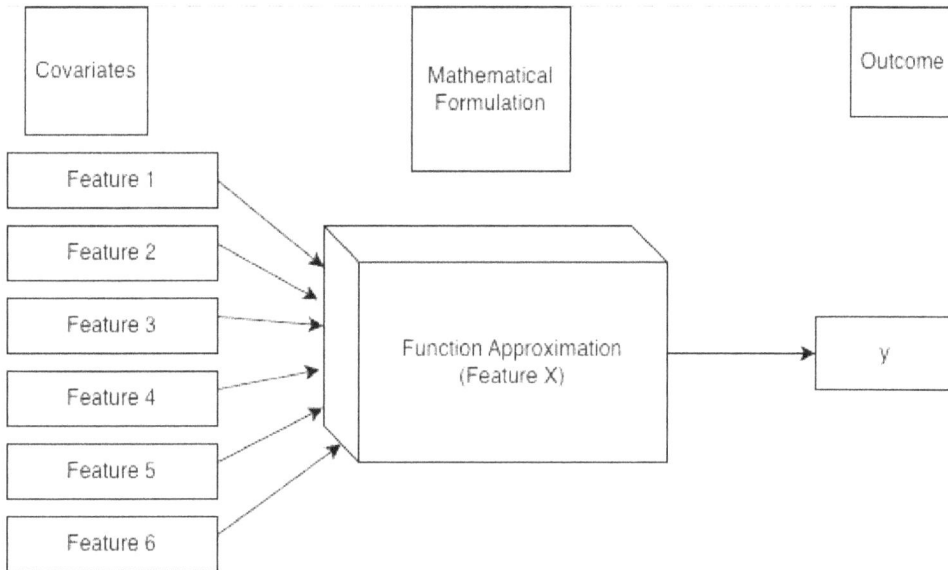

Figure 8.2: A predictive model performs function approximation, mapping X to y

The preceding figure explains that a typical machine learning model is primarily responsible for function approximation for a given input set of features, X tries to predict the outcome, y.

It's a critical distinction. A standard predictive model is built to answer, "What will happen?"

Example: "Who is most likely to sign up as a paid customer after a trial membership?"

In this model, all inputs, user features (x1, x2…) and any treatment (T), are treated as a bag of features. The model is great at finding correlations and making accurate predictions, but it fundamentally confuses correlation with causation. It can't tell you whether a trial discount caused a conversion, or whether the users who got the discount were simply more engaged to begin with, by virtue of being more engaged online.

On the other hand, a causal model is built to answer a completely different question: "What if we do something? What would be counterfactual if this had happened?" The following figure illustrates this concept:

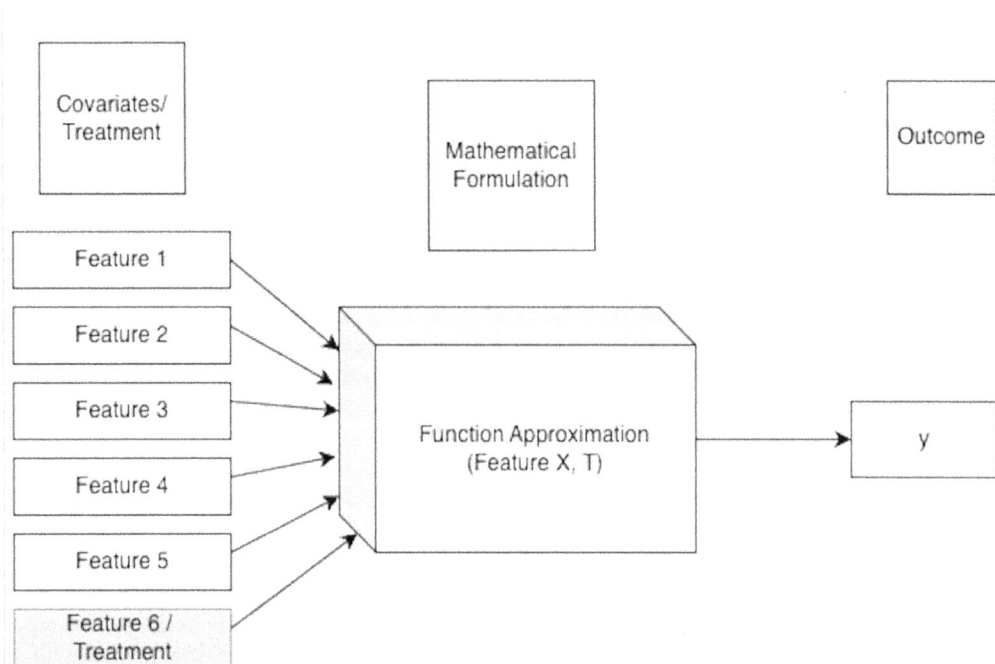

Figure 8.3: A causal model explores "what if" scenarios, examining counterfactual outcomes of interventions

Example: "What is the effect of giving a 10% discount on the membership signup rate?"

To answer this, the treatment (T), i.e., the "discounts" in the diagram described as "T", can no longer be just another feature. It must be treated as a "first-class citizen." The entire goal of the model shifts from predicting an outcome to isolating the precise, independent impact of T on that outcome.

If we apply machine learning here for function approximation, it won't treat the "discount" as a first-class citizen and consider all features the same, which undermines the entire goal of isolating the effect of treatment on outcome.

So, what do causal models need (besides just data)? The following figure shows the answer:

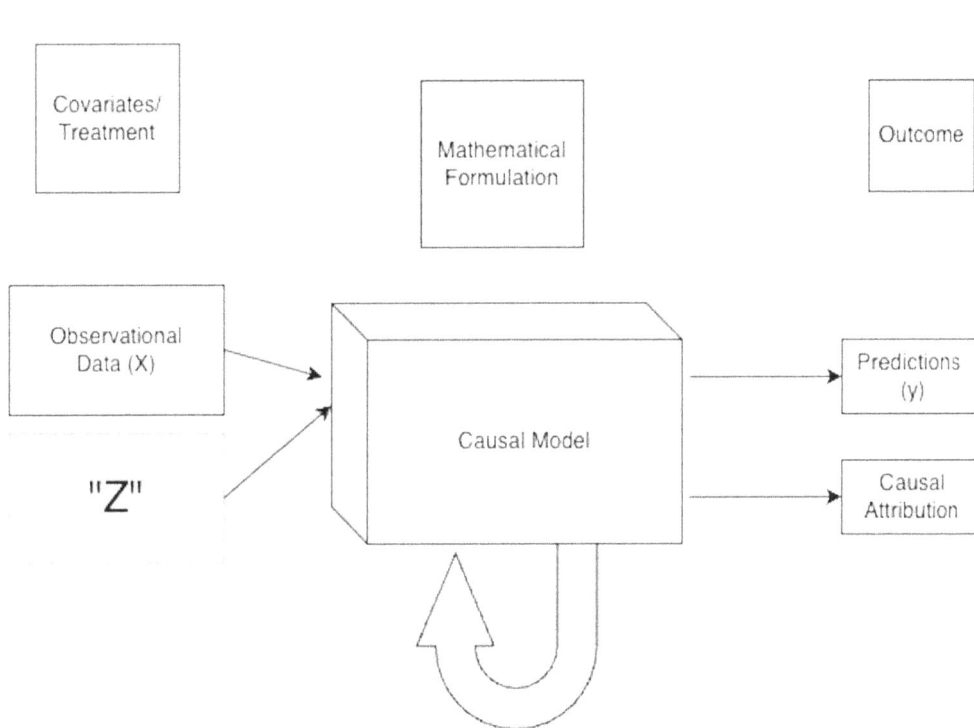

Figure 8.4: Causal modeling extends beyond function fitting, requiring data plus causal assumptions (Z)

This shift means a causal model needs more than just function approximation, which we can get from fitting the model model.fit(X, y). As the preceding diagram shows, the model needs data and an explicit "Z" factor. This "Z" represents our causal assumptions, that is, our understanding of how the system works.

Now, let's recap all that we need before we can even run this causal model. We must define the following:

1. **The causal question**: What is the treatment (T) and what is the outcome (y)?
2. **Confounders**: What other variables (x) affect both the treatment and the outcome? For example, a user's "engagement level" might affect whether they receive a discount (T) and whether they sign up for paid membership (y). We must explicitly identify and control these.

3. **The causal structure**: What do we believe causes what? This is often mapped out in a diagram before any analysis begins.

These assumptions are the "quasi-experimental" part of the design. We are using our knowledge to build a structure that attempts to statistically "design" an experiment from data that was never experimental.

What's "Z" here? Our understanding of the system is beyond data. This understanding determines the approach we want to experiment with:

- If the understanding is the network, what causes what, then the method we can try is the Bayesian network

- If the understanding is common with confounders (confounders are defined as variables that impact treatment (assignment) and outcome at the same time), then the methods we can try are DoWhy + EconML

- If understanding is the prior belief, then the method we can try is the Bayesian filter

This need for an explicit structure has led to two major families of causal methods. We'll begin by exploring the foundational observational methods, many of which originated in econometrics. These techniques use clever "designs" to isolate causal effects. After that, we will cover the new wave of advanced ML models that leverage machine learning's power to handle complex, high-dimensional data and find personalized causal effects.

Observational methods — statistical approaches

The aim is to isolate the effect of a treatment (e.g., a discount) on an outcome (e.g., a paid signup). These statistical approaches generally fall into two categories: matching methods that create comparable groups (such as PSM, synthetic control, and DiD) and modeling approaches that exploit specific data structures to estimate the effect (such as RDD and IV).

- **Propensity score matching (PSM)**: Attempts to create a "control group" from observational data. It calculates the probability (propensity) that any given individual would have received the "treatment" (e.g., based on their income, age, location) and then matches treated and untreated individuals who had a similar propensity score.

- **Synthetic control matching**: Creates a "synthetic" control group by finding a weighted combination of non-treated units (e.g., other cities) that best matches the pre-treatment trend of the treated unit (e.g., the city where you launched a new ad campaign).

- **Difference-in-differences (DiD)**: A powerful technique used when you have data from before and after an intervention for both a treated group and an untreated group. It subtracts the pre-to-post change in the control group from the pre-to-post change in the treatment group, isolating the treatment's effect from the underlying trend.

- **Regression discontinuity design (RDD)**: Used when a treatment is assigned based on a sharp cutoff (e.g., students with a score >80 get a scholarship). By comparing the outcomes of individuals just above and just below that cutoff, we can estimate the causal impact of the scholarship.

- **Instrumental variables (IV)**: A complex but powerful method that finds a third variable (the "instrument") that is correlated with the treatment but not the outcome (except through the treatment). This helps isolate the true causal effect from confounding variables.

These classical methods are powerful but often rely on specific data structures (such as a sharp cutoff for RDD) and can struggle with very high-dimensional or non-linear data. Next, we'll see how the principles of machine learning can be combined with these causal goals to create even more flexible and powerful models.

Observational methods — advanced ML approaches

A new class of methods uses modern machine learning to handle the high-dimensional and non-linear nature of causal problems, especially for personalization.

- **Causal tree and forest**: These are (random) forests adapted for causal inference. They partition the data to find subgroups with the most significant differences in treatment effects, helping to uncover heterogeneous (uneven) effects.

- **Double machine learning (DML)**: Uses two ML models, one to predict the outcome and one to predict the treatment, and then uses the residuals (errors) from both models in a final estimation step. This is a robust way to control many confounding variables.

- **Uplift modeling**: This is the key to true personalization. Instead of modeling the outcome (e.g., "Will this user convert?"), uplift models directly model the treatment effect itself (e.g., "What is the additional probability this user will convert if I show them this ad?"). This allows you to target only the "persuadables" and avoid wasting resources on those who would convert anyway ("sure things") or will never convert ("lost causes").

- **Bayesian Structural Time Series (BSTS)**: A method popularized by Google for time-series data. It builds a model of what would have happened to a metric (e.g., sales in California) in the absence of an intervention, and then compares that "synthetic" prediction to what actually happened.

- **Causal deep learning (neural networks for causal inference)**: An emerging field using the power of neural networks to model complex causal relationships, especially in data with unstructured features such as images or text.

The causal methods we've just covered are incredibly powerful for learning from historical data and understanding complex, "what if" questions. They excel at post-hoc analysis, thereby looking back to understand what worked and why. Now, let's shift our focus from offline analysis back to online optimization. When we're running live experiments, our goal is not just to learn, but to learn as fast as possible and adapt our decisions in real time.

The next sections will explore advanced methods for this exact challenge. We'll first look at sequential A/B testing to make our experiments more efficient and then delve into reinforcement learning as a powerful framework for continuous, automated decision-making, which is a sophisticated evolution of the bandit problem.

Sequential A/B testing and its advantages over RCTs

Traditional A/B tests require a fixed sample size before analysis, leading to wasted time and resources if one variation is significantly better early on. Sequential A/B testing improves efficiency by allowing continuous evaluation.

Why choose sequential A/B testing?

1. **Early stopping**: If a new feature is clearly outperforming, testing can be halted early, saving resources.

2. **Lower sample requirements**: By stopping tests early when results are conclusive, the required sample size is reduced.

3. **More efficient experimentation**: Instead of waiting for an entire test period, decisions can be made dynamically.

Example: Sequential A/B versus A-B-C testing

Consider a company testing three variations (A, B, and C) of a landing page. A-B-C testing requires collecting enough data for all three variations before drawing conclusions. A sequential approach (e.g., A-B testing first, then testing the best against C) ensures significant sample sizes and faster iteration.

Interesting take: reinforcement learning versus model predictive control

Both **reinforcement learning (RL)** and **model predictive control (MPC)** focus on adaptive learning, but differ in approach.

RL is an approach where an agent learns by interacting with an environment, receiving rewards, and updating its policy over time.

Key properties include the following:

- Learn optimal policies through trial and error
- Updates policy based on observed rewards
- Adaptively refined strategies over time

Example: A recommendation system improving its personalization based on continuous user feedback.

MPC is a control method that predicts future system states and optimizes decisions accordingly.

Key properties include the following:

- Uses a model of the system to forecast outcomes
- Optimizes actions over a rolling horizon
- More stable than pure RL but requires domain knowledge

Example: A self-driving car adjusting acceleration and braking based on predicted traffic flow rather than learning purely from experience.

Here are the key differences between the two:

Feature	Reinforcement learning (RL)	Model predictive control (MPC)
Adaptation method	Trial and error	Predictive optimization
Use of prior data	Limited	Strong reliance on models
Stability	May experience instability	More stable control

Why choose one over the other?

- Use RL when the environment is uncertain, and long-term learning is beneficial
- Use MPC when a good system model exists, and stability is critical

Note

Measurement techniques are essential for evaluating machine learning models, guiding optimization strategies, and ensuring business impact. Randomized control trials remain a foundational approach but have limitations in certain contexts, requiring causal inference methods. Multi-arm bandits offer real-time optimization, especially for dynamic environments such as search engines. Sequential A/B testing improves efficiency by dynamically adjusting sample sizes and stopping tests early. Finally, reinforcement learning and model predictive control provide distinct approaches to adaptive learning, each with specific advantages. By selecting the appropriate measurement and adaptation techniques, organizations can achieve robust, data-driven decision-making processes that drive continuous improvement.

Summary

This chapter provided a comprehensive guide to causal inference, which is the essential science of proving that an ML system *caused* a specific business outcome, moving us beyond simple correlation. This is the critical third step, building directly on our previous work of defining metrics (*Chapter 6*) and operationalizing models (*Chapter 7*).

We began our journey with the "gold standard" of experimental methods, focusing heavily on A/B testing (RCTs). We explored its entire lifecycle, from the fundamentals of defining a solid hypothesis and selecting metrics, to the practicalities of execution, such as calculating the sample size and closely watching pitfalls such as **sample ratio mismatch** (**SRM**). We saw how to choose the right statistical test, how cohort analysis can uncover hidden insights, and contrasted the frequentist and Bayesian testing philosophies. We also explored more efficient methods, such as sequential A/B testing for early stopping and **multi-armed bandits** (**MABs**), which are perfect for dynamically testing many variants.

From there, we moved on to observational methods, the toolkit for when a randomized experiment is impossible, seeing how techniques such as **Difference-in-Differences (DiD)** and **propensity score matching (PSM)** statistically *approximate* a control group. We then explored the new frontier of advanced ML models, such as uplift modeling, which moves us from measuring an average effect to personalizing an intervention. Finally, we contrasted the adaptive learning approaches of **reinforcement learning (RL)** and **model predictive control (MPC)**.

Having established these rigorous frameworks for *measuring impact* and *making data-driven decisions*, we are now equipped to evaluate the next major wave of technological change. The tools we've just learned about, A/B testing, MABs, and causal inference, are precisely what enterprises will need to validate the value of the most transformative technology of our time, generative AI. In the next chapter, we will explore this new landscape, examining how GenAI is reshaping business, acting as a decision-making copilot, and creating entirely new opportunities for innovation.

Subscribe for a free eBook

New frameworks, evolving architectures, research drops, production breakdowns—*AI_Distilled* filters the noise into a weekly briefing for engineers and researchers working hands-on with LLMs and GenAI systems. Subscribe now and receive a free eBook, along with weekly insights that help you stay focused and informed.

Subscribe at `https://packt.link/80z6Y` or scan the QR code below.

Part 4

Emerging Topics: Generative AI and AI Agents

In *Part 4* of this book, we will explore the new frontier of AI technologies that are transforming enterprises. We will begin by explaining generative AI and **large language models (LLMs)** in business-friendly terms, covering key use cases across various functions, from marketing and customer service to code generation, as well as practical adoption considerations. Following this, we will define LLMOps and detail how it extends traditional MLOps to handle the unique operational life cycle of LLMs, including prompt orchestration, fine-tuning, and specialized monitoring. Finally, we will explore the emerging world of AI agents, discussing what they are, their potential to automate complex multi-step tasks, and the frameworks for building and governing these autonomous systems safely.

This part contains the following chapters:

- *Chapter 9, Generative AI in the Enterprise: Unlocking New Opportunities*
- *Chapter 10, Understanding GenAI Operations*
- *Chapter 11, AI Agents Explained*

9

Generative AI in the Enterprise: Unlocking New Opportunities

The rise of ChatGPT has been transformational for all of us, impacting our lives in various ways. While **generative AI (GenAI)** existed in the past and was widely used for applications such as synthetic data generation, this time it is different. ChatGPT provides us with an intuitive user interface to interact with these advanced models, revolutionizing the way we search for information and offering an effortless method to learn and retrieve knowledge. GenAI has proven to be transformational by reshaping how we work, decide, and innovate.

It enhances productivity by making information retrieval easier than ever, while also automating routine tasks, such as drafting emails and creating summaries, leading to a significant boost in productivity.

Beyond productivity, it strengthens decision-making by serving as a reliable copilot, helping individuals brainstorm fresh ideas, uncover insights, and identify patterns that drive faster and more informed choices.

On the enterprise front, multiple processes, such as customer engagement, new hire orientation, and brand strategies, are being transformed using GenAI. Technology is also being used to create intelligent apps that enable natural language interaction, personalized experiences, and quick delivery of new features.

Keeping all of this in mind, we explore the following key topics in this chapter:

- When to consider GenAI

- When not to consider GenAI

- Best practices for building GenAI solutions

Here are some important definitions and disclaimers before we get started:

- GenAI is a field within AI that specializes in generating new data in the form of text, images, and other media.

- **Large language models (LLMs)** are advanced machine learning models designed to understand and generate human language. They are trained on vast amounts of text data. They are based on transformer architecture.

- Transformers use a mechanism called self-attention to focus on different parts of the input text, allowing the model to understand the context and relationships between words. This architecture enables LLMs to process longer sequences of text more efficiently than previous models.

- *Solution* and *system* in the context of LLMs are synonyms if you are using small or medium-sized models for your enterprise application.

We are covering the most common use cases, so we may miss a few unique to your organization.

When to consider GenAI

Evaluating potential GenAI use cases is challenging. We get the urge to solve everything using GenAI, but obviously, that is impossible. We have been researching multiple frameworks to decide on meaningful GenAI use cases. We have divided the use cases into comprehension and generative applications, as follows:

- Comprehension applications cover tasks that involve sentiment analysis, relationship extraction, intent classification, summarization, and so on. The focus area around these tasks is interpreting, organizing, and tagging data.

- Generative applications are more prevalent in an enterprise setting and involve generating new artifacts such as text or images. With the right prompts and fine-tuning, LLMs can produce the desired output through new code, images, text, and so on.

In the next section, we list some use cases.

Use cases of GenAI

Let's explore a few use cases to understand the preceding classification:

- **5-star customer engagement**: Imagine this scenario: you are trying to book a flight through a chatbot, and the chatbot keeps misunderstanding your message. Wouldn't that bother you? Wouldn't you try talking to a human as soon as possible? I know I would! If this kept happening to all customers, the company would have to employ multiple human customer service representatives and might even lose a few customers.

  Along with this, there is also a possibility that some representatives might be less experienced than others and might not know the answer to all questions. To get to those edge cases, they might go to their supervisor, who then needs to leave their current task at hand to answer the burning question from the customer. This is a common scenario in most call centers. If we look closely, this operating model has multiple problems:

  - Higher costs associated with employing different representatives and a few supervisors

  - Information is not democratized, which means a few reps might know more than others, leading to a non-uniform customer experience

  - Longer wait times for customers during holidays or busy seasons lead to chaos and decreased customer satisfaction

  Now imagine a world where you don't know whether you are talking to a human or AI, and your questions will be answered in seconds without a "human" in the loop. This is the definition of world-class customer service. With the advent of LLMs, this is achievable. The sophisticated technology allows you to build chatbots that can interpret human text accurately and provide the expected response in seconds. On top of that, LLMs can provide multilingual support.

  An AI-based solution reduces the traffic to customer service representatives, who can then provide 100% attention to only a few customers with complicated questions or situations. To achieve this within your organization, here are a few things you can start doing today:

  - LLM systems are as good as their underlying data. Building a robust chatbot means training it on accurate and reliable internal documentation to reap the benefits of your investments. If you plan to deploy a chatbot in 2026, data strategy must be the top priority in 2025. This should include, but not be limited to, documentation on FAQs, edge cases, updated policy information, and price.

- When deploying LLM-based solutions for customer experiences, it is best to perform detailed testing with a few customers before deploying a full-blown solution. This means starting with a few customers and analyzing their experiences through customer surveys or employing a human in the loop to monitor those conversations. This will help you identify the gaps and improve upon them. This should be paired with the LLM as a judge mechanism to ensure that you have robust evaluations that include humans in the loop as well as the LLM as a judge.

- Along with the accuracy of the responses, it is also essential to monitor your LLM solution's reactions to bad actors with malicious intent who, for example, try to get users' credit card information or use inappropriate words. Monitoring responses for edge scenarios will help you tweak your system to block out such content and ensure a seamless customer experience.

- AI-based LLM solutions can't replace all your customer service representatives on day 1. Think about an AI solution as a staff augmentation for the first few months or years. For example, an AI solution might reduce traffic to your human reps only by 3 to 5% when you start, but as the AI becomes smarter with constant feedback, this percentage will increase and you will experience productivity gains.

- **Data democratization:** According to Accenture, businesses that adopt AI for data analysis report a 30% improvement in decision-making speed and a 20% increase in data-driven insights. Let's take a scenario to understand this use case. Consider a data organization within your team that crunches data to produce results. You are an airline company interested in seeing the number of bookings, cancellations, and customer ratings during Thanksgiving for the last five years to be better prepared for the holiday season. One way for you to do this is to go to your data organization and ask them to prioritize this request. Often, data organizations are inundated with such requests and will usually put your request in a queue and provide a timeline, such as one week, to get back to you on the request. This puts you in a tight spot as the senior leadership might have asked for the analysis, and you might not have a week for this.

Instead, think about an alternate world where all this information is fed into an LLM-based solution; any business user could ask these easy questions and get responses immediately. This is the definition of data democratization. You can also take this experience forward and provide visual representations from existing reports.

Another application within this realm is Text2SQL. It is also possible that your organization is not ready to launch the copilot solution discussed previously due to multiple reasons, such as a lack of clean data or resources. In that case, you can provide a copilot to your data team, which can write a SQL query for them based on inputs provided by the user through natural language. This will accelerate the process of getting data quickly and efficiently.

To achieve a Text2SQL use case within your organization, here are a couple of things you can do:

- If you plan to build the solution in the cloud, the data must also reside there. Though it's not mandatory, it can accelerate the development process, making it easier to connect to diverse data sources.

- Identify the tables, BI reports, and their respective metadata that will be fed into the copilot solution. This is a great way to identify updated information for your LLM-based solution.

- **Democratizing information**: If your team members are still spending a lot of time getting the correct information (such as data, internal documentation, or email), it might be time to rethink whether that is the best use of everyone's time. With the internet, information is already available in abundance and for free. However, with LLMs, it is available in a friendly user interface and in the most compact way possible. Deploying copilots within your organization and training them on your company's data can ensure that information is available quickly, enhancing productivity.

Let's understand this with an example. You employed five new customer reps and provided them with appropriate training, but you can't expect everyone to learn and grasp everything on day 1. If all the information were available to them via a copilot, where a customer asks a question they don't know about and could quickly type it into the copilot chat to get a response, it would increase their learning curve and eliminate the need for another supervisor. Since your company created all the documentation and deployed copilots, the same information is available to everyone without the need to scour through hundreds of documents. This would also lead to faster customer responses, hence increasing brand loyalty.

To begin implementing this within your organization, you can start with these actions:

- Collect all the critical documentation and ensure it's updated with the most recent information. Make sure there is a data ingestion pipeline that ensures that the most up-to-date information is fed to the AI system.

- Such copilots can be deployed enterprise-wide, but always start with the team that has the least sensitive data to get comfortable with the technology and then scale to all the teams.

- **Operational efficiency**: As per Forbes, 64% of businesses expect AI to increase productivity. We all know that some specific reports and processes must be run simultaneously and during the day. I have also seen analysts sending reports even while they are on vacation or, worse, at their weddings. This kind of dependency can prove to be catastrophic for an organization. With the availability of AI agents, they can quickly produce these defined reports and even send them to the right audience.

  Companies such as Tableau leverage LLMs to automate report generation and data visualization. By integrating LLMs such as Tableau GPT into their platform, Tableau users can automate report generation and data visualization effectively.

  Here's how you can start applying this approach within your organization today:

  - Identify the top 3 or 4 workloads that are low risk but can be automated using LLM or agentic workloads by breaking them into well-defined steps.

    For example, every Monday, marketing files are dropped from an external vendor to a location, which is then loaded into your database. Some predefined questions are calculated from that data and sent to a specific group. This is a workflow with 3 or 4 fixed steps and can be automated via an agentic workload.

  - The analyst who runs the identified workloads should be the person who validates the process and responses, so that they will be your SME.

- **Ramping up marketing efforts**: Marketing is an expensive undertaking for any company. But we all know it's the secret driver behind the company's revenue. Content creation and video editing take days and sometimes hours to strategize and implement. AI can help fast-track those efforts. Here is how:

  - Text-to-speech and text-to-video technologies can be used to create customized avatars of the CEO/famous personalities, saving time and costs.

- Video editing/creation and content creation can be achieved in just a few hours rather than days. GenAI is great at "generating" any kind of data, such as images and video, hence this is a classic example where they can shine.

- Hyper-personalization is enabled as personalized recommendations can be sent to customers more straightforwardly. This can be achieved by traditional machine learning recommendation systems or training a large/small language model through methods such as fine-tuning and agents, to name a few. We will cover this in detail in the upcoming chapters.

If you're ready to put these ideas into action, here are some practical steps to get started:

- Identify the top 3 or 4 marketing workloads that require intensive resources or are challenging to implement. Analyze whether LLMs can be leveraged to automate these.

- To implement personalization, ensure that data containing past user behaviors is available in the proper format.

- **Machine learning workloads**: Historically, for any predictive or forecasting use case, machine learning and statistical algorithms such as Random Forest, linear regression, ARIMA, and Holt-Winters were popular choices. However, with the advent of LLMs, they are being used to identify trends and patterns. LLMs can identify trends, correlations, and anomalies that might be elusive to traditional statistical models, providing businesses with a competitive advantage.

What are the reasons that enterprises prefer LLMs over machine learning for such use cases? Here are a few reasons:

- If the data is unstructured (e.g., customer reviews, chat logs, or legal documents) and you need to extract insights or generate predictions.

- When the relationships in the data require understanding nuanced language or complex dependencies.

- When there is labeled data for training, LLMs can be used without extensive custom training. For example, Salesforce uses LLMs to predict customer churn based on factors such as historical purchase data and customer support interactions. This information is then used to identify customers at risk of churning and take action to prevent them from leaving.

To make this actionable in your organization, consider the following:

- If the data is structured, you might not even need LLMs, and you can stick to machine learning for traditional prediction and classification workloads
- LLMs can be pretty resource-intensive, so keep that in mind before committing to any solution

- **Research and development**: Research can be a lonely field for many researchers. Think of AI as a smart intern who can discuss ideas, find similar research papers, perform complex mathematical computations, write proposals, and so on. It can share the burden of a researcher so that they can focus on high-value tasks. LLMs can also help solve complex challenges, which can fast-track the solution for complex problems.

Now that we have discussed some everyday use cases, here are a few best practices you can follow to implement the AI-based solution within your organization:

- Decide on the underlying platform (cloud provider) to build the solution as early as possible. This will help you make decisions regarding the data, API management, the scale of the solution, and so on. Most enterprises leverage model as a service from cloud platforms so that they don't have to worry about the underlying infrastructure.

- Your first LLM-based solution can break your trust with internal or external users. Choose the early adopters wisely and scale your solution slowly. Launching the solution to thousands of users can do more harm than good.

- Provide your users with a list of questions (prompts) for each use case. This will help them craft better prompts and get accurate responses. You can be creative and supply them through the user interface, such as "You may want to ask…" followed by a list of questions.

- Make your application model agnostic. As you have seen, providers launch new models, but that means they sometimes decommission older models, so you should not over-rely on one model. Choose a model that is within your reach and makes it easy to switch to a new model, if required. LLMs are commoditized now; it is how you provide the relevant context that determines the success of the application. Examples of context include your enterprise data or appropriate prompts.

- Build your A-team on day 1. This will include your human testers, data scientists, app developers, and the infrastructure/cloud team.

- When building LLM solutions, consider data anonymization, strict access controls, and extreme measures such as confidential computing. These can help you safeguard your customers' data and give auditors and legal authorities more confidence.

- Set clear expectations for your business users. Though LLM solutions ease multiple pain points within the organization, they are still not a solution to all problems. Be clear about the launch timeline and the solution's capabilities.

These best practices will ensure you get the required ROI for your GenAI solution. But how do you measure the "value" of this solution? In the next section, we will deep dive into how to achieve this.

Measuring the business value of your GenAI solution

Understanding the business value of your GenAI solution is critical to getting appropriate funding and creating solutions that give us the required **return on investment** (**ROI**). Here are a few factors to quantify your gains:

- **Cost savings**: Measure hours recovered through automation and reduced errors. Here, the KPI can be the automation rate (percentage of automated tasks).

- **Revenue increase**: Increased customer lifetime value and acquisition of new customers are identified by 5-star customer engagement and satisfaction.

- **Employee experience**: Internal surveys on satisfaction and productivity show that more time for creative work leads to happy employees and an improved retention rate. Here, the KPI could be the number of hours saved with the implementation of GenAI.

In this section, we examined a range of GenAI use cases that hold potential value for enterprises. While we aimed to present a broad spectrum, the list is intended as a general guideline rather than an exhaustive catalog. Recognizing the importance of securing funding and stakeholder interest, we also addressed the need to measure the ROI for these use cases. To that end, we discussed quantifiable factors such as cost, revenue impact, and employee experience.

Next, we will cover when not to consider GenAI for your enterprise workloads.

When not to consider GenAI

People often talk about how GenAI can be transformational for your organization; while that is true, there are also use cases where GenAI won't add value to your firm. Here are a few scenarios to consider:

- Purely mathematical analysis may not be the best fit for GenAI. Limited mathematical reasoning exists within models, but it is best to stick with predictive AI if you are trying to achieve large volumes of statistical data processing. GenAI best describes insights from numerical analysis or creates SQL queries in plain English. Still, you might not get value on running regression analysis or optimization from prompts alone. This was one of the first discoveries of model hallucinations when it was used for logical reasoning or numerical analysis. With the advent of advanced models, reasoning capabilities might improve over time, but where we stand now, it is best to avoid LLMs for mathematical analysis. Even though LLMs are becoming smarter every day with advanced reasoning capabilities, for solutions such as multi-variate data forecasting, it is important to either stick with classic machine learning or build a hybrid solution where machine learning is used for inferencing and LLMs are used for explanation of the inferencing and deriving additional information based on the results of the machine learning model.

- LLM-based solutions shouldn't be treated as an end solution but rather as an ingredient to enhance existing solutions or workflows. It is easy to get attracted to "shiny new toys" and start building flashy demos to get funding, but the end goal is not to use AI because it's trendy; rather, use it if it adds real business value. Hence, it is essential to always align your GenAI solution with the business goals to measure the ROI and show tangible impact. One of the examples of how LLM-based solutions aid traditional workflows is through improved product search due to metadata augmentation for products on retail websites.

- When integrating LLMs with the existing application, create a robust integration plan. Your integration plan should include timelines for rollout and testing and a mitigation plan in case of last-minute failures and any future decommissioning of features that might be required. If the plan is not executed correctly, it can lead to poor customer experience and even loss of customers.

- GenAI may also be a poor fit for your use case if the risks that come with it are unacceptable and cannot be effectively mitigated. These include unreliable outputs, data privacy, intellectual property, liability, cybersecurity, and regulatory compliance, alone or in combination.

- When making critical decisions, relying on GenAI can be risky. Current GenAI models are not built for reliable decision-making. Their outputs can be unpredictable, they often lack explainability, and they can't model decisions clearly and explicitly to achieve desired outcomes. Traditional decision-making tools are more appropriate for tasks that require high-stakes decisions, such as financial investments or strategic business moves.

- Planning tasks such as inventory optimization, field workforce scheduling, route optimization, financial portfolio optimization, pricing optimization, and resource allocation demand exact calculations and explicit decision modeling. GenAI models struggle with this level of precision and complexity. You'll likely need optimization algorithms or simulation models for these use cases to handle detailed calculations and offer reliable solutions.

In this section, we explored how GenAI may not be suitable for tasks requiring precise mathematical reasoning, high-stakes decision-making, or exact optimization. It should be used to enhance existing workflows, rather than serve as a standalone solution, and must align with business goals to demonstrate ROI. Additionally, risks such as unreliable outputs, privacy concerns, and poor integration planning can outweigh its benefits in certain scenarios. In the next section, we will discuss a case study of building a successful GenAI solution.

Scenario — building a "chat with the data" use case

Consider a Fortune 500 company deciding to build an internal chatbot to democratize data and its insights for business stakeholders. With this solution, business stakeholders can ask questions pertaining to the data, such as "What was the revenue for XYZ month for ABC product?" This "chat with the data" application can help them quickly get insights by conversing in natural language without the need for writing complex queries or code. This revolutionary approach eliminates the need for analysts to drop everything and prioritize queries from business stakeholders, freeing them from being available 24/7 to answer business queries. This way, any business user can get data on demand and feel empowered about their own business line.

The following are the challenges of deploying such a solution:

- Crafting prompts is crucial in these cases. Providing users with sample prompts, especially during the initial rollout, helps them get comfortable with prompting.

- The solution improves based on user feedback, but not all users are proactive in providing feedback. Identifying a few power users in the initial months to gather feedback on responses is essential.

- Monitoring data drift is extremely important. Refreshing the data based on the original source's refresh cadence ensures users receive the most updated information.

- Involving stakeholders throughout the process is vital, but when gathering requirements, avoid boiling the ocean. Collect all requirements and create a phased approach to accommodate them as much as possible. Classify the requirements as "nice to have" and "must have." As a data scientist, making that judgment call is crucial.

- LLMs are great at understanding unstructured data, but sometimes understanding complex tables can be challenging as the AI system might not be able to capture the relationships between different columns within a table.

Here is what would make the solution successful:

- Even though analysts are not involved 100%, they will still monitor the application to ensure it operates at the highest standards.

- User feedback is collected diligently, and analysts spend time performing appropriate error analysis to determine which questions are answered correctly by the model and which are not. This helps them tweak the prompts, models, and so on.

- The solution is rolled out in a phased manner, giving more control over the changes and allowing measurement of the lift from each change.

- When chunking and indexing structured data, ensure you use the right technique to preserve the semantic relationship of the table.

- Continuous measurement of business metrics ensures the AI system is heading toward the ROI. In this case, the ROI can be measured in terms of productivity, that is, the number of hours saved for each analyst to focus on other innovative tasks.

- Set up data refresh pipelines to ensure data is refreshed at a fixed cadence and users always get the most relevant information.

- Rolled out in a phase-wise manner to ensure adequate buy-in and involvement from business stakeholders.

In this scenario, we discussed how a Fortune 500 company can build an internal chatbot to simplify data access for business users, reducing analysts' workloads. Success hinges on prompt design, phased rollout, stakeholder involvement, and continuous feedback. The ROI is measured through productivity gains and reliable data refresh pipelines. Now, let's conclude the chapter with some best practices for building such AI solutions.

Best practices for building GenAI solutions

Let's end this chapter by discussing a few best practices for building GenAI solutions. We covered a few at the start of the chapter, but here are some additional things to consider:

- **Non-deterministic**: GenAI solutions are non-deterministic, so responses will not be 100% accurate. Set these expectations proactively with the users. You can reduce the hallucinations by grounding your model on your data or fine-tuning it, but you cannot completely eliminate the hallucinations. There are techniques that you can use, such as semantic caching for more deterministic output, but still, LLM-based systems are probabilistic systems.

Semantic caching is an advanced caching technique that stores and retrieves data based on meaning (semantics) rather than exact text matches. Unlike traditional caching, which only works when the query string is identical, semantic caching uses embeddings (vector representations of text) to understand the intent behind a query and match it to previously cached responses, even if the wording differs.

Take the following example:

- **Traditional cache:**

  "What is AI?" ≠ "What's artificial intelligence?" Cache miss

- **Semantic cache:**

  "What is AI?" ≈ "What's artificial intelligence?" Cache hit

- **Data strategy**: This is still a critical element in the overall AI strategy. Spend time crafting the data strategy, ensuring the input data is in the right format, and set up data refresh before proceeding to build GenAI solutions.

- **Model testing**: Test different models based on your use case. LLMs are great, but small language models might suffice for your use case, saving you time and resources. Start with LLMs to establish baseline performance for your AI application, then try small language models. Compare the performance, and if small language models are not significantly off, you can choose them for your GenAI system.

- **Safety measures**: Implement robust safety measures to protect your applications against malicious attacks. Be proactive here.

- **Scalability**: Design the solution for scalability. You might start with 10 users but could have 10,000 in later years. Your GenAI solution should be nimble enough to accommodate this growth.

All these best practices will help you succeed in your GenAI journey and have a seamless experience with your users.

Summary

This chapter introduced key GenAI concepts, including LLMs and their architecture, and explored practical enterprise use cases, such as customer engagement, data democratization, and operational efficiency. It outlined when GenAI may not be suitable, shared a case study on chatbot deployment, and emphasized best practices for implementation. We now understand how measuring the ROI through cost savings, revenue impact, and employee experience is essential for success.

In the next chapter, we will cover GenAI operations in detail and uncover how to bring GenAI applications to life.

References

- Bourne, K. (2024). *Unlocking Data with Generative AI and RAG.* Packt Publishing. `https://www.packtpub.com/en-it/product/unlocking-data-with-generative-ai-and-rag-9781835887905`

- Bustos, J. P., & Soria, L. L. (2024*). Generative AI Application Integration Patterns.* Packt Publishing. `https://www.packtpub.com/en-be/product/generative-ai-application-integration-patterns-9781835887608`

- Gartner. (2024). *When Not to Use Generative AI.* LinkedIn Pulse. `https://www.linkedin.com/pulse/when-use-generative-ai-gartner-cna6c/`

- Google Developers. (n.d.). *Introduction to Large Language Models.* Google. `https://developers.google.com/machine-learning/resources/intro-llms`

- Sahin, S. (n.d.). *When to Avoid Using Gen AI and When to Adopt it: A Comprehensive Analysis.* Medium. `https://medium.com/@sahin.samia/when-to-avoid-using-gen-ai-and-when-to-adopt-it-a-comprehensive-analysis-7a453483b888`

- Turing. (n.d.). *How LLMs Are Changing the Face of Business Analytics.* Turing. `https://www.turing.com/resources/how-llms-are-changing-the-face-of-business-analytics`

10
Understanding GenAI Operations

Large language models (LLMs) gained popularity in 2018 with the launch of BERT. Even though "GPT" has existed since 2019, it was leveraged in an application called "ChatGPT" and launched in 2022. This is when the internet blew up, gaining one million users within five days of being available (yahoo.com/news/chatgpt-gained-1-million-followers-224523258.html). This signals the fact that there is the right kind of excitement within the market. However, building something similar within an enterprise or an application where you expect users to commercialize is an entirely different ball game.

Enterprise AI is hard. Choosing a suitable model, optimization technique, and evaluation metrics can be difficult. The choice can make or break your enterprise solution, which can affect the overall adaptation within the firm. This is where GenAI **operations (Ops)** come into play. Implementing GenAI Ops can help you make the right choice related to the model, data, evaluation metrics, and optimization technique, and deploy a production-ready solution. In this chapter, we will explore the what, why, and how of GenAI Ops.

We will cover the following key topics:

- The what and why of GenAI Ops
- Life cycle of GenAI Ops
- Case study – behind the scenes of an enterprise LLM solution
- Case study – intelligent claims processing platform

Important definitions and disclaimers

- **LLM systems:** Any application, workflow, or system powered by an LLM. This is important as we will highlight the LLM system's evaluation in detail in this chapter, not the evaluation of the actual large language model.

- **Mixed precision training:** A technique used in deep learning to improve computational efficiency by combining different numerical precisions in a single model. Typically, it involves using **16-bit floating-point (FP16)** precision for most operations to reduce memory usage and increase speed while retaining **32-bit floating-point (FP32)** precision for critical calculations to maintain accuracy.

- **User prompts:** Specific questions given by the user to the AI system to guide the AI to perform a particular task.

- **System prompts:** A set of instructions provided by the developers to define an AI model's overall behavior and role.

- **Knowledge distillation:** A technique in machine learning where a smaller, simpler model (the "student") is trained to replicate the behavior of a larger, more complex model (the "teacher"). The goal is to transfer the knowledge from the teacher to the student model, enabling the student to achieve similar performance with reduced computational resources.

In this chapter, we are assuming you have a background in GenAI, particularly LLMs and **small language models (SLMs)**, as we will not deep dive into the architecture but share practical tips and tricks to build successful GenAI systems.

Please note that *GenAI Ops* and *LLMOps* are often used interchangeably, though the intent behind them is the same.

What is GenAI Ops?

GenAI Ops (LLMOps) is a process meant to accelerate and optimize model creation, development, evaluation, and monitoring throughout its lifespan.

Why GenAI Ops?

Let's explore why GenAI Ops is an important concept while building GenAI applications. Here are a few reasons:

- GenAI Ops is essential to optimizing the performance of your LLMs, which could involve fine-tuning models, adding new data points, and so on, to improve accuracy and achieve the required ROI
- It helps you monitor your model actively, find potential pitfalls, and mitigate them immediately
- It reduces risk and ensures that users get the most reliable experience
- It helps you scale up or down, depending on your application's usage, enabling you to save costs and ensure that your users get the highest level of experience
- GenAI is an expensive undertaking; GenAI Ops ensures that you can reap the maximum benefits of GenAI through a defined process within your enterprise

How is GenAI Ops different from MLOps?

AI practitioners often question the need for GenAI Ops when MLOps have existed in the past. Though there are similarities between LLM and ML-based applications, such as both being probabilistic applications, there are also underlying differences that lead to separate processes. The following table highlights some of the differences:

Features	MLOps	GenAI Ops
Talent	Data scientists and ML engineers	Data scientists, AI engineers, and application developers
Metrics	Model metrics such as accuracy and precision	Model metrics such as groundedness and coherence; operation metrics such as latency and tokens per minute
Training process	Built from scratch	Fine-tuned on foundation models or API calling
Human feedback	Optional	Non-negotiable

Table 10.1: Differences between MLOps and GenAI Ops

GenAI Ops is not just about using the latest AI technology but about the confluence involving the right people, platform, and process. The right people include the business and technical folks, compliance, legal, and early adopters or business users. The right platform is about hosting it robustly and providing end users with the best-in-class experience. The process is about having a streamlined system to measure and monitor the performance of your LLM system so that you can be proactive rather than reactive as soon as you notice slight model degradation or any kind of performance issues.

In this section, we introduced the concept of GenAI Ops, why it is necessary, and how it is different from MLOps. In the next section, we will explore the life cycle of GenAI Ops in detail.

Life cycle of GenAI Ops

Organizations perceive GenAI Ops differently. No one path is a holy grail and is highly customizable for your organization and use case. The following subsections provide a high-level flow of all the steps you need to consider when building your AI application.

Ideation

This is the first step; the process starts with ideation. Companies start exploring the idea of a use case where they want to leverage language models. AI practitioners or data scientists often explore the possibility of SLMs or LLMs in this step to build their application in an optimized and cost-effective way. This is the step where you also involve other stakeholders, such as product or project managers, to design the vision of your overall product. The designated team then frames an initial use case and also defines what success looks like for that use case. Once the use case has been identified, data scientists will start thinking about user prompts and system prompts and select a foundation model. It is highly recommended to seek expert advice from solutions architects, advisors, and experts within the company during this phase.

The result is a defined use case with an execution plan and model selected for building the use case.

Building

This is the step where you refine the initial plan and evaluate whether the chosen model, user prompts, and meta prompts/system messages work for you. The best way to see whether something works is to evaluate it in action. In this stage, you will be leveraging the sandbox/innovation environment of your company to build the solution and see whether it is working as expected. There is a strong possibility that you will want to tweak certain elements of the solution. So, part of this step is to experiment with different LLM optimization techniques, such as prompt engineering, **retrieval-augmented generation** (**RAG**), or fine-tuning, to get the desired results. Based on the chosen method, you will also need an evaluation plan, which could include adding **subject matter experts** (**SMEs**) to evaluate your response, using an LLM as a judge, and so on. We will cover this in detail in the upcoming sections.

Before we move to the third phase of GenAI Ops, let's discuss all the optimization techniques in detail.

When thinking of optimizing LLM-driven solutions, there are usually three techniques: RAG, prompting, and fine-tuning. Usually, AI developers start with prompting and then move on to RAG. The important question to ask while choosing between RAG, prompting, and fine-tuning is what you wish to optimize. LLM optimization is not a linear flow, meaning that, more often than not, enterprise LLM solutions require either a combination of these techniques or all three at once, depending on the complexity of the use case. We will unpack this in the upcoming sections.

Prompting

Prompting is a way for you to provide detailed instructions for your AI solution to achieve the desired output. Like humans, models also require meticulous instructions to give high-quality output.

Prompting can be classified into two types:

- **Crafting system messages**: These provide models with a persona or tone to behave accordingly. System messages are also a great way to introduce guardrails and reduce hallucinations. Developers configure these on the backend. For example, you are a coder who writes accurate Python code. If you don't know something, say it.
- **Crafting user prompts**: These are user-driven, so they are basically how a user interacts in natural language with the LLM. We have all been doing this since the launch of ChatGPT.

Advantages of prompting are as follows:

- Prompting is easy to implement and doesn't require advanced technical skills
- It is cost-effective as you are utilizing pretrained models
- Prompts can be quickly adjusted based on evaluation results without the need for retraining the model (refer to `https://medium.com/@myscale/prompt-engineering-vs-finetuning-vs-rag-cfae761c6d06`)

Best practices for prompting

Here are some best practices to craft effective prompts:

- Designing accurate meta prompts is an iterative process. Creating a spreadsheet with different meta prompts and responses is essential to tracking how tweaking different meta prompts affects system performance.

- Developing reusable prompt templates or patterns to help users easily and quickly adapt to different use cases.

- **Chain of thought (CoT)** prompting is when the model outputs its thought process and answers the final question. This prompting technique is perfect for complex reasoning questions. Let us understand further with an example:

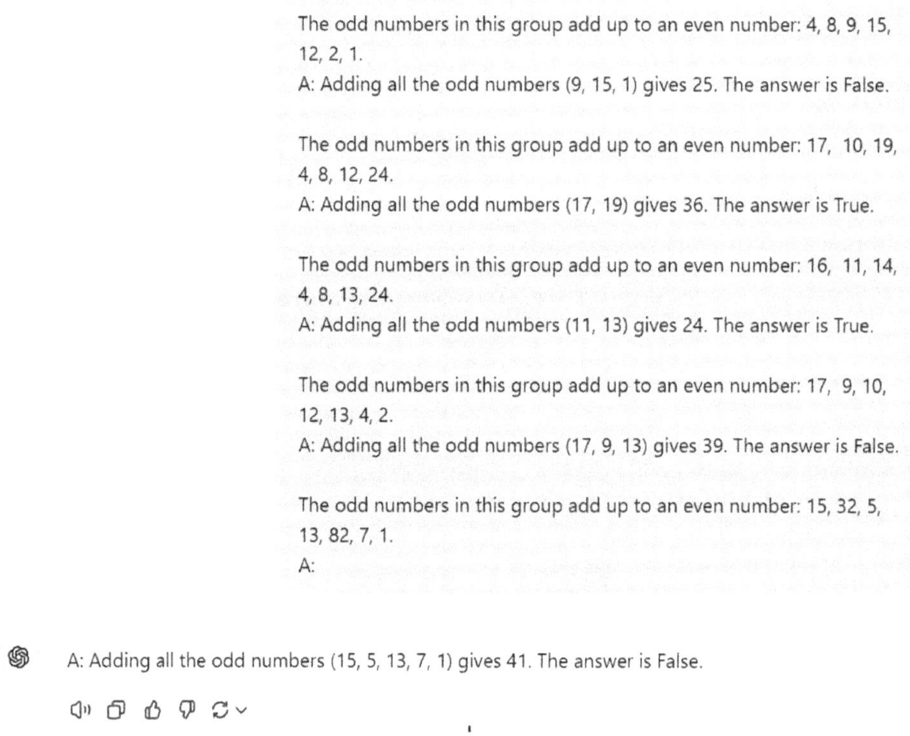

> The odd numbers in this group add up to an even number: 4, 8, 9, 15, 12, 2, 1.
> A: Adding all the odd numbers (9, 15, 1) gives 25. The answer is False.
>
> The odd numbers in this group add up to an even number: 17, 10, 19, 4, 8, 12, 24.
> A: Adding all the odd numbers (17, 19) gives 36. The answer is True.
>
> The odd numbers in this group add up to an even number: 16, 11, 14, 4, 8, 13, 24.
> A: Adding all the odd numbers (11, 13) gives 24. The answer is True.
>
> The odd numbers in this group add up to an even number: 17, 9, 10, 12, 13, 4, 2.
> A: Adding all the odd numbers (17, 9, 13) gives 39. The answer is False.
>
> The odd numbers in this group add up to an even number: 15, 32, 5, 13, 82, 7, 1.
> A:

> A: Adding all the odd numbers (15, 5, 13, 7, 1) gives 41. The answer is False.

Figure 10.1: Illustration of a sample CoT prompt

Here, I provided relevant examples through the prompt so that it could adapt my thought process and then answer the question. So, it produced the correct output. It didn't just print 41; it also showed you how it arrived at the solution.

Another essential thing to note here is that since I provided a few examples, it's called **few-shot learning**. Let's decode what few-shot learning is; it refers to the ability of the model to perform a new task by being given just a few examples in the prompt. Here is an example of a few-shot prompt:

- **Task**: Classify sentiment as Positive or Negative
- **Example 1 input**: "I love this product!"
- **Output**: Positive
- **Example 2 input**: "This is terrible."
- Output: Negative

The important thing to note here is that even as part of CoT prompting, you are doing few-shot learning as you are providing examples in the prompt, but the major difference is that chain of thought prompting is generally used for reasoning/logical use cases, such as mathematical workloads, as it encourages the model to **reason step by step** before giving the final answer.

RAG

RAG is a way of optimizing LLMs to make them more grounded so that they can access the knowledge through an authoritative knowledge base. The vital part is to know that the authoritative knowledge base is validated to ensure that the information is accurate and updated. To draw an analogy, think about RAG as an "open-book" exam. In an open-book exam, students are allowed to bring reference materials, such as textbooks or notes, which they can use to look up relevant information to answer a question. The idea behind an open-book exam is that the test focuses on the students' reasoning skills rather than their ability to memorize specific information. Similarly, the factual knowledge is separated from the LLM's reasoning capability and stored in an external knowledge source, which can be easily accessed and updated.

Here are the advantages of RAG:

- **Cost-effective**: Fine-tuning a foundational model is expensive, but introducing new information to the RAG within LLMs is cheaper
- **Enhanced user trust**: RAG provides accurate information along with the sources, such as footnotes in the research papers, improving user trust in the retrieved information
- **Maintain relevance**: GenAI models are usually trained with outdated information, but RAG allows you to train them with the most recent and relevant information about your use case

RAG introduces an information retrieval component that first utilizes user input to pull information from a new data source. The user query and the relevant information are given to the LLM, which uses the latest knowledge and training data to create better responses.

The following steps provide an overview of the process:

1. **Data collection**: Pull all the relevant data needed for your application. For example, for an internal chatbot, it could mean all the knowledge manuals on internal data sources

    > **Pro tip**
    >
    > Ensure that the data used in the RAG application is relevant and updated to limit hallucinations and incorrect responses.

2. **Data chunking**: Data chunking is breaking your data into smaller, bite-sized pieces of information. This allows the model to retrieve relevant data chunks efficiently. How you perform chunking can also affect the model's performance. For example, if you are dealing with a 1,000-page manual, the chunking should be so that each chunk talks about a particular topic. This way, the model can quickly retrieve the required chunk when the user asks a question. The following list contains a few chunking strategies you can select based on the use case.

3. The list needs to be more comprehensive, but the most relevant ones work in an enterprise:

    - **Fixed token overlap**: In this technique, documents are split into chunks to overlap information between two different chunks. This is important so that there is no information loss while chunking, and it ensures that all data is retained.

    - **Semantic**: In this technique, documents are split based on semantic similarity. Documents are first divided into sentence groups of three sentences using a sliding window (usually the sentence, the previous sentence, and the following sentence). Embeddings are generated for each sentence group, and similar groups in the embedding space are merged to form chunks. The similarity threshold for merging is determined using metrics such as percentile, standard deviation, and interquartile distance. As a result, the chunk size can vary across chunks.

    - **Hybrid chunking**: This combines multiple strategies based on content type and document structure. For instance, text can be chunked by sentences, while tables and images are handled separately. It is helpful for technical reports, business documents, or product manuals.

4. **Document embedding**: Once you have performed data chunking, converting them into vector representations through embeddings is essential. Embeddings are numeric representations of text data that also retain the semantic meaning behind the text. While choosing a suitable embedding model, remember that the effectiveness of retrieval via similarity search heavily depends on the quality of the embeddings used to represent the documents and queries. Consequently, choosing an embedding model will significantly impact the retrieval precision, affecting the quality of the LLM responses and the overall RAG application.

5. **Handling user queries**: Once the user enters the query, it is also converted into embeddings. Then, query embeddings are compared with document embeddings using cosine similarity (or similar methods) to find the most relevant chunks of information.

6. **Generating responses with an LLM**: The retrieved text chunks and the initial user query are fed into a language model. The algorithm will use this information to respond coherently to the user's questions through a chat interface.

Next, we will look at the example use cases for RAG:

- Chatbots with an internal knowledge base to help employees find information faster and be more productive.

- Personalized recommendation engines for external customers to improve customer service and user experience.

- An intelligent companion for doing research studies and solving complex reasoning-based problems. For instance, it can assist doctors and researchers by quickly retrieving the latest research findings or clinically pertinent data for a patient's case or medical condition.

Best practices for implementing RAG

Now that we have understood the workings and advantages of RAG, here are a few best practices we have learned after building and deploying several RAG solutions:

- **Data preprocessing**:

  - Ensure that you include metadata in your data for RAG. This will provide additional contextual information. Some examples of metadata could be date or year if the user can ask any time-sensitive questions.

  - Ordering the documents can help LLMs better understand the context. Let's say you are retrieving several chunks from a document that only makes sense if ordered properly; then, inserting the chunks in that order is essential.

- Filter the data based on specific criteria before performing a vector search, such as using regular expressions or metadata to narrow the search space. If the use case is about getting the latest information, then it is best to filter the data, let's say in 2024, before performing the vector search. This will help retrieve relevant information and also improve latency.

- Ensure that the data is clean and updated before feeding it to the RAG system. Deploy systems that can detect data drift so that practitioners know when to update the data or the underlined model. Chatbots fail because the old data doesn't give the users the correct information, resulting in a loss of user base.

- Robust data pipelines are essential for adapting to changes in source data. This adaptability ensures that the RAG system remains efficient and effective, even as the nature of the input data evolves.

- Experiment with different models to ensure optimal accuracy and speed. Sometimes, starting with SLMs might be beneficial if your use case is more straightforward to save cost and increase speed.

- Start with a simple RAG architecture and customize it as you evaluate the performance. If you tweak the chunking strategy and embedding model all at once, you won't be able to know the drivers behind the model's performance.

- Define evaluation metrics early, such as groundedness, coherence, and so on, and prepare baseline evaluations to compare against.

- Scalable design in RAG systems is about anticipating and addressing potential latency issues in production. This will ensure that your users get a constant throughput, hence a great user experience.

- Always follow a phase-wise roll-out approach for your RAG system. Start with a limited user base and increase the users as you gain more confidence in your AI application.

- Establish strict protocols for data privacy, security, and compliance with data protection laws. It is essential to have a robust system to prevent against prompt injections and bad actors. Refer to `https://nexla.com/ai-infrastructure/retrieval-augmented-generation/`.

- Use hybrid search wherever possible; keyword and context-based search techniques combine the best of both worlds. This improves the accuracy and relevance of search results. Refer to `https://medium.com/@juanc.olamendy/rag-best-practices-enhancing-large-language-models-with-retrieval-augmented-generation-6961c8b834ff`.

The following figure illustrates the workings of the RAG method:

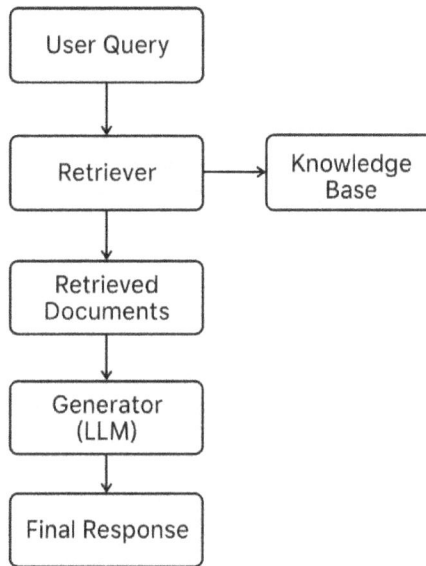

```
          ┌──────────────┐
          │  User Query  │
          └──────────────┘
                 │
                 ▼
       ┌──────────────┐        ┌──────────────┐
       │   Retriever  │───────▶│  Knowledge   │
       └──────────────┘        │     Base     │
                 │             └──────────────┘
                 ▼
        ┌──────────────┐
        │  Retrieved   │
        │  Documents   │
        └──────────────┘
                 │
                 ▼
        ┌──────────────┐
        │  Generator   │
        │    (LLM)     │
        └──────────────┘
                 │
                 ▼
       ┌──────────────┐
       │ Final Response │
       └──────────────┘
```

Figure 10.2: Steps in RAG

We hope this section has given you a deeper understanding of the workings of RAG, when to use it, and things to keep in mind while building it. Now, let's explore another powerful technique called fine-tuning.

Fine-tuning

Fine-tuning involves training a pretrained model on a domain-specific dataset to prepare it for a specific task. Think of the pretrained model as a student who has learned general knowledge in school (e.g., language, math, and science). Fine-tuning is like giving that student specialized training for a specific profession, such as law or medicine, where they apply what they've already learned but with additional practice in a particular area.

Here are the steps for fine-tuning:

1. Prepare your dataset:

    - **Training examples**: These are specific instances or data points used to teach the model how to respond correctly.
    - **Targeting undesired behavior**: Some examples should focus on situations where the model's current responses are not ideal or incorrect. By identifying these problematic cases, you can provide better guidance.

- **Ideal responses**: For each of these targeted examples, include the perfect response you want the model to produce. Comparing its current response to the desired one helps the model learn the correct behavior.

You should have at least 50 demonstrations to see whether the model improves after fine-tuning.

2. Split the data into a training and a test set:

    - Feed both train and test data into the fine-tuning job; this will help you get statistics on both datasets and calculate how much the model improves with fine-tuning.

    - After training the model, you will use this test set to evaluate its performance. By comparing the model's predictions on the test set to the actual correct responses, you can measure its accuracy and effectiveness.

3. Create the new fine-tuned model. Determine the suitable model for your use case. Running experiments or consulting experts might help choose an appropriate model.

4. Evaluate the results and go to *step 1* if necessary. This is the most crucial step. Determine the evaluation metrics before you start fine-tuning. OpenAI, by default, provides you with training loss, training token accuracy, valid loss, and valid token accuracy. This serves as a good benchmark, but you should also have a way to compare the results with prompt engineering and RAG to calculate the LIFT that you got after implementing the RAG or prompt engineering solution..

The reasons to fine-tune are as follows:

- If you want to own the model and ensure that data doesn't leave the four walls of your infrastructure, it is best to fine-tune.

- Fine-tuning might be the right choice when an SLM is enough for your use case. It is a quality versus latency trade-off.

- Fine-tuning might be better if the use case or domain is highly narrow. An example of this is that your enterprise uses a highly complicated syntax to retrieve information from databases; there is a possibility that fine-tuning the model to learn your syntax might be an appropriate choice.

- If the use case is so complicated that prompt engineering is impractical, as you cannot teach all the workings of this specific use case and contain it in a prompt, fine-tuning might be the right choice.

Best practices for fine-tuning

By now, you should have understood the why and how behind fine-tuning. Now, let's explore key pointers to keep in mind while fine-tuning for your enterprise use case:

- The success of fine-tuning depends on the quality of the pretrained model. When selecting a pretrained model, it's essential to consider its size, the type of data it was trained on, and the task it was trained to perform. For example, if you're fine-tuning an image recognition model, you may want to select a pre-trained model that was trained on a large dataset of images (refer to `https://saturncloud.io/blog/a-comprehensive-guide-to-fine-tuning/`).

- For smaller models, more data length and breadth are needed to achieve optimized fine-tuning performance. It is important to iterate over different models and see what best suits your use case. For the data length, consider at least 100 good examples with diverse examples, including edge cases, so the model can learn better.

- Iteratively adjust hyperparameters to optimize the model's performance. Hyperparameters such as the learning rate, the batch size, and the number of epochs can significantly affect the model's performance. Note that epochs affect the training the most. Standard epochs are 4, the batch size is usually 256, and the recommended learning rate multiplier is 0.1 or 0.2.

- Ensure that the fine-tuning data is of both optimal quality and quantity:

  - The dataset should be diverse and include both correct and incorrect responses

  - The dataset shouldn't have grammatical, logical, or style issues; otherwise, it will degrade the model's performance

  - Ensure that all your training examples are in the same format, as expected, for inference

Fine-tuning can be a powerful technique to explore, but it might be expensive for organizations to implement. Now, let's explore another powerful technique to optimize your GenAI solutions: prompting.

Combining RAG, prompt engineering, and fine-tuning: the perfect trifecta

These three techniques are not mutually exclusive; you don't have to choose one over the other. Depending on the use case, you might want to use them in pairs, individually, or all three together.

Let's understand this with an example. Imagine you are building a chatbot for customer service for XYZ company:

- **Prompt engineering/prompting**: You can use prompts to define the chatbot's persona, tone of voice, and how it should handle different inquiries.
- **RAG**: You can integrate a knowledge base containing the company's documentation, FAQs, and product information. This allows the chatbot to access and utilize relevant information to answer customer questions accurately.
- **Fine-tuning**: You can fine-tune the chatbot on a dataset of customer interactions, teaching it to understand common customer issues, provide helpful solutions, and maintain a positive and professional tone (refer to `https://www.linkedin.com/pulse/prompt-engineering-rag-fine-tuning-benefits-when-use-deependra-verma-7g8dc/`).

To summarize the preceding discussion, here is a table to help you choose the correct technique for optimization:

Parameter	Potential scenarios	Optimization technique	Word of caution
Accuracy	Missing context Outdated/biased information	RAG Prompting Data preprocessing	The golden rule is to try RAG, prompting, or combining both while improving accuracy. Fine-tuning can't be helpful if RAG and prompting fail to enhance the use case.
Consistency	Inconsistent results Tone is not as per the expectation Reasoning is not followed correctly	Fine-tuning Prompting	RAG might not be useful here, as "inconsistent results" usually mean an issue with the meta prompts. So, always start by tweaking meta prompts, and if it doesn't work, then move on to fine-tuning.

Cost	High tokens per minute (TPM) High model cost Data type processing	Model optimization (mixed precision training and knowledge distillation) Choosing an SLM over an LLM	
Performance	High latency Data leakage	Choose a different model Prompt optimization	

Table 10.2: Choosing the correct technique for optimization

Choosing the most suitable technique among RAG, prompting, or fine-tuning can be a challenging decision. More often than not, it is a combination of two or three techniques that creates impactful AI solutions. Now, let's explore some best practices for this phase of GenAI Ops.

Best practices for the building phase

Here are a few best practices for the building phase:

- The rule of thumb is to avoid fine-tuning as much as possible. It is expensive and might not provide value for your buck.
- Start with prompt engineering and evaluate your results. The results from prompt engineering can serve as a baseline to see whether fine-tuning improves the situation.
- If the results from prompt engineering are to your satisfaction, there is a 90% chance fine-tuning will make it better. If it doesn't work with prompting, there is a 25% chance it will work with prompting.
- Fine-tuning requires extensive labeled datasets specific to the task. If this is scarce, then stick to RAG.
- Fine-tuning can be computationally intensive, whereas RAG leverages existing databases to supplement the generative model, potentially reducing the need for extensive training.
- The result is a strong **proof of concept** (**POC**) with an execution plan to deploy and monitor the application in production.

In this section, we explored three key techniques for building GenAI solutions (RAG, fine-tuning, and prompting), and how they can be combined to create robust enterprise applications. We also covered best practices for each approach to ensure effective implementation. Next, we'll dive into the operationalization phase in detail.

Operationalization

Once you have a POC, it is time to deploy your application in production. The operationalization stage comprises a few main steps: build CI/CD pipelines and monitor your application for ethical, operational, and cost metrics. Remember, this is an LLM-based solution and can become costly quickly; hence, it is important to monitor TPM, cost usage trends, and so on. This section will focus on uncovering how to build a robust LLM system's evaluation strategy and how to optimize the performance of the GenAI solution once it is in production.

Evaluations

Evaluations are an essential part of the GenAI Ops life cycle. Given the probabilistic nature of LLMs, continuously monitoring and evaluating your LLM application's performance is necessary. Another thing to note here is that evaluations are performed at two levels: one is the LLM performance, and the other is the LLM system performance. We will discuss the performance of the LLM system here.

Let's look at why GenAI system evaluation is hard:

- Different versions of system prompts and user prompts can change the model's responses, making performance variable and difficult to track.
- There is a lack of good benchmarks. We will discuss this in the upcoming section.
- The need for humans in the loop introduces unwanted bias.
- It is hard to define the right metric for a particular use case.

Let's explore some practical techniques for evaluation.

Offline and online evaluations

Offline evaluation is where you benchmark the performance of the LLM against preselected datasets. It is an effective method to evaluate aspects such as groundedness and factuality. Here are a couple of strategies to perform offline evaluation:

- **Golden datasets**: These are curated datasets, preferably by SMEs, that cover a diverse set of input and output examples, serving as a benchmark to evaluate LLMs' capabilities. The golden dataset should have the "ground truth" label to measure the performance of the

LLM evaluation template. This is a great way to begin your evaluation journey and prove the feasibility of your minimum viable product; however, this approach is not scalable and can introduce human-induced bias.

- **Model as a judge**: AI evaluating AI is a scalable evaluation method. It is faster and more cost-effective. But as we know, LLMs can also make mistakes; hence, having humans in the loop can prove beneficial when evaluating your models.

Once your solution is in production, you can leverage models as a judge along with humans in the loop for a few months to monitor the performance. Have a certain threshold in place where if the predecided metrics go below a certain threshold, it should be flagged to the developer so they can take action on it.

Online evaluation is another critical aspect of evaluation, where you leverage authentic user data to assess live performance through direct and indirect feedback. The **thumbs-up** and **thumbs-down** feature in ChatGPT is an online evaluation feature.

There was a study conducted by Chatbot Arena (`https://arxiv.org/html/2403.04132v1`) where users could submit questions and receive responses from two anonymous LLMs. Once they received the responses, they could provide thumbs up or thumbs down for the response. The voting process was anonymous and random to ensure fairness. These responses were collected into a rich dataset of user prompts and human preferences. This is a great example of how online evaluation can be simulated within an enterprise as well.

Best practices for evaluations

Here are a few best practices to keep in mind for evaluations:

- When using the model as a judge, use the most powerful model you can afford.
- Continuously monitor the LLM system and iterate as needed.
- Have humans in the loop to validate the information. Include use case experts to provide feedback. No one knows better than they what "good" looks like.
- Don't wait until the end to evaluate the model; evaluations should be part of the development cycle.
- Understand the goal of the LLM-based application clearly; this will help you define and prioritize the metrics that make the most sense for your application. For example, some applications prioritize fluency and coherence in language generation, while others prioritize factual accuracy or domain-specific knowledge (refer to `https://medium.com/data-science-at-microsoft/evaluating-llm-systems-metrics-challenges-and-best-practices-664ac25be7e5`).

- Building evaluations can be tricky. Start by exploring out-of-the-box evaluation SDKs to save time and effort. If they don't work for you, then you can build your own evaluation frameworks.

Here are a few general guidelines on choosing the right metric for evaluation, given your use case:

- **Extracting structured information**: You can look at how well the LLM extracts information. For example, you can look at completeness (is there information in the input that is not in the output?).

- **Question answering**: How well does the system answer the user's question? You can look at the answer's accuracy, politeness, or brevity.

- **RAG**: Are the retrieved documents and final answer relevant, grounded, and so on?

This section served as an introduction to evaluations and covered practical methods to perform them in an enterprise. In the next section, we will explore logging and monitoring for your LLM system.

Logging and monitoring

Another important step within operationalization is logging and monitoring. This mechanism helps to capture the prompts, responses, evaluation scores, as well as the metadata, such as the model versions, input data, and so on. This data is important for debugging, maintaining an audit trail, and detecting drift within the data or the underlying model. This is also a great way to monitor the cost of your LLM system as well as the changing user needs.

An organization doesn't need to build a new logging and monitoring system; you can leverage any existing system and integrate the AI application alerts. Ensure that any significant deviations or anomalies are promptly flagged and sent to the concerned teams for remediation. You can read about this in detail in the book, *Generative AI Application Integration Patterns* (https://www.packtpub.com/en-mx/product/generative-ai-application-integration-patterns-9781835887615).

Best practices for once the solution is deployed in production

The goal is to deploy the GenAI solution into production. Here are a few best practices to keep in mind when the solution is in production:

- **Cost threshold**: It's best to set up thresholds once the AI solution is in production. For developers, it is important to receive notifications on their allocated budget. There should also be an IT admin continuously receiving updates on the cost. If the cost surpasses the threshold, it might be time to analyze the workings of your AI system; it could be the choice of model leading to higher cost, more traffic than expected, and so on.

- **Caching**: By storing frequently accessed data, you can improve response times without needing to make repeated calls to our API. Your application will need to be designed to use cached data whenever possible and invalidate the cache when new information is added. There are a few different ways you could do this. For example, you could store data in a database, filesystem, or in-memory cache, depending on what makes the most sense for your application. Refer to `https://platform.openai.com/docs/guides/production-best-practices`.

- **Load balancing**: Consider load-balancing techniques to ensure requests are distributed evenly across your available servers. Refer to `https://platform.openai.com/docs/guides/production-best-practices`.

- **Human feedback loop**: Implement a system where users can flag incorrect responses, helping improve the model over time.

- **Toxicity and bias mitigation**: Regularly test for biases and inappropriate outputs using tools such as OpenAI's Moderation API, Perspective API, or custom safety classifiers.

- **Ethical compliance**: Ensure compliance with regulations (GDPR, HIPAA, etc.), maintaining transparency in how the model generates responses.

- **Content filtering**: Apply prompt engineering techniques, **reinforcement learning from human feedback (RLHF)**, or fine-tuning to prevent hallucinations and misinformation.

- **Autoscaling and load management**: Implement autoscaling for cloud deployments and optimize inference costs by leveraging quantization, pruning, or knowledge distillation. We are not covering it in detail here, but attaching resources for anyone to review (`https://medium.com/@sahin.samia/llm-inference-optimization-techniques-a-comprehensive-analysis-1c434e85ba7c`).

In this section, we explored the operationalization phase, including evaluation, logging, and monitoring, as well as best practices to keep in mind once the solution is in production. In the next section, we will explore a case study in detail to see how GenAI Ops comes to life in enterprises.

Case study — behind the scenes of an enterprise LLM solution

LexCorp (a fictitious company), a leading legal firm specializing in corporate law, recognized the potential of AI to revolutionize its operations. With a team of over 200 lawyers, LexCorp handles a vast array of contracts daily, ranging from mergers and acquisitions to intellectual property agreements. The firm's commitment to innovation led it to invest in developing a domain-specific LLM tailored to its unique needs.

Building the domain-specific chatbot involved the following steps:

1. The development of LexCorp's chatbot began with defining the business goal to quantify the potential impact of the chatbot. The goal was simple: provide tools that could help lawyers become more efficient and focus on important tasks.

2. The development started with extensive data collection and identifying experts who would validate the output, as well as provide support during the entire development process.

3. The next step involved the identification of the method they would use to build the chatbot. In their case, they were confused between RAG and fine-tuning, but decided to start with RAG for an efficient and cheaper optimization option.

4. They built a simple UI and grounded the chatbot with the identified data sources. They decided to choose the GPT-4o model as it is affordable and yet can handle multi-modal data.

5. Next, they identified the metrics they would like to measure the performance of the chatbot and did thorough testing over a few weeks to ensure that the chatbot was generating appropriate responses.

6. To keep the LLM up to date, the Ops team implemented a robust feedback loop. Lawyers using the AI provided continuous feedback on the drafts generated. This feedback was meticulously analyzed to identify areas for improvement. Regular updates were rolled out, incorporating the latest legal precedents and refining the model's understanding of complex legal concepts. The Ops team also monitored the model's performance, ensuring that it met the firm's high standards for accuracy and reliability.

7. Reliability was a critical concern for LexCorp. The Ops team employed several strategies to ensure that the LLM's outputs were dependable. They conducted rigorous testing, simulating various legal scenarios to evaluate the model's performance. Additionally, they established a system for human oversight, where senior lawyers reviewed the AI-generated drafts before finalization. This dual-layer approach ensured that the LLM's outputs were both accurate and legally sound.

8. LexCorp's commitment to excellence drove the continuous improvement of its LLM. The Ops team leveraged advanced techniques such as transfer learning and reinforcement learning to enhance the model's capabilities. They also explored integrating external legal databases to expand the model's knowledge base.

9. Regular training sessions were conducted for lawyers to familiarize them with the AI's functionalities, fostering a collaborative environment where human expertise and AI innovation coexisted harmoniously.

We can learn the following from LexCorp:

1. Through meticulous data collection, continuous feedback, rigorous testing, and ongoing improvements, the firm successfully harnessed the power of GenAI to streamline its legal drafting process.

2. They built robust testing and evaluation frameworks from day one, which led them to perform incremental updates.

3. They started with one team and then rolled out to other teams. Performing a phase-wise launch is extremely beneficial when it comes to GenAI development.

4. They involved business stakeholders from day one and defined what "success" would look like. This helped them get the required sponsorship for their product. With the help of stakeholders, they were also able to create a golden dataset for evaluation.

5. They built a process-oriented product rather than a model-focused one. What that means is they didn't go for the most fancy model, but the one that was cheap and could also benefit them for their use case.

6. They baked responsible AI practices into their product to be proactive about any malicious attacks.

7. They built a simple UI instead of investing tons of resources to integrate into their legacy applications on day one. Integration could be managed later, but the first step was to get users comfortable with the technology.

This case study highlights the importance of collaboration between AI experts and domain professionals in achieving reliable and impactful AI solutions.

Case study – intelligent claims processing platform

An insurance company wants to automate claims handling for auto accidents. The process involves the following:

- **Structured data**: Policy details, customer demographics, historical claims, and coverage limits
- **Unstructured data**: Images of damaged vehicles, free-text accident descriptions, and repair invoices

Manual review is slow and inconsistent. The goal is to build a web-based UI that combines ML inference and LLM reasoning to deliver fast, transparent decisions.

Let's look at the solution overview. The platform uses the following:

- **Computer vision ML model** for image-based damage detection
- **Predictive ML model** that predicts the estimated cost for claims and fraud probability
- **LLM reasoning layer** to synthesize ML outputs and unstructured text into a coherent explanation for the claim decision

Through the following diagram, we can visualize the architecture workflow:

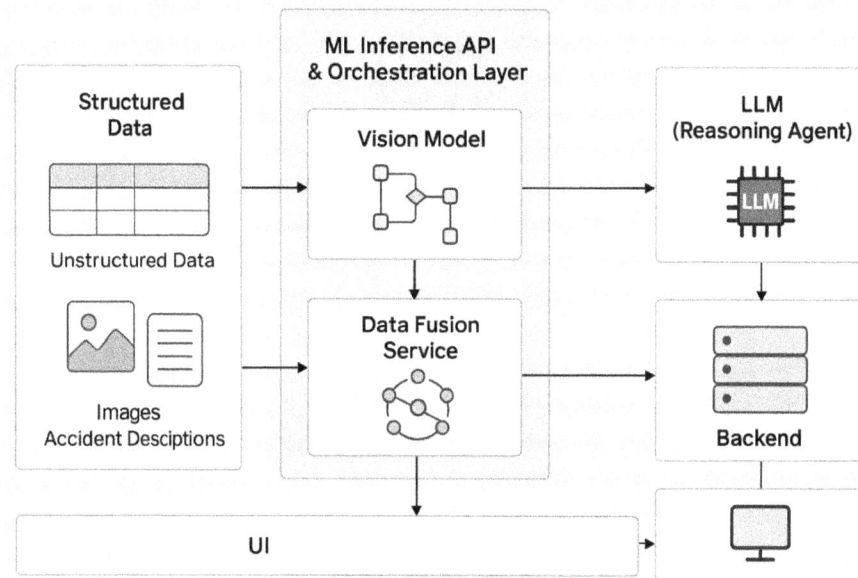

Figure 10.3: Solution architecture workflow

With this visualization in mind, let's discuss the architecture workflow in detail:

1. **Data layer:**

    - **Structured data**: Policy details, coverage limits, and historical claims (stored in relational DB)
    - **Unstructured data**: Images (stored in object storage) and accident descriptions (text)

2. **ML model development:**

    - **Vision model**: Train a convoluted neural network (CNN) based model (e.g., EfficientNet or YOLO) for damage detection and severity scoring

- **Tabular model**: Train a gradient boosted tree or a neural network for claim cost estimation and fraud risk prediction

- **Output standardization**: Ensure that every model outputs data using the same field names and structure. For example, if one model returns severity_score and another returns damage_severity, the orchestration layer must perform additional work to interpret them. Standardizing the keys ensures all downstream components like the API layer can process the results reliably without additional mapping or transformation.

3. **ML inference API**:

- **Containerize models**: Use **FastAPI** or **Flask** to build REST endpoints.

- **Endpoints**: Have an endpoint for accepting an image and returning damage analysis. Also, have an endpoint for accepting structured data, returning cost, and fraud risk.

- **Deployment**: Host on **Azure App Service** or **AWS Lambda** for scalability.

- **Authentication**: Secure with OAuth or API keys.

4. **Orchestration layer**: The data fusion service combines outputs from both ML APIs and user inputs. Also, it creates a unified JSON payload for reasoning.

5. **LLM reasoning agent**: Here's a prompt template or example:

```
Context:
- Damage: {damage_area}, severity {severity_score}
- Estimated cost: ${estimated_cost}
- Fraud risk: {fraud_risk}
- Coverage limit: ${coverage_limit}
- Customer statement: "{customer_statement}"

Task:
Generate a professional claim decision summary explaining approval/
rejection and reasoning.
```

6. **LLM integration**: Use **Azure OpenAI** or **OpenAI GPT API**. Then, wrap in an agent that does the following:

- Calls ML APIs

- Builds a reasoning prompt

- Returns structured and natural language output

7. **UI layer:**

   - **Frontend**: React or Angular dashboard; upload images, enter text, view ML and LLM outputs
   - **Backend gateway**: Handles API calls to ML services and LLM agent

8. **Logging, compliance, and evaluation:**

   - Store ML outputs, LLM reasoning text, and final decision for audit and regulatory compliance
   - Robust evaluations for measuring the performance of the agents through task adherence, intent resolution

Based on the architecture flow, let's now discuss the core design principles:

1. **Agent-centric orchestration:**

   - The LLM acts as the decision-maker, not just a text generator
   - It decides when to call the ML tool, how to interpret outputs, and how to combine structured and unstructured data

2. **Tool exposure via API:**

   - Each ML model (vision and tabular) is wrapped in a REST API
   - These APIs are registered as tools for the agent using a schema (name, description, and input/output format)
   - The agent can dynamically invoke these tools during reasoning

3. **Data fusion layer:**

   - Before reasoning, outputs from ML tools and user inputs are normalized into a single JSON payload
   - This ensures that the LLM sees a clean, structured context for reasoning

4. **Prompt engineering for reasoning:** The agent uses a template prompt that includes the following:

   - ML outputs (damage area, severity, cost, and fraud risk)
   - Structured data (coverage limits)
   - Unstructured text (customer statement)

Here is an example:

```
Context:
Damage: {damage_area}, severity {severity_score}
Estimated cost: ${estimated_cost}
Fraud risk: {fraud_risk}
Coverage limit: ${coverage_limit}
Customer statement: "{customer_statement}"

Task:
Generate a professional claim decision summary explaining approval/
rejection and reasoning.
```

5. **UI integration:**

   - The UI interacts only with the Agent API, not directly with ML models
   - This keeps the workflow simple for the user while enabling complex orchestration behind the scenes

Why use this approach?

- **Scalability**: Adding new tools (e.g., fraud detection and cost optimization) is easy
- **Transparency**: LLM reasoning provides human-readable explanations
- **Compliance**: Logs every ML output and LLM decision for audit

The following challenges emerge:

- **Data integration**: Combining structured (policy tables) and unstructured (images and text) data for coherent reasoning
- **Model interoperability**: Vision and tabular models must output standardized formats for LLM consumption
- **Prompt robustness**: LLM must handle edge cases (e.g., missing data and conflicting signals)
- **Bias and fairness**: Avoid decisions skewed by demographic data
- **Latency**: Real-time inference and reasoning without degrading user experience
- **Explainability**: Regulatory compliance requires clear reasoning for every decision

Here are the added complexities:

- **Multi-modal reasoning**: LLM interprets numeric scores, textual descriptions, and image-derived insights
- **Dynamic prompts**: Adjust based on missing fields or anomalies
- **Audit trail**: Store ML outputs and LLM reasoning for compliance

This solution demonstrates how combining structured and unstructured data with ML and LLM reasoning can transform traditional workflows into intelligent, transparent systems. By leveraging multi-modal AI, the platform not only accelerates decision-making but also builds trust through clear explanations. Ultimately, it sets the stage for scalable, compliant, and customer-centric automation in the insurance industry.

Summary

In this chapter, we introduced GenAI Ops, focusing on how enterprises can successfully build, deploy, and manage LLM systems. We explained the differences between GenAI Ops and traditional MLOps, emphasizing the unique challenges of operationalizing GenAI in business environments. The chapter covered the GenAI Ops life cycle, from ideation and building (including optimization techniques such as RAG, fine-tuning, and prompting) to operationalization, evaluation, and monitoring. It also provided best practices and a case study illustrating how a legal firm implemented a domain-specific LLM solution to streamline contract management.

In the upcoming chapter, we will take this one step forward and discuss AI agents.

References

- Abideen, Z. (2024, October 15). 15 *Chunking Techniques to Build Exceptional RAG Systems.* Analytics Vidhya. `https://www.analyticsvidhya.com/blog/2024/10/chunking-techniques-to-build-exceptional-rag-systems/`
- Amazon Web Services (AWS). (n.d.). *What is Prompt Engineering?* `https://aws.amazon.com/what-is/prompt-engineering/`
- Amazon Web Services (AWS). (n.d.). *What is Retrieval-Augmented Generation?* `https://aws.amazon.com/what-is/retrieval-augmented-generation/`
- Bustos, J. P., & Soria, L. L. (2024). *Generative AI Application Integration Patterns. Packt Publishing.* `https://www.packtpub.com/en-mx/product/generative-ai-application-integration-patterns-9781835887615`

- Chiang, W.-L., Zheng, L., Sheng, Y., et al. (2024). *Chatbot Arena: An Open Platform for Evaluating LLMs by Human Preference.* arXiv. https://arxiv.org/abs/2403.04132

- DataCamp. (n.d.). *LLM Evaluation: Metrics, Methodologies, Best Practices.* DataCamp Blog. https://www.datacamp.com/blog/llm-evaluation

- Ferrer, J. (2024, August 9). *Optimizing Your LLM for Performance and Scalability.* KDnuggets. https://www.kdnuggets.com/optimizing-your-llm-for-performance-and-scalability

- Forbes Technology Council. (2024, September 20). *How LLMs Are Transforming The Customer Support Industry.* Forbes. https://www.forbes.com/councils/forbestechcouncil/2024/09/20/how-llms-are-transforming-the-customer-support-industry/

- Google Cloud. (n.d.). *GenAI Ops: What it is and how it works.* Google Cloud. https://cloud.google.com/discover/what-is-llmops

- Huang, J. (2024, March 5). *Evaluating Large Language Model (LLM) systems: Metrics, challenges, and best practices.* Data Science at Microsoft (Medium). https://medium.com/data-science-at-microsoft/evaluating-llm-systems-metrics-challenges-and-best-practices-664ac25be7e5

- Microsoft Azure. (n.d.). *GenAI Ops with Azure AI* [Video]. YouTube. https://www.youtube.com/watch?v=rdShYiURnmM

- MongoDB. (n.d.). *How to Choose the Right Chunking Strategy for Your LLM Application.* MongoDB Developer Center. https://www.mongodb.com/developer/products/atlas/choosing-chunking-strategy-rag/

- MyScale. (n.d.). *Prompt Engineering vs Finetuning vs RAG.* Medium. https://medium.com/@myscale/prompt-engineering-vs-finetuning-vs-rag-cfae761c6d06

- Nexla. (n.d.). *Retrieval-Augmented Generation (RAG) Tutorial, Examples & Best Practices.* Nexla. https://nexla.com/ai-infrastructure/retrieval-augmented-generation/

- Olamendy, J. C. (n.d.). *RAG Best Practices: Enhancing Large Language Models with Retrieval-Augmented Generation.* Medium. https://medium.com/@juanc.olamendy/rag-best-practices-enhancing-large-language-models-with-retrieval-augmented-generation-6961c8b834ff

- OpenAI. (n.d.). *Optimizing LLM Accuracy.* OpenAI API Documentation. https://platform.openai.com/docs/guides/optimizing-llm-accuracy

- OpenAI. (n.d.). *Production Best Practices.* OpenAI API Documentation. https://platform.openai.com/docs/guides/production-best-practices

- Saturn Cloud. (n.d.). *A Comprehensive Guide to Fine-Tuning.* Saturn Cloud Blog. `https://saturncloud.io/blog/a-comprehensive-guide-to-fine-tuning/`

- Verma, D. (n.d.). *Prompt Engineering, RAG, and Fine-tuning: Benefits and When to Use.* LinkedIn Pulse. `https://www.linkedin.com/pulse/prompt-engineering-rag-fine-tuning-benefits-when-use-deependra-verma-7g8dc/`

Subscribe for a free eBook

New frameworks, evolving architectures, research drops, production breakdowns—AI_Distilled filters the noise into a weekly briefing for engineers and researchers working hands-on with LLMs and GenAI systems. Subscribe now and receive a free eBook, along with weekly insights that help you stay focused and informed.

Subscribe at `https://packt.link/80z6Y` or scan the QR code below.

11

AI Agents Explained

Imagine joining a new company, being inundated with new information, feeling like an imposter, and being scared to ask your colleagues for information or help with understanding the processes. You don't want to be that new person who bugs your manager with every small question, and your colleagues are grappling to meet their deadlines, so you don't want to be an additional burden. Sound relatable? Imagine a new world where you join a company, have your initial orientation, and are told about this copilot that could answer your questions, big or small, and even provide you with the sources for that information. That is the power of AI agents. They can automate complicated, repetitive, and time-consuming tasks so that you can focus your energy on something productive.

AI agents are not new, but they have gained popularity, with LLMs being more accessible now. The agentic workflows powered with LLMs make agents powerful.

In this chapter, we will explore the following key topics:

- Understanding AI agents and their components
- AI agents – when to apply them and when to avoid them
- Types of AI agents
- Agentic frameworks
- Agent observability
- Challenges related to AI agents
- Enterprise agent AI use cases
- Model Context Protocol and Agent2Agent protocols
- Best practices for implementing agentic AI

Understanding AI agents and their capabilities

Agents are software programs that perform tasks autonomously based on the configuration provided by the user through code or prompts. The beauty of agentic systems is that they are dynamic and can interact with and improve their behavior over time. For instance, an AI agent planning a vacation could assess the weather, budget, and user preferences to recommend the best tour options. It can consult external tools, adjust suggestions based on feedback, and refine its recommendations over time.

Capabilities of AI agents

Four capabilities of AI agents make them unique and capable of handling complex workflows:

- **Understanding complex instructions**: This is for the user to type the request and for the model to understand the user's needs and ultimately carry out each task. For example, if a user types, "Book a flight to New York and arrange accommodation," LLMs can grasp this request by interpreting location, preference, and logistical nuances.

- **Planning and reasoning frameworks**: These help agents break the task into smaller, manageable steps. This is great for use cases such as those of a financial advisor or trip-planning agent.

- **Enhanced tool interaction**: LLMs can interact with external tools and APIs. This capability enables AI agents to perform tasks such as executing code, interacting with databases, and performing web searches.

- **Memory and context management**: LLMs use different types of memory systems. Episodic memory helps agents recall specific past interactions, aiding in context retention. Semantic memory stores general knowledge, enhancing the AI's reasoning and application of learned information across various tasks. Working memory allows LLMs to focus on current tasks, ensuring they can handle multi-step processes without losing sight of their overall goal.

AI agents thrive at solving complex workflows with their unique capability to understand the problem, call the right tools, and remember context from previous conversations. In the next section, we will dive deep into the "why" behind AI agents.

Why AI agents?

By now, you should have a good understanding of what AI agents are, their capabilities, and the impact they could have on your enterprise. Let's discuss a few reasons why enterprises should consider building AI agents:

- **Improved productivity**: Organizations use AI agents to achieve specific goals and more efficient business outcomes.

- **Reduced costs**: Businesses can use intelligent agents to reduce unnecessary costs arising from inefficiencies, human errors, and manual processes.

- **Informed decision-making**: Advanced intelligent agents use **machine learning** (ML) to gather and process massive amounts of real-time data. This allows business managers to make better predictions at pace when strategizing their next move.

- **24/7 availability**: AI agents are available around the clock, ensuring that customer inquiries are addressed promptly, regardless of time zones or business hours.

- **Improved customer experience**: Integrating AI agents allows businesses to personalize product recommendations, provide prompt responses, and innovate to improve customer engagement, conversion, and loyalty.

In this section, we learned that AI agents are autonomous software programs that perform tasks based on user input and improve over time through interaction and feedback. They consist of components such as instruction understanding, planning frameworks, tool integration, and memory systems that enable complex workflows. Businesses use them to boost productivity, reduce costs, enhance decision-making, and improve customer experience with 24/7 availability. In the next section, we will explore when and when not to use agents.

AI agents — when to apply them and when to avoid them

Real-world tasks are complicated, cumbersome, and non-deterministic. Imagine you run a travel company. A customer logs on to your website and submits this request: "Book me a three-day trip to Malibu in October. I am flexible on the dates. Plan the activities based on the weather. The hotel should be a mile away from downtown, and I need a Mercedes car to pick me up from the airport. If my flight is delayed by an hour, cancel the car booking."

This request involves multiple layers:

- Checking availability for a specific month
- Evaluating cancellation options
- Selecting the right activities based on the weather
- Understanding personal schedules and logistical details

In situations where workflows can't be neatly defined in advance, agents offer the flexibility needed to respond to complex requests. An agentic system could handle this request by dynamically accessing various tools and APIs:

- **Weather API**: To provide accurate forecasts
- **Google Maps API**: For calculating travel distances
- **Renting car availability portal**: To rent cars
- **Employee availability dashboard**: To check staff schedules
- **RAG system**: To retrieve relevant answers from your knowledge base

In this section, we learned that AI agents allow systems to break free from rigid workflows, adapting to user requests on the fly. This makes them ideal for solving problems in unpredictable or high-variability domains.

When to avoid AI agents

While agents can handle complexity, they're not always the best choice. Overusing them can introduce unnecessary risks and costs. You should avoid agents in the following situations:

- **The workflow is not expected to perform an action**: If the AI workflow that you are building does not involve an action such as writing a report, booking a ticket, or sending an email, it is recommended to start with a simple chatbot and then scale to an agentic system.
- **Error tolerance is low**: Agents, powered by LLMs, are probabilistic systems, meaning they may occasionally make incorrect decisions. For applications where accuracy is critical, avoid relying on agents.
- **High-volume, low-latency pipelines**: Agents rely on LLM calls, which introduce latency and cost. For real-time classification at scale, for example, a classic ML model or deterministic approach would be better.
- **No tool integration**: If the workflow has no external tools and is just calling an API, you don't need an agent but an API directly. Agents are useful when they can choose between multiple tools or combine reasoning with actions.

In this section, we explored how AI agents are ideal for handling complex, dynamic tasks where workflows can't be predefined, such as travel planning with multiple variables and contingencies. However, they should be avoided for well-defined, low-error-tolerance, or cost-sensitive tasks where deterministic systems are more efficient and reliable. In the next section, we will explore the type of agents and agentic frameworks.

Types of AI agents

Based on the complexity of the use case, you can build a single agent or multiple agents. Let's dive deep into each of them to explore them further.

Single agent versus multi-agent

Single agents are one entity or agent performing a particular task. In single-agent models, a single AI entity is responsible for all decision-making processes. It makes managing and understanding the system's behavior easier. They are also easier to implement and can be optimized for an organization. Examples of single agents include chess-playing agents and image recognition.

The limitations of a single agent are as follows:

- Single agents struggle to solve complex tasks and increased computational loads
- Single points of failure can lead to overall system breakdowns, making these models less robust in dynamic and unpredictable environments

Multi-agents or multiple entities work together to accomplish a task. Multiple agents share the workload, distributing tasks based on specialization and capability, which can enhance efficiency and performance. Different agents can be designed to specialize in various tasks, making the system more flexible and adaptable to diverse challenges.

Examples include autonomous vehicles, such as Waymo. Traditional single-agent models may struggle to navigate complex urban environments efficiently. However, a multi-agent system can divide the tasks among specialized agents, such as the following:

- One agent focuses on real-time traffic data analysis and route optimization
- Another agent handles obstacle detection and collision avoidance
- A third agent manages passenger interactions and in-vehicle services

By collaborating, these agents can ensure a smoother, safer, and more efficient ride, demonstrating the tangible advantages of multi-agent systems.

The limitations of multi-agents are as follows:

- **Complexity**: Developing and managing multiple agents requires sophisticated coordination and communication protocols, increasing the overall system complexity
- **Resource management**: Efficiently allocating resources among agents and ensuring optimal performance can be challenging and requires advanced optimization techniques

In this section, we saw that single-agent systems are simpler and easier to manage but struggle with complex tasks, while multi-agent systems offer flexibility and specialization for handling dynamic workflows. The choice between a single- or multi-agent framework is dependent on your use case. Both can offer unique benefits and possess certain limitations. In the next section, we will explore frameworks to build agents.

Agentic frameworks

Building agents from scratch is hard. Frameworks simplify the process and allow developers to focus on their application rather than creating a framework from scratch. A framework is designed to help define tools, an orchestration mechanism, and memory, to name a few.

Frameworks enable the collaboration of different agents to solve complex tasks. They provide processes with which agents can talk to each other, coordinate, and achieve a common goal. They also equip agents to understand context and adapt to changing environments.

Let's discuss a few popular frameworks:

- **LangChain**: A framework for developing applications and agents powered by language models. It is robust and adaptable as it has extensive tools and abstractions. LangChain provides an easier way to integrate with data sources and external tools and is flexible in designing complex agent behaviors.

- **AutoGen**: This is an open source framework by Microsoft that enables the development of LLM applications using multiple agents that can converse with each other to solve tasks. AutoGen is a great way to perform experimentation and spin a quick prototype to showcase the art of the possible. It also supports both autonomous operation and human oversight. One important element that distinguishes AutoGen is its multi-agent communication structure. Because of this, developers can design systems in which many specialized agents work together to solve complicated issues or carry out difficult jobs.

- **LlamaIndex**: A framework for connecting custom data sources to LLMs.

- **Agentverse**: Designed to facilitate the deployment of multiple LLM-based agents in various applications.

- **Agents**: An open source library/framework for building autonomous language agents. The library supports long-term and short-term memory, tool usage, web navigation, multi-agent communication, and brand-new features, including human-agent interaction and symbolic control.

- **Crew AI**: An AI agent framework reimagined for engineers, offering powerful, simple capabilities to build agents and automation. This allows developers to create a "crew" of AI agents, each with specific responsibilities to work together on complex tasks. The unique aspect of this is that it creates more realistic simulations of human team dynamics.

- **Semantic Kernel**: This framework, developed by Microsoft, is designed to make it easier to integrate LLMs into existing applications. It is lightweight and modular, which makes it easier to update the code. The framework is highly secure and scalable and promotes code reusability.

How to choose the right agentic framework

Agentic frameworks are an evolving field, so it is important to ensure that there is a strong community associated with it that can provide valuable resources, support, and innovation.

It is important that the framework is stable and suitable for production environments. You can always confirm this by sending a note to the developer community.

Different frameworks excel in different areas, such as conversational agents, multi-agents, and autonomous decision-making; hence, it is important to clearly define the outcome you would like to achieve through these agents so that you can make the right choice.

It is also important to consider combining multiple frameworks to build robust applications.

You should also consider the expertise of your team while choosing the right framework; some require software engineering expertise, while others, such as Crew AI, can be configured via prompt engineering.

In this section, we explored agentic frameworks such as LangChain, AutoGen, and Semantic Kernel that simplify development and enable collaboration, tool integration, and context awareness. In the next section, we will learn what agent observability is and why it is important.

Agent observability

Agent observability is the practice of achieving deep, actionable visibility into the internal workings, decisions, and outcomes of AI agents throughout their life cycle, that is, from development and testing to deployment and ongoing operation. Key aspects of agent observability include the following:

- **Continuous monitoring**: Tracking agent actions, decisions, and interactions in real time to surface anomalies, unexpected behaviors, or performance drift.

- **Tracing**: Capturing detailed execution flows, including how agents respond through tasks, select tools, and collaborate with other agents or services. This helps answer not just what happened but why and how it happened.

- **Logging**: Records agent decisions, tool calls, and internal state changes to support debugging and behavior analysis in agentic AI workflows.

- **Evaluation**: Systematically assessing agent outputs for quality, safety, compliance, and alignment with user intent using both automated and human-in-the-loop methods. Some evaluation methods include, but are not limited to, the following:

  - **Human annotation**: This includes human evaluators who directly score LLM results across different application aspects, such as honesty, helpfulness, engagement, and unbiasedness.

  - **Turing test**: Human evaluators are asked to compare results from real humans and agents, whereas indistinguishable results mean that agents can achieve human-like performance.

  - **Protocols**: Correspond to standard evaluation protocols that determine how the metrics are used. Examples include real-world simulation, social evaluation, multi-task evaluation, and software testing.

  - **Evaluation SDKs and frameworks**: Companies such as Microsoft have invested heavily in building Evaluation SDKs that automate the process of agent evaluation. You can calculate how well the agent is adhering to the task, planning the task, and executing it. It is best to leverage these evaluation frameworks to escalate the development.

- **Open source framework**: You can also leverage open source frameworks such as the Microsoft evaluation framework. Microsoft introduced two new roles during the evaluation process: the examiner and the judge. The task description is first given to the examiner for each test case. The examiner then asks the agent questions and supervises the conversation. The evaluation target is allowed to ask the examiner questions to clarify the task. The examiner can only provide the task description and cannot provide any hints or solutions. When the evaluation target provides a solution, the examiner will stop the conversation and pass the solution to the judge. The judge will then evaluate the solution based on the ground truth.

- **Governance**: Enforcing policies and standards to ensure agents operate ethically, safely, and in accordance with organizational and regulatory requirements.

Agent observability is a critical aspect of building agentic applications. It is important to spend substantial time designing the agent architecture in a way that you are able to evaluate and monitor it continuously. In the next section, we will explore some other best practices for observability.

Best practices for agent observability

Let's now dive deep into best practices for observability that you can implement within your organization when building observability for your agents. These are based on the practical experiences that we have had building agents day in and day out:

- Pick the right evaluation method and evaluate continuously. One size does not fit all. It is possible that for your organization or use case, out-of-the-box methods won't work. It is always a good idea to start with them, so you don't have to invest in building, but if one iteration proves that it is not providing adequate information, it is best to build your own evaluation framework. This can be done by building an agent for evaluating and providing it with instructions such as: "You are an evaluation agent and your job is to evaluate on XYZ parameters."

- It is imperative to evaluate your agent continuously, both in development and production, to be able to monitor it and be proactive about low performance.

- Integrate evaluations and logging capabilities in your **continuous integration** (**CI**) and **continuous deployment** (**CD**) pipelines. Automated evaluations and tracing should be part of your CI/CD pipeline, so every code change is tested for quality and safety before release. This approach helps teams catch regressions early and can help ensure agents remain reliable as they evolve. Logging helps you monitor all the conversations for auditing and safety purposes. If a drift is detected, you can always go back to the logs to see what caused it. It is also a good idea to have alerts in place, so if the performance is below a threshold, you can get informed.

- Scan for vulnerabilities before the launch. Before deployment, proactively test agents for security and safety risks by simulating adversarial attacks. This will help you to test your application and be prepared for unfortunate events such as an attack by a malicious actor.

In this section, we explored the different dimensions of agent observability, tracing, evaluation, and logging, and their importance for enterprise-grade applications. In the next section, we will uncover challenges associated with building AI agents.

Challenges related to AI agents

As AI systems evolve from static models to autonomous agents capable of planning, reasoning, and acting, organizations face a new set of challenges that go beyond traditional ML concerns. In this section, we will discuss these challenges in detail:

- **Lack of high-quality data**: AI systems can leverage generalized data, but agents require highly specialized data to learn and execute tasks. For instance, training an AI agent to perform complex, nuanced tasks in dynamic environments demands detailed, context-rich data that is often not readily available. The absence of such targeted data can lead to ineffective training, where agents either fail to generalize or exhibit suboptimal performance due to gaps in their learning. Issues of data privacy, high collection costs, and the inherent biases in available datasets compound this challenge.

- **Lower accuracy**: Since multiple LLM calls are needed for agents to perform, if one of the LLMs is hallucinating, it is possible that the outcome of the agent will be inaccurate. High accuracy at every stage is essential to prevent these errors from escalating and for the agent to achieve its goals.

- **Lack of stable agentic frameworks**: Though there are multiple agentic frameworks available in the market, it can be challenging to choose one for production workloads. The reason is that most frameworks are still evolving and can prove to be unstable for enterprise workloads.

- **Autonomy challenges**: Agents can perform tasks autonomously, but that can prove to be tricky in highly regulated environments where each step needs to be monitored and validated. In such cases, it is best to either avoid agents altogether or have humans in the loop. Examples of these scenarios could be prescribing medication to a patient or approving someone's loan application.

In this section, we discussed the challenges of building agents, such as a lack of high-quality data and lower accuracy. In the next section, we will discuss how AI agents can help with enterprise AI use cases.

Enterprise agent AI use cases

In this section, let's deep dive into some interesting enterprise AI agent use cases:

- **Agentic workflow for data tasks**: Let's say the user asks the question about the difference between revenue for a company from 2023 to 2024. If you have deployed a simple RAG application, the LLM has to first retrieve the data for 2023 and then 2024, and then find the difference. It may not see the revenue for 2023 or 2024, as you might have grounded it only on the latest data. In this case, agentic frameworks can be helpful as they can dynamically plan this task and leverage the RAG pipeline, and memory modules can handle the subsequent questions.

Along with that, data is no longer limited to text; it can take multiple forms, such as images and audio files. Agents for data curation, processing, collection, and domain expertise can all be used to build enterprise-ready applications.

- **Swarm of agents for marketing campaigns and coding workflows**: This refers to a collection of agents working together to solve a common problem. Frameworks such as ChatDev enable you to build a team of engineers, designers, product managers, a CEO, and agents to build essential software cheaply. With this, you can populate an entire marketing campaign for a company or achieve complex coding workflows.

- **Dynamic pricing systems**: These power services such as ride-sharing apps. These agents adjust prices in real-time based on factors such as demand, competition, and time of booking. This is why your Uber ride might cost more during rush hour or in bad weather.

- **Modern irrigation systems**: Modern model-based irrigation systems are powered by model-based reflex agents. These agents can collect data and create informed decisions around water needs and which part of the field might require more attention.

These use cases are just a few examples of how AI agents can impact enterprises. In the next section, let's explore the **Model Context Protocol** (**MCP**) and **Agent2Agent** (**A2A**) protocols.

Model Context Protocol and Agent2Agent protocols

As enterprises shift toward multi-agent AI architectures, two foundational protocols, MCP and A2A, are emerging as critical enablers of scalable, interoperable, and intelligent systems.

MCP – tool access and execution

MCP, introduced by Anthropic, standardizes how AI agents discover and invoke external tools, APIs, and data sources, making it smarter and more helpful. It acts as a "USB-C port" for AI applications, providing a universal interface between models and the outside world.

MCP follows a client-server architecture with the following key components:

- **MCP hosts**: Programs using LLMs (such as Claude Desktop or IDEs) that initiate connections to access external data and tools

- **MCP clients**: Protocol clients embedded within the host application that maintain a 1:1 connection with servers

- **MCP servers**: Lightweight programs that expose specific capabilities through the standardized protocol

- **Data sources**: Both local (files, databases) and remote services (APIs) that MCP servers can access

A2A – collaboration and interoperability

The **Agent-to-Agent (A2A)** protocol, spearheaded by Google, focuses on enabling agents to communicate and collaborate across platforms, vendors, and frameworks. It defines structured interactions using agent cards, which describe an agent's capabilities, endpoints, and authentication requirements. A2A supports decentralized orchestration, allowing agents to dynamically discover and coordinate tasks without centralized control, which is ideal for complex workflows involving multiple specialized agents.

A2A architecture centers around facilitating communication between agents with these key components:

- **Client agent**: Formulates tasks and communicates them to remote agents
- **Remote agent**: Acts on tasks to provide information or perform actions
- **Agent card**: JSON metadata file describing an agent's capabilities and endpoint
- **Task management**: Defines task objects with life cycle stages and outputs
- **Messaging system**: Allows agents to exchange context, replies, and artifacts

While MCP provides vertical integration (agent-to-tool), A2A enables horizontal integration (agent-to-agent). Together, they form a robust ecosystem for building modular, multi-agent systems. In the next section, we will explore best practices for building agentic AI systems.

Best practices for implementing agentic AI

In this last section, we want to bring all the knowledge home and share practical tips and tricks for building AI agents. Since this space is rapidly evolving, we would recommend not just learning from these but also building fast and learning from your mistakes so you can evolve quickly in this space:

- Clearly define the objectives of your agentic workload. Defining clear goals will help you define success, which could be reducing response times, enhancing customer satisfaction, or cutting operational costs; this will help you decide between single- or multi-agent and choose appropriate agentic frameworks for the development process.

- When choosing the use case for agents, focus on the process that needs to be automated instead of the underlying model or tools. Being process-focused will help you derive business value.

- The quality of your agent is dependent on the quality of your data. Before starting the development process, ensure that you have robust data management practices.

- Consider integrating your agentic workflow into your legacy systems for optimal results and increasing the intelligence of your existing system.

- Ensure that the UI is intuitive and responses are timely and accurate, providing a positive customer experience. Test your AI agents thoroughly to identify and address potential issues before deployment, ensuring they meet customer expectations.

- Regularly monitor your agent to adapt to the changing user needs, as well as for any safety threats.

- In the initial stages, plan to have a human in the loop for agentic oversight to ensure the process works as expected.

- Implement robust data privacy and security measures to protect customer information handled by your AI agents.

- Have a "trust but verify" approach. When starting the journey, it is normal to spend hours on the performance of agents, analyzing their responses, and having humans in the loop. As the trust builds up, you can reduce the human oversight.

- If you just started your Gen AI as an organization, don't immediately jump to agentic workflows; start slow and then create more complex workflows.

- Inform users where AI is involved, how it works, and how to give feedback.

- Aim for consistent, multi-modal experiences across devices and endpoints. Use familiar UI/UX elements where possible (e.g., microphone icon for voice interaction) and reduce the customer's cognitive load as much as possible (e.g., aim for concise responses, visual aids, and "Learn More" content).

- Ensure you have set up robust logging for each action done by an agent. A log entry should store information on the agent that took the action, the action taken, and the outcome of the action. This is necessary for any debugging required.

- Performance metrics can help you track the effectiveness of the multi-agent system. For example, you could track the time taken to complete a task, the number of tasks completed per unit of time, and the accuracy of the recommendations made by the agents.

- Though it is tempting to use MCP or A2A for agentic workloads, it is important to think about whether you need it for your use case or whether it is the next shiny new object. Using any of these protocols demands maintenance; hence, only use what you need.

- Take a phased approach to your Gen AI journey. Start simple with **retrieval-augmented generation (RAG)** and gradually evolve toward agentic RAG capabilities. Begin with foundational use cases to build confidence, then scale into more advanced agentic workflows as your maturity and infrastructure grow.

From Roomba (a smart vacuum cleaner) to adaptive thermostats, we are surrounded by agents in our homes and offices. Now it's time to adapt them on an enterprise level to transform the way you cater to your customers and make your employees more productive. Agents will bring a change to the way we operate. It may transform jobs, but hopefully for the better.

In this section, we explored how enterprise AI agents are used for dynamic data tasks, marketing campaigns, pricing systems, and smart irrigation, leveraging multi-agent collaboration and external tools. We also discussed that successful implementation requires clear objectives, robust data practices, intuitive UI, human oversight, and continuous performance monitoring to ensure reliability and business value.

Case study — agent-based architecture for counterparty credit risk assessment

Counterparty credit risk (CCR) refers to the possibility that the counterparty in a financial transaction may default before the final settlement of the contract. This risk is especially critical in **over-the-counter (OTC)** derivatives, securities lending, and other bilateral financial agreements. Traditional CCR models often struggle to capture the dynamic and nonlinear nature of financial markets, especially during stress periods.

The goal of this project is to build a **modular, intelligent, and scalable system** that can do the following:

- Ingest and process client and trade data

- Analyze credit risk using contextual and market-aware reasoning

- Provide actionable insights to financial analysts and risk managers

- Be agent framework-agnostic, so developers can use any framework to orchestrate the agent and host these agents anywhere

Here's an overview of the solution. The repository implements a **full-stack application** combining the following:

- **Frontend**: Built with **Next.js**, offering a modern UI for user interaction
- **Backend**: Powered by **FastAPI (Python)**, handling API requests, data processing, and orchestrating AI agents
- **AI agents**: Can be deployed using any agent framework, such as Azure AI; each agent specializes in a distinct aspect of the credit risk workflow

Let's dive deep into the agentic architecture.

Agent-based architecture

The system is composed of **five specialized agents**, each with a unique role:

1. **Client data agent:**

   - **Role:** Retrieves and processes client-specific information from internal or external data sources
   - **Functionality:** Extracts financial ratios, credit ratings, and historical default data
   - **Purpose:** Establishes a foundational profile for credit risk evaluation

2. **Trade data agent:**

   - **Role:** Gathers and processes trade-related data
   - **Functionality:** Analyzes exposure, trade types, and contractual terms
   - **Purpose:** Quantifies potential exposure and risk from active trades

3. **Reasoning agent:**

   - **Role:** Performs detailed credit risk analysis
   - **Functionality:** Uses client and trade data, along with market indicators, to assess risk
   - **Purpose:** Generates insights and recommendations based on complex reasoning and probabilistic models

4. **Orchestrator agent:**

   - **Role:** Acts as the central coordinator
   - **Functionality:** Interfaces with users, gathers additional information via Bing Search, and delegates tasks to other agents

- **Purpose**: Ensures smooth workflow execution and integrates results from all agents

The following table lists the frameworks and technologies used:

Component	Technology	Purpose
Frontend	Next.js	UI and interaction
Backend	FastAPI (Python)	API handling and agent orchestration
AI agents	Azure AI or any cloud for hosting and executing	Intelligent task execution and reasoning
DevOps	npm, virtualenv	Dependency management and environment setup

Table 10.1: Frameworks and technologies used

Impact and use case

This architecture allows financial institutions to do the following:

- Automate and scale credit risk assessments
- Improve accuracy by leveraging contextual and market-aware reasoning
- Reduce manual effort and operational risk

You will find the full project at https://github.com/rom212/counterparty_credit_risk. This agent-based system offers a modular and intelligent approach to CCR assessment, leveraging specialized agents for data ingestion, contextual modeling, and reasoning. The architecture exemplifies how autonomous agents can transform complex risk workflows into efficient, explainable, and adaptive solutions.

Summary

In this chapter, we covered how AI agents can automate complex tasks, improve productivity, and enhance user experience through dynamic, autonomous workflows. It covered when and how to use agents, types of agent systems, popular frameworks, such as LangChain, AutoGen, and Semantic Kernel, evaluation methods, and enterprise use cases such as data tasks, marketing, and pricing. The chapter concluded with best practices for implementation, emphasizing clear goals, robust data, human oversight, and continuous monitoring, as well as a real-life case study.

In the next chapter, we will discuss responsible AI practices for building enterprise AI solutions.

References

- Analytics Vidhya. (2024, July). *Top 7 Frameworks for Building AI Agents in 2025.* https://www.analyticsvidhya.com/blog/2024/07/ai-agent-frameworks/

- Ardent Venture Partners. (2024, September). *AI Agents Show Huge Promise, But Face Technical Barriers to Wide Adoption.* Medium. https://medium.com/@ardent-vc/ai-agents-show-huge-promise-but-face-technical-barriers-to-wide-adoption-68e90e01bab1

- Botpress. (n.d.). *36 Real-World Examples of AI Agents.* https://botpress.com/blog/real-world-applications-of-ai-agents

- Chatbase. (2025). *11 Real-World AI Agent Examples in 2025.* https://www.chatbase.co/blog/ai-agent-examples

- Jain, A. (n.d.). *Agentic MCP and A2A Architecture: A Comprehensive Guide.* Medium. https://medium.com/@anil.jain.baba/agentic-mcp-and-a2a-architecture-a-comprehensive-guide-0ddf4359e152

- Microsoft. (n.d.). *AI agents — what they are, and how they'll change the way we work.* Microsoft Source. https://news.microsoft.com/source/features/ai/ai-agents-what-they-are-and-how-theyll-change-the-way-we-work/

- Microsoft. (n.d.). *AI Agents for Beginners: Agentic Design Patterns.* GitHub. https://github.com/microsoft/ai-agents-for-beginners/tree/main/03-agentic-design-patterns

- Microsoft Azure. (n.d.). *Agent Factory: Top 5 agent observability best practices for reliable AI.* Azure Blog. https://azure.microsoft.com/en-us/blog/agent-factory-top-5-agent-observability-best-practices-for-reliable-ai/

- Nigro, V. (n.d.). *Do you really need AI Agents?* Medium. https://veronicanigro.medium.com/do-you-really-need-ai-agents-82457f550ac1

- Nuvi. (n.d.). *Choosing the Right AI Agent Framework: LangGraph vs CrewAI vs OpenAI Swarm.* https://www.nuvi.dev/blog/ai-agent-framework-comparison-langgraph-crewai-openai-swarm

- NVIDIA. (n.d.). *Introduction to LLM Agents.* NVIDIA Technical Blog. https://developer.nvidia.com/blog/introduction-to-llm-agents/

- Prompt Engineering Guide. (n.d.). *LLM Agents.* https://www.promptingguide.ai/research/llm-agents

- Salesforce. (n.d.). *What Are AI Agents?* https://www.salesforce.com/agentforce/ai-agents/

- Shakrapani. (n.d.). *Traditional Single-Agent vs Multi AI Agents Models using Azure AI Studio & Semantic Kernel.* LinkedIn Pulse. `https://www.linkedin.com/pulse/traditional-single-agent-vs-multi-ai-agents-models-using-shakrapani-x66fe/`

- TaskWeaver. (n.d.). *How to evaluate a LLM agent?* Microsoft TaskWeaver Blog. `https://microsoft.github.io/TaskWeaver/blog/evaluation/`

- Unite.AI. (n.d.). *Agentic AI: How Large Language Models Are Shaping the Future of Autonomous Agents.* `https://www.unite.ai/agentic-ai-how-large-language-models-are-shaping-the-future-of-autonomous-agents/`

Get This Book's PDF Version and Exclusive Extras

UNLOCK NOW

Scan the QR code (or go to `packtpub.com/unlock`). Search for this book by name, confirm the edition, and then follow the steps on the page.

Note: Keep your invoice handy. Purchases made directly from Packt don't require an invoice.

Part 5

Responsible AI and Governance

In *Part 5* of this book, we will provide a crucial framework for ensuring that AI solutions are ethical, fair, compliant, and sustainable, starting by defining **responsible AI (RAI)** and its core pillars (FEAT). We will then provide a practical guide to operationalizing these principles through governance committees, risk assessment checklists (***Risk Score = Likelihood*Impact***), and strategic human-in-the-loop approaches. The part also addresses the unique challenges of trustworthy LLMs, such as "hallucinations," and surveys the evolving global regulatory landscape, including the EU AI Act, before concluding with a look at future trends such as quantum computing and a vision of the fully optimized, AI-driven enterprise of 2030.

This part contains the following chapters:

- *Chapter 12, Introduction to Responsible AI*
- *Chapter 13, Implementing RAI Frameworks, Metrics, and Best Practices*
- *Chapter 14, Building Trustworthy LLMs and Generative AI*
- *Chapter 15, Regulatory and Legal Frameworks for Responsible AI*
- *Chapter 16, The Future of AI Optimization: Trends, Vision, and Responsible Implementation*

12

Introduction to Responsible AI

Responsible AI (RAI) is a practical approach that requires **Artificial Intelligence (AI)** systems to be developed and deployed in alignment with an organization's values, supporting both business and ethical goals. RAI emphasizes the responsible, fair, and transparent use of AI tools, focusing on accountability and structured governance.

Indeed, RAI is indispensable for truly optimizing AI solutions within a business context. By establishing robust frameworks and prioritizing human values, RAI guides organizations in using AI responsibly, bridging intentions with real-world impact, and creating AI products that serve both business objectives and social responsibility.

RAI is vital for building trust in AI, as it reduces risks such as bias, privacy issues, and unanticipated harms that can lead to legal, financial, and reputational damage. Such failures in responsibility directly hinder the optimization of AI solutions by limiting their reach, eroding user trust, and creating operational challenges. By addressing these risks, RAI empowers organizations to use AI confidently and ethically, promoting growth and innovation. Proactively addressing ethics through RAI can also be a significant differentiator in the market, contributing to long-term business success and longevity.

This chapter explores the foundational principles of RAI, its significance in business, and the roles of various stakeholders in building RAI solutions.

We will cover the following key topics in this chapter:

- Understanding related terms – responsible AI, ethical AI, and trustworthy AI
- The pillars of RAI and ethical business practices
- The significance of RAI in business practices

- Who is responsible for making "AI responsible"?
- Why does RAI matter for optimizing machine learning models?

By the end of the chapter, you will be able to distinguish between responsible, ethical, and trustworthy AI; understand the foundational pillars of an ethical AI framework; and recognize the roles of various stakeholders in building a collaborative RAI ecosystem.

Understanding related terms – responsible AI, ethical AI, and trustworthy AI

While the terms RAI, ethical AI, and trustworthy AI are often used interchangeably, they have distinct focuses:

- **Ethical AI**: Ethical AI focuses on the moral principles guiding AI development, such as fairness, transparency, and the avoidance of harm. It is concerned with the philosophical and normative aspects of AI, ensuring that AI systems are designed and used in ways that are morally acceptable. Ethical AI addresses questions of what is right and wrong in AI practices, emphasizing the importance of fairness and inclusivity, and is free from bias.

- **Trustworthy AI**: Trustworthy AI involves making AI systems reliable and secure and ensuring they do what they are supposed to do without errors or risks. It focuses on the technical robustness and reliability of AI systems, making sure they perform consistently and safely. Trustworthy AI is similar to a trustworthy car that works reliably, doesn't break down, and keeps you safe.

- **Responsible AI**: RAI is a framework that ensures AI development and deployment are done accountably, with a focus on practical governance. It involves creating AI systems with clear lines of responsibility, robust risk management processes, and transparent decision-making capabilities. RAI addresses the operational aspects of implementing ethical principles in AI systems, aligning them with organizational values and societal expectations. It is RAI that makes sure the system is ethical, meaning it's fair to everyone, doesn't discriminate, is free of bias, respects privacy, and aligns with human values.

RAI serves as the overarching framework that operationalizes the principles of both ethical AI and trustworthy AI into practical business and technical practices.

The following is the key difference between these concepts:

- **Ethical AI**: Focuses on the foundational moral principles that guide AI's purpose and design (fairness and non-maleficence)
- **Trustworthy AI**: Focuses on how well the AI works (safe, secure, and reliable)

- **RAI**: Focuses on how ethically the AI behaves (fair, inclusive, and aligned with societal values) and the governance needed to implement all three practices are in place

All three are important. A car (or AI) needs to be ethical (doesn't cause harm), trustworthy (works well), and responsible (does good for society) to be a successful and sustainable product.

To illustrate the difference, imagine a medical diagnostic system used in a hospital that is AI-powered:

- An ethical medical diagnostic system is built on moral principles, primarily focusing on the core idea of non-maleficence (doing no harm). For example, the developers validate that the algorithm design respects patient autonomy and that the data supply chain for training is ethically sourced and respects privacy. This is about the moral design of the system.

- A trustworthy medical diagnostic system is one that works reliably, consistently, and securely. It has been technically validated to have a consistently high technical success rate, low false positives/negatives, robust security against cyberattacks, and clear error handling to prevent system failure. This is about the technical performance and reliability of the system.

- A responsible medical diagnostic system goes beyond just being ethical and trustworthy. It is governed by a framework that makes sure its real-world application is fair and accountable. For example, the hospital's ethics board verifies the system's technical results are equitable across all demographics (fairness), that its decisions are explainable to doctors (transparency), and that there are clear lines of accountability if a misdiagnosis occurs. RAI operationalizes the principles of both ethical and trustworthy AI in a real-world setting. In AI terms, RAI makes sure the system is ethical, meaning it's fair to everyone, doesn't discriminate, respects privacy, and aligns with human values.

The pillars of RAI and ethical business practices

Business practices involving AI should help build trust among users and stakeholders, mitigate risks, and promote innovation. The core principles of ethical AI practices, i.e., **Fairness, Ethics, Accountability, and Transparency** (**FEAT**), are the fundamental pillars of RAI. Many organizations are now turning to the FEAT principles to develop RAI for ethical business practices (for more information, see https://www.mas.gov.sg/news/media-releases/2018/mas-introduces-new-feat-principles-to-promote-responsible-use-of-ai-and-data-analytics):

The following figure visually represents how the FEAT principles for an AI governance framework are intertwined and supported by these core pillars:

Figure 12.1: An overview of the FEAT principles for an AI governance framework,

Exhibit from "Using the FEAT approach to avoid biased AI," April 2022, McKinsey & Company, www.mckinsey.com. Copyright © 2025 McKinsey & Company. All rights reserved. Reprinted by permission

- **Fairness** in AI development strives to ensure that certain AI systems do not discriminate against any individuals or marginalized groups and provide equitable treatment. Implementing techniques for detecting and mitigating biases in AI models, using diverse and representative training data, and designing AI systems with inclusivity in mind are key steps. These practices contribute to preventing discrimination and achieving equitable outcomes, enhancing their performance and reliability for all users.

- **Ethics** involves embedding ethical considerations into every stage of AI development to align with societal values and not cause harm. Developing and adhering to ethical guidelines and providing ethics training for AI developers and stakeholders promotes RAI development by creating trust and acceptance among users and stakeholders.

- **Accountability** requires establishing clear lines of responsibility for the outcomes of AI systems. This includes conducting impact assessments to evaluate the potential effects of AI systems on individuals and society and establishing oversight mechanisms such as ethics committees and independent review boards. These measures help identify and mitigate risks, promote ethical outcomes, and align AI development with societal values.

- **Transparency** is about making the workings of AI systems understandable to stakeholders, and explainability is a critical component of this. Making AI systems explainable not only builds trust but also allows stakeholders to comprehend how decisions are made, fostering accountability and confidence in the technology. This includes clear documentation of how AI models are trained, the data used, and the decision-making processes. By creating detailed documentation such as datasheets, model cards, system cards, and transparency notes, and maintaining open communication with stakeholders, businesses can build trust and facilitate regulatory compliance. A practical guide on how to create and operationalize these cards and notes is provided in the next chapter.

In addition to the core FEAT pillars, a robust RAI framework must also address privacy and safety as these are the surrounding pillars upholding the core principles. **Privacy** requires that AI systems strictly follow the data protection laws and ethical standards, so the personal information used to train, test, and run the models is handled securely, anonymized effectively, and used only for its intended purpose. Protecting user privacy is a crucial aspect of RAI, ensuring ethical data handling and building user trust. Simultaneously, **safety** requires that AI systems are not only technically robust and secure against malicious attacks but also free from unintended harms. This includes conducting safety assessments and implementing safety mechanisms such as fail-safes and redundancy; these are essential for reducing risks and protecting users. For example, **Failure Modes and Effects Analysis (FMEA)** can be used to systematically identify potential failure points in an AI system, preventing dangerous or discriminatory outputs and establishing clear emergency protocols for safe system shutdowns, thereby mitigating all potential risks to users as well as to the organization. Mechanisms such as watchdog timers can be implemented in production to automatically restart a system if it becomes unresponsive, while redundant systems can guarantee a backup is available if the primary AI fails.

The following diagram expands on the FEAT principles, outlining the specific components and practices that contribute to each pillar when developing RAI:

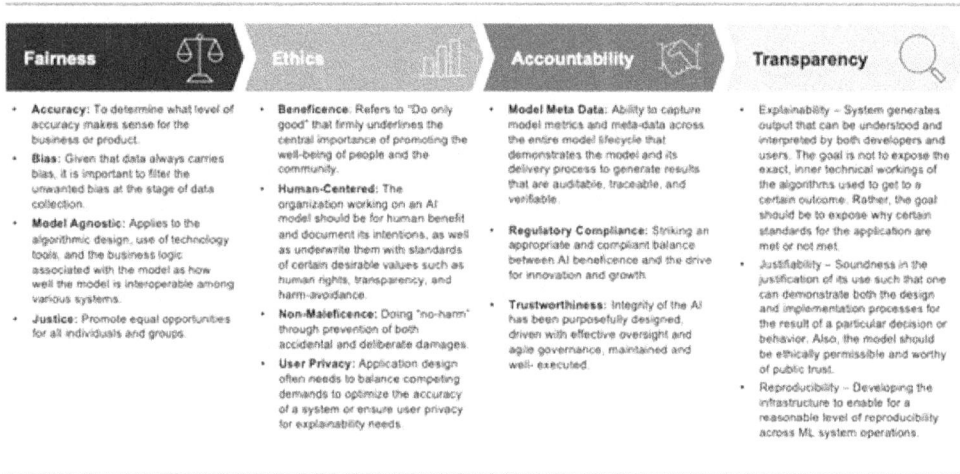

Fairness

- **Accuracy:** To determine what level of accuracy makes sense for the business or product.
- **Bias:** Given that data always carries bias, it is important to filter the unwanted bias at the stage of data collection.
- **Model Agnostic:** Applies to the algorithmic design, use of technology tools, and the business logic associated with the model as how well the model is interoperable among various systems.
- **Justice:** Promote equal opportunities for all individuals and groups.

Ethics

- **Beneficence:** Refers to "Do only good" that firmly underlines the central importance of promoting the well-being of people and the community.
- **Human-Centered:** The organization working on an AI model should be for human benefit and document its intentions, as well as underwrite them with standards of certain desirable values such as human rights, transparency, and harm-avoidance.
- **Non-Maleficence:** Doing "no-harm" through prevention of both accidental and deliberate damages.
- **User Privacy:** Application design often needs to balance competing demands to optimize the accuracy of a system or ensure user privacy for explainability needs.

Accountability

- **Model Meta Data:** Ability to capture model metrics and meta-data across the entire model lifecycle that demonstrates the model and its delivery process to generate results that are auditable, traceable, and verifiable.
- **Regulatory Compliance:** Striking an appropriate and compliant balance between AI beneficence and the drive for innovation and growth.
- **Trustworthiness:** Integrity of the AI has been purposefully designed, driven with effective oversight and agile governance, maintained and well-executed.

Transparency

- Explainability – System generates output that can be understood and interpreted by both developers and users. The goal is not to expose the exact, inner technical workings of the algorithms used to get to a certain outcome. Rather, the goal should be to expose why certain standards for the application are met or not met.
- Justifiability – Soundness in the justification of its use such that one can demonstrate both the design and implementation processes for the result of a particular decision or behavior. Also, the model should be ethically permissible and worthy of public trust.
- Reproducibility – Developing the infrastructure to enable for a reasonable level of reproducibility across ML system operations.

Figure 12.2: An overview of expanding Expanding on the FEAT approach to develop RAI.

Exhibit from "Using the FEAT approach to avoid biased AI," April 2022, McKinsey & Company, www.mckinsey.com. Copyright © 2025 McKinsey & Company. All rights reserved. Reprinted by permission

Privacy is all about protecting the personal data and privacy of individuals interacting with AI systems. By using techniques such as data anonymization and encryption and ensuring compliance with privacy regulations such as the **General Data Protection Regulation (GDPR)**, businesses can enhance user trust and avoid legal issues.

Safety is paramount when AI systems operate reliably and safely, minimizing potential harm. Conducting safety assessments and implementing safety mechanisms such as fail-safes and redundancy are essential for reducing risks and protecting users. Ethical AI practices have a significant business impact. They enhance a company's reputation by demonstrating a commitment to responsible and ethical technology development, reducing risks associated with AI deployment, and fostering innovation by creating a trustworthy environment for experimentation and development. Companies that prioritize ethics in AI are more likely to attract top talent and gain a competitive edge.

Let's take an example of a medical diagnostic system leveraging AI in a hospital to illustrate the successful implementation of ethical and RAI practices across the project life cycle. A hospital is implementing an AI system to analyze medical images (X-rays and CT scans) to help doctors identify early signs of a specific condition, aiming to improve the speed and consistency of diagnosis while not compromising patient safety and trust.

Here are the implementation steps:

1. **Establishing ethical guidelines**: The AI project begins with the RAI steering committee setting a foundational ethical principle: the model must perform equitably for all patients. They mandate that the training data must represent the full diversity of the target patient population (across demographics such as age, gender, and ethnicity) to prevent algorithmic bias. This proactive step shows that a commitment to fairness and patient safety is built into the system's design from day one.

2. **Conducting bias audits**: During the development and testing phase, the focus shifts to trustworthy AI. The system is subjected to rigorous bias audits where performance is not measured by overall technical success rate alone, but by consistency across specific demographic slices. If the model's success rate drops for a particular group, it is retrained or augmented until performance is equitable and reliable, confirming that the initial ethical guideline is met.

3. **Maintaining transparency**: For successful deployment, the principle of transparency is operationalized. The hospital validates that every physician who uses the system is provided with model cards and transparency notes. These documents clearly explain the model's purpose, its known limitations, the data that was used for training, and, most importantly, how it reached a specific diagnostic recommendation. This clarity fosters trust and enables the human doctor to effectively interpret the AI's output.

4. **Protecting privacy and enhanced safety**: The final governance framework upholds ongoing privacy and safety. Technical measures include robust encryption and access protocols to protect sensitive patient data (privacy). In addition, a governance policy is enforced that requires a human physician to always review and approve a final diagnosis, thereby ensuring accountability and providing a human-in-the-loop safeguard for ultimate patient safety. This continuous oversight completes the framework for responsible implementation.

After implementing the preceding steps, the hospital achieves the following results:

*   **Increased trust**: The hospital gains increased trust from customers and stakeholders due to its commitment to ethical AI practices

*   **Improved performance**: Their AI models perform more accurately and reliably, thanks to regular bias audits and inclusive design practices

- **Regulatory compliance**: They successfully comply with relevant regulations, avoiding legal issues and penalties

By integrating these ethical business practices into AI development, companies can create AI systems that are not only powerful and efficient but also aligned with societal values and ethical standards. This approach allows AI technologies to contribute positively to society while limiting potential harm.

RAI is a fundamental principle guiding ethical AI development by prioritizing human values, transparency, fairness, privacy, safety, and accountability. Measuring its impact includes quantifying fairness, transparency, and trust through various metrics and assessments. Embedding RAI in businesses can foster a culture of innovation and ethics, elevating brand reputation and driving long-term success. With AI's continually evolving landscape, a vigilant and adaptable approach is a valuable investment for both businesses and society.

RAI is more of a framework making sure AI systems are built with clear lines of responsibility, robust risk management processes, and transparent decision-making capabilities. It is RAI that bridges the "why" and "how" of ethical AI development, turning principles into practice.

The significance of RAI in business practices

AI adoption in businesses has grown exponentially, especially in the last two years, transforming industries and accelerating innovation. AI technologies are being used to improve healthcare, advance research, enable sustainable practices, and develop climate solutions, among many other applications. This widespread adoption has brought about significant benefits, but it has also raised concerns about the ethical implications of AI systems. As a result, there is an increasing demand for ethical AI solutions that prioritize transparency, fairness, accountability, and privacy. Ultimately, the integration of RAI practices is not merely a matter of ethical compliance but a strategic imperative that fosters trust, mitigates long-term risks, and cultivates a sustainable foundation for business optimization and longevity in an increasingly AI-driven world.

Businesses are recognizing the importance of integrating RAI practices into their operations to address these concerns. Companies such as Microsoft and other major cloud providers have developed comprehensive frameworks and guidelines stressing the need for transparency, accountability, fairness, and privacy, and assisting with actionable steps for businesses to follow.

Stakeholders' expectations, including customers, regulators, and investors, for RAI practices are higher than ever. Customers are becoming more aware of the ethical implications of AI and are demanding greater transparency and accountability from businesses. They want to know how AI systems are making decisions, what data is being used, and how their privacy is being protected. This shift in customer expectations is driving businesses to adopt RAI practices to build trust and maintain their reputation.

Regulators are also playing a key role in shaping the fast-paced AI adoption landscape. Governments and regulatory bodies are introducing new laws and guidelines; for example, the EU's GDPR has set stringent requirements for data privacy and protection, which businesses must comply with when developing AI systems, and the EU AI Act enforces legally binding regulation with penalties for non-compliance. Similarly, the **National Institute of Standards and Technology (NIST)** in the United States is working on developing standards for AI risk management. These regulatory requirements are pushing businesses to adopt RAI practices to comply with and avoid legal repercussions.

Investors are increasingly considering the ethical implications of AI when making investment decisions. They are looking for businesses that prioritize RAI practices and demonstrate a commitment to ethical AI development. Companies that adopt RAI practices are seen as more trustworthy and sustainable, making them more attractive to investors. This shift in investor expectations is encouraging businesses to integrate RAI into their operations to secure funding and drive long-term growth.

Adopting RAI practices can provide a significant competitive advantage for businesses. By differentiating themselves as leaders in ethical AI, companies can enhance their reputation, build trust with customers, and attract top talent. Ethical AI practices can also drive innovation by creating a trustworthy environment for experimentation and development.

Businesses that prioritize RAI are better positioned to navigate the complex regulatory landscape and avoid legal issues. They can also mitigate risks associated with AI deployment, such as bias, discrimination, and privacy breaches, which can lead to reputational damage and financial losses. By addressing these risks proactively, businesses can enhance the reliability and safety of their AI systems, which will also enhance their overall performance and reliability.

Moreover, companies that adopt RAI practices can foster a culture of innovation and ethics within their organization. This culture can drive employee engagement and satisfaction, as employees are more likely to be motivated and committed to working for a company that prioritizes ethical considerations. This, in turn, can lead to higher productivity and better business outcomes.

This chapter reinforces the profound impact of RAI in today's businesses, which cannot be overstated. The current surge in AI adoption, paired with the increasing focus on ethical AI, makes it imperative for businesses to adopt RAI practices. Also, in aligning with stakeholder expectations and capitalizing on the benefits of RAI, companies can foster trust, stimulate innovation, and enable long-term success.

Who is responsible for making "AI responsible"?

A key question in the development and deployment of AI is: Who is responsible for making "AI responsible"? Responsibility for RAI is not confined to a single team; it is a shared and distributed duty across the organization's ecosystem. Successful RAI requires continuous oversight and collaboration from all stakeholders involved in the AI life cycle, from design to deployment. The successful operationalization of Responsible AI requires clearly defined roles and accountability. The following structure outlines key roles adapted from leading industry governance models.

Key roles and their responsibilities in implementing RAI include the following:

- **Executive leadership and the board of directors**: Responsible for defining the high-level ethical vision and setting the tone for ethical AI practices within their organizations. They are responsible for establishing ethical guidelines, allocating resources for RAI initiatives, and fostering a culture of responsibility and transparency. They carry ultimate accountability for systemic harm caused by AI systems.

- **Ethics committee and independent review boards**: These bodies (whether ethics committees or formal councils) provide oversight and guidance on ethical AI practices. The councils engage with both internal and external stakeholders to shape the company's ethical framework and promote RAI culture. Ethics committees develop specific policies, conduct risk assessments, review AI projects to align with ethical guidelines, and maintain accountability and transparency in AI development.

- **AI developers and data scientists**: These professionals are responsible for designing, building, and testing AI models ethically. They are at the forefront of AI development. Their role includes implementing technical mitigations to detect and prevent bias, documenting model decisions (using model cards), and protecting user privacy and data rights. Industry consensus and leading standards recommend that developers should conduct impact assessments early in the system's development.

- **Deployment and business unit leaders (product owners and last-mile vendors)**: These people are responsible for guardrails and the real-world deployment of AI. They ensure the AI system is used as intended, establish clear human-in-the-loop protocols, and monitor the model's performance and impact on customers and stakeholders. Last-mile vendors carry a significant responsibility for how AI is packaged, deployed, and used in real-world scenarios. They are the entities that implement the final system into a business process and are responsible for setting guardrails, applying AI safely, and conducting regular audits to maintain compliance and ethical standards in the operational environment.

- **Legal and compliance teams**: These teams are responsible for translating external rules into internal action. They validate that systems comply with all relevant regulations (such as GDPR, sector-specific laws, and emerging AI acts). They advise on data privacy protocols and ensure that legal guardrails are in place.

- **Policymakers and regulators**: Governments and regulatory bodies are responsible for creating and enforcing laws and guidelines that govern AI development and deployment, protecting public interest and upholding human rights. Policymakers must stay informed about advancements in AI technology and continuously update regulations to address emerging ethical challenges.

- **End users (external stakeholders)**: End users also have a role to play in making AI responsible. They provide valuable feedback on AI systems, which can help developers improve their models. Users should be informed about how AI systems work and how their data is being used, fostering transparency and encouraging the responsible use of AI technologies.

The following table outlines these responsibilities by mapping each key role to the relevant phase of the RAI lifecycle:

RAI lifecycle phase	Key role/ stakeholder (Who)	Core responsibility (Why/What)
1. Planning and strategy (vision and governance)	Executive leadership and board of directors	Define the high-level ethical vision, set the organizational tone, allocate resources for RAI, and carry ultimate accountability for systemic harm.
	Ethics committee and independent review boards	Provide oversight and guidance, develop specific policies, review AI projects for ethical alignment, and conduct risk assessments.
2. Build and test (development)	AI developers and data scientists	Design, build, and test models ethically, implement technical bias mitigations, conduct AI impact assessments (AIA) early in the lifecycle, and provide documentation (e.g., model cards).

RAI lifecycle phase	Key role/ stakeholder (Who)	Core responsibility (Why/What)
3. Deployment and operation (accountability and compliance)	Deployment and business unit leaders	Implement guardrails, manage real-world deployment, establish human-in-the-loop protocols, and make sure models maintain compliance in operation.
	Last-mile vendors	Carry significant responsibility for how the AI is packaged and deployed, set client-facing guardrails, and conduct regular audits.
	Legal and compliance teams	Advise on data privacy protocols and enforce legal and regulatory guardrails, translate external rules into internal action, and validate system compliance.
4. Post deployment and feedback (external stakeholders)	Policymakers, regulators, and end users	Policymakers create/enforce laws. End users provide vital feedback on performance, fairness, and safety to help developers improve models and update regulations.

Table 12.1: Roles and responsibilities across the RAI lifecycle

The preceding table summarizes the interconnected roles and responsibilities of various stakeholders across the entire RAI lifecycle. This lifecycle is divided into four distinct phases: **planning and strategy** (vision and governance in setting ethical scope and defining risk), **build and test** (development, i.e., building and mitigating bias with thorough stress testing), **deployment and operation** (accountability and compliance setting guardrails and oversight), and **post deployment** (managing external stakeholders, i.e., monitoring, updating, and collecting feedback). The table highlights how different stakeholders are involved in these stages, emphasizing the continuous and connected nature of RAI governance.

To foster a truly collaborative approach to RAI, it is highly imperative to avoid responsibility gaps. This requires stakeholders to work together and contribute to ethical AI practices by taking the following actions, as discussed in the upcoming sections.

Avoiding responsibility gaps

It is imperative to avoid responsibility gaps, where stakeholders assume that responsibility lies solely with another group. Each stakeholder must understand their part in fostering RAI and actively contribute to ethical AI practices. It's essential for stakeholders to collaborate and communicate effectively throughout the AI life cycle and post-deployment.

For example, AI developers should work closely with ethics committees to align their models with ethical guidelines. Business leaders should engage with policymakers to stay informed about regulatory requirements and maintain compliance. Last-mile vendors should implement safety mechanisms and conduct regular audits to maintain ethical standards in AI deployment. End users should provide feedback to developers and be informed about the ethical implications of AI technologies.

By working collaboratively and actively fulfilling these responsibilities, stakeholders can create a robust ecosystem for RAI. This collective effort ensures that AI systems are not only technically advanced but also ethically sound.

Collaborative effort in RAI

Consider a scenario where InnovAIte LLC, a forward-thinking tech company committed to developing RAI solutions across multiple sectors, is developing an AI system for healthcare diagnostics. The company establishes an ethics committee to oversee the project and align it with ethical guidelines. AI developers conduct impact assessments to evaluate the potential effects of the AI system on patients and healthcare providers. Business leaders allocate resources for RAI initiatives and engage with stakeholders, including patients, healthcare professionals, and regulators, to understand their expectations and concerns. Policymakers provide guidelines for the ethical use of AI in healthcare, making sure the AI system complies with relevant regulations. Last-mile vendors package and deploy the AI system, implementing safety mechanisms and conducting regular audits to uphold ethical standards. End users, including healthcare providers and patients, provide feedback on the AI system, helping developers improve their technical performance and reliability.

This effort also means the AI system is built responsibly, protecting patient privacy, promoting fairness, and maintaining transparency. Continuous monitoring and improvement of the AI system post-deployment addresses new challenges and keeps the system effective and ethical. Training and educating all stakeholders on the ethical use of AI builds a culture of responsibility and awareness.

Such effort helps build trust, drive innovation, and put into force AI technologies to serve the greater good, demonstrating that success hinges on all stakeholders fulfilling their shared responsibility for ethical AI. This example illustrates InnovAIte LLC's foundational commitment to RAI, a commitment that will shape its trajectory to become a leading AI-driven enterprise.

Next, we will explore why this commitment is not just a matter of ethics but a fundamental driver of true model optimization.

Why does RAI matter for optimizing AI systems?

In the rapidly evolving field of **Artificial Intelligence** (**AI**), optimizing AI systems for performance and efficiency is a primary goal. However, true optimization extends beyond mere technical metrics and necessitates a careful balance with ethical considerations. RAI practices are absolutely vital for achieving this holistic optimization by confirming that AI systems are fair, transparent, and accountable, ultimately leading to more robust and impactful solutions. This section explores why RAI is essential for AI optimization and how it directly enhances their real-world value and long-term viability.

The importance of ethical considerations

Dr. Joy Buolamwini's work, particularly her book *Unmasking AI*, highlights the profound gaps and biases present even in gold-standard training datasets. For instance, a system could achieve a high-performance rate on a benchmark dataset while failing on all women of color in the dataset. This example reinforces the need to look beyond mere model optimization and consider the end-to-end process from data to model to impact. Focusing solely on technical performance metrics (such as accuracy) is insufficient; we must also address subjective costs and ensure that the models do not perpetuate biases at scale.

Ignoring these broader ethical considerations and focusing solely on benchmark success can lead to models that fail in real-world scenarios, thus undermining any perceived optimization based on limited datasets. RAI compels us to optimize the AI system for improved performance and equitable outcomes, not just abstract metrics.

Beyond narrow optimization

As organizations mature, optimization moves beyond just achieving the best model accuracy or F1 score. True optimization requires a strategic view of the entire AI lifecycle from data usage to infrastructure cost and drives alignment with measurable business value. This broader view is necessary for scaling AI successfully.

Here are the new dimensions of optimization:

1. **Optimize AI system performance**: This goes beyond testing the model's mathematical scores on test data. It involves optimizing the AI application's real-world latency, through-put, and decision-making speed in production environments. This helps achieve a system that is not only accurate but fast enough to deliver value.

2. **Optimize resource allocation (cost and efficiency)**: This is a core AIOps concern. It means continuously monitoring the cost-to-serve (inference cost, GPU hours, cloud storage) versus the generated business value. Techniques like model compression and efficient deployment aim to optimize the AI system to run with the lowest possible infrastructure expenses.

3. **Optimize ethical and human-centric outcomes**: This aligns with the RAI principles discussed later. Optimization must include minimizing bias, promoting fairness, and maximizing explainability. An AI system that is technically perfect but ethically harmful is not optimized for long-term business viability.

4. **Optimize feedback loops**: Implement a process for continuous learning. This means optimizing the process of collecting user feedback, monitoring drift in real-world data, and using this information to automatically or semi-automatically update the AI system to maintain its value proposition over time.

Real-world applications and impact

In healthcare, AI is revolutionizing the way we diagnose and treat diseases, manage healthcare systems, and optimize resource allocation. For example, AI algorithms can analyze patient data to detect early signs of diseases, craft personalized treatment plans, and predict patient admissions. These applications demonstrate the true potential of AI systems when combined with RAI practices that can enhance their real-world impact and improve patient outcomes.

When combined with RAI practices, the optimization of AI systems in healthcare not only improves efficiency and performance but also builds patient trust and promotes equitable access to care, thereby maximizing the positive impact and long-term value of these advancements. RAI aims for the optimization of AI in critical domains to align with societal well-being and ethical standards.

Challenges and best practices

Optimizing AI systems involves several challenges, including data quality, computational demands, and bias mitigation. Reliable outcomes depend on high-quality data, while efficient resource management is essential to counteract computational demands. Addressing bias through tech-niques such as bias detection and corrective algorithms is not just an ethical imperative but also a crucial step in optimizing AI system performance for all user groups, leading to wider adoption and more reliable outcomes. Fairness, therefore, becomes a key dimension of effective AI optimization. Regular evaluation and tuning of AI systems are necessary to maintain their performance and generalizability in real-world environments.

The role of continuous learning

Continuous learning and AI system updates are vital for keeping AI systems relevant and accurate. As more data becomes available, AI systems can improve over time through incremental learning techniques that not only improve performance against a balanced set of metrics but also evolve responsibly, optimizing their long-term utility and alignment with societal values. This iterative process of learning and ethical refinement is essential for sustained AI optimization that enhances both efficiency and performance. Keeping AI systems in check remains valuable and actionable.

Ethical considerations and bias mitigation

Ethical considerations are central to RAI. By actively identifying and mitigating biases and establishing transparency, we are not just being ethical; we are building more robust and reliable AI systems that are optimized for fair and equitable outcomes, ultimately leading to greater trust and wider acceptance. Ethical considerations are therefore integral to achieving true and sustainable optimization in AI systems.

RAI is fundamental for AI optimization, making sure AI systems are not only powerful and efficient but also ethically sound and aligned with societal values. By addressing biases, implementing comprehensive evaluation practices that include fairness and transparency, and fostering continuous learning with ethical considerations in mind, we can enhance the real-world value and long-term sustainability of AI systems.

This approach fosters trust, drives innovation that benefits all, and helps ensure that using AI contributes positively to society while minimizing potential harms. As we continue to push the boundaries of what's possible with AI, integrating RAI practices is vital for achieving sustainable and ethical advancements that truly optimize outcomes for both businesses and society.

Ethical considerations are therefore integral to achieving true and sustainable optimization in AI systems. In the next section, we will move from theory to practice, providing a practical guide for operationalizing these RAI principles within organizations, complete with frameworks, metrics, and best practices.

Earning trust through RAI — real-world case studies

Consider these experiences of companies that have successfully implemented RAI practices and witnessed positive outcomes.

Case study 1: Google's inclusive image recognition

Google faced criticism for biases in its early image recognition AI, which struggled to accurately identify individuals with darker skin tones. Recognizing the ethical implications and the limitations imposed on their products' usability, Google proactively addressed this issue. They invested in more diverse training data and refined their models to reduce these biases. This commitment to fairness not only improved the technical performance and inclusivity of their image recognition technology but also enhanced user trust and broadened the appeal of their products to a wider audience. By taking responsibility for addressing bias, Google optimized its AI for a larger market and improved user experience.

Case study 2: a financial institution's fair underwriting model

A financial institution sought to improve its loan underwriting process using AI. Initially, their model inadvertently exhibited biases against certain demographic groups, limiting access to credit and potentially leading to regulatory scrutiny. By prioritizing fairness as a core tenet of their RAI strategy, the institution undertook efforts to identify and mitigate these biases. They analyzed the data used to train the model, removed or adjusted discriminatory features, and implemented fairness metrics to evaluate the model's output. As a result, they developed a more equitable underwriting model that expanded their customer base to previously underserved segments. This not only aligned with ethical principles but also optimized their business by tapping into new markets and mitigating potential legal and reputational risks associated with discriminatory practices.

These examples illustrate that RAI isn't just about compliance or avoiding negative consequences; it can be a powerful driver of business optimization, leading to more inclusive products, greater user trust, and expanded market opportunities.

Summary

In this chapter, we embarked on a journey to understand the foundational principles of RAI and its indispensable role in achieving true and sustainable optimization of AI solutions. We began by defining RAI, emphasizing the importance of developing and deploying AI technologies in an ethical, transparent, and accountable manner. This sets the stage for exploring the broader societal implications and the necessity of integrating ethical considerations as a core component of effective AI optimization.

We then discussed ethical business practices in AI development, highlighting the core principles of transparency, accountability, fairness, and privacy. By adopting these practices, businesses can build trust, mitigate risks, and foster innovation, ultimately enhancing their reputation and operational efficiency.

The significance of RAI in today's business practices was reinforced by examining the current landscape of AI adoption and the increasing demand for ethical AI solutions. We discussed how meeting stakeholder expectations and leveraging the competitive advantages of RAI can position businesses as leaders in ethical AI, driving long-term success.

Understanding who is responsible for making AI "responsible" revealed that it is a collective effort involving AI developers, data scientists, business leaders, last-mile vendors, ethics committees, policymakers, and end users. Each stakeholder plays a vital role in ensuring that AI systems are developed and deployed responsibly, with clear lines of accountability and collaboration to avoid responsibility gaps.

Finally, we explored why RAI is not just an ethical consideration but a fundamental driver of optimizing AI systems. By proactively addressing biases, implementing comprehensive evaluation practices that include fairness and transparency, and fostering continuous learning with ethical considerations, we can significantly enhance the real-world value, user trust, and long-term viability of AI applications, leading to more impactful, trustworthy, and sustainable AI solutions.

With new AI advancements and reasoning models on the rise, understanding and establishing trust in AI systems to build products and services responsibly is more important than ever. RAI is the end outcome that ensures AI systems are not only technically robust and reliable but also ethically sound and aligned with societal values. By adopting RAI practices, organizations can navigate the complexities of AI development, mitigate risks, and foster trust as this fluid AI landscape requires continuous adaptation and innovation.

This chapter has laid a solid foundation for understanding the principles and practices of RAI. As we move forward, we will dive deeper into practical frameworks for implementing RAI and examine real-world examples and case studies that illustrate its impact.

Subscribe for a free eBook

New frameworks, evolving architectures, research drops, production breakdowns—AI_Distilled filters the noise into a weekly briefing for engineers and researchers working hands-on with LLMs and GenAI systems. Subscribe now and receive a free eBook, along with weekly insights that help you stay focused and informed.

Subscribe at `https://packt.link/80z6Y` or scan the QR code below.

13

Implementing RAI Frameworks, Metrics, and Best Practices

The preceding chapter laid out the essential groundwork for understanding the principles and significance of **Responsible AI (RAI)**. However, translating these guiding ideals into tangible practice requires a structured and deliberate approach. This chapter serves as a practical roadmap for operationalizing RAI, moving beyond theoretical discussions to provide actionable strategies and tools that organizations can implement throughout the AI life cycle. Effectively embedding ethical considerations is not a passive aspiration but an active process that demands the establishment of clear frameworks, the application of relevant metrics, and the adoption of proven best practices.

This chapter will guide you through the essential components of an ethical AI implementation strategy. We will begin by exploring various frameworks for ethical AI governance, such as the establishment of a dedicated RAI governance committee and the utilization of ethical risk assessment checklists. These frameworks provide the foundational structure for oversight and risk mitigation (Mucci & Stryker, 2024). Building upon this, we will delve into tangible ethical governance structures and processes, including the formation of AI ethics boards and the crucial practice of routine bias audits, which promotes ongoing vigilance and accountability.

Recognizing that AI systems are not infallible, this chapter will also examine the strategic integration of **Human-in-the-Loop (HITL)** approaches. We will explore where and how human oversight can be effectively incorporated, particularly in high-stakes decision-making scenarios where ethical considerations and nuanced judgment are paramount. Furthermore, to move beyond qualitative assessments, we will present key metrics for quantifying RAI, encompassing fairness, explainability, robustness, privacy, and safety. These metrics provide a tangible way to evaluate and track progress toward more RAI systems.

Finally, the chapter will outline essential best practices for implementing RAI, including techniques for data anonymization, strategies for inclusive dataset curation, and the critical importance of comprehensive model documentation and transparency. By adopting these practices, organizations can proactively build ethical considerations into their AI development and deployment workflows. To illustrate the practical application of these concepts, a real-world case study will detail a company's journey in establishing and executing a comprehensive RAI program, highlighting the steps taken and the tangible outcomes achieved.

The key topics to be covered include the following:

- Framework for ethical AI governance
- Regulatory compliance in a global context
- Human-in-the-loop approaches
- Metrics for RAI
- Best practices for implementing RAI
- Real-world applications of RAI

By the end of this chapter, you will be equipped with the knowledge and practical guidance necessary to move from understanding the why of RAI to effectively implementing the how, fostering trust in AI systems, and paving the way for their sustainable and ethical integration into business and society.

Framework for ethical AI governance

Organizations seeking to operationalize RAI need robust governance frameworks. These frameworks provide the essential structure and guiding principles for ensuring ethical considerations are integrated throughout the entire AI life cycle, from ideation and development to deployment and ongoing monitoring. Establishing clear lines of responsibility, documented processes, and mechanisms for oversight are critical for building trustworthy and sustainable AI systems. This section introduces several key frameworks and components that organizations can adopt to establish effective ethical AI governance.

One fundamental element of ethical AI governance is the establishment of RAI governance committees. These committees typically comprise individuals with diverse expertise, including AI developers, ethicists, legal counsel, business stakeholders, and representatives from relevant user groups. The primary role of an RAI governance committee (the organization's strategic policy-setting and oversight body) is to provide guidance on all aspects of AI development and deployment from an ethical perspective.

Their responsibilities may include the following:

- **Defining ethical guidelines and policies**: Establishing clear principles and rules that govern the development and use of AI within the organization

- **Reviewing AI project proposals**: Assessing the potential ethical implications of new AI initiatives before development begins

- **Evaluating model design and architecture**: Instilling that ethical considerations are embedded in the technical design of AI systems

- **Monitoring model performance and impact**: Continuously tracking the real-world effects of deployed AI systems for potential ethical concerns, including bias and fairness issues

- **Providing recommendations for mitigation and remediation**: Identifying and suggesting corrective actions for any ethical risks or harms that arise

- **Upholding compliance with regulations and standards**: Keeping abreast of and adhering to relevant legal and ethical guidelines

The RAI governance committee provides the essential policy oversight and strategic direction for all AI activities. Their primary responsibilities include establishing the ethical thresholds (e.g., maximum allowable bias), reviewing and approving the system cards, and deciding on mitigation strategies for high-risk models identified in the ethical risk Assessment.

Crucially, while the committee establishes the monitoring requirements and reviews the results, it typically does not participate in day-to-day model performance monitoring. That operational responsibility falls to the **ML Operations** (**MLOps**) teams and data scientists, who use automated tools (covered later in the *Metrics for RAI* section) to continuously track model performance, data drift, and fairness metrics against the standards set by the committee.

Ethical risk assessment checklist: quantifying risk

Another crucial framework component is the implementation of ethical risk assessment checklists. These checklists operationalize the identification of potential ethical risks across the entire AI life cycle. By prompting developers and stakeholders to consider a range of ethical dimensions, these checklists help safeguard that potential harms are proactively addressed.

In the ethical risk assessment checklist, the risk severity score is a critical calculation used to prioritize mitigation efforts. The formula to determine the risk score is as follows:

Risk Score = Likelihood (L) * Impact (I)

The **Likelihood** (**L**) rates the probability of the harm occurring (e.g., 1=Rare, 5=Almost Certain), and the **Impact** (**I**) rates the degree of harm (e.g., 1=Minor, 5=Catastrophic). This clear quantification allows the RAI governance committee to focus resources on the highest-scoring risks.

We will now go through a concrete risk assessment example.

Consider the healthcare AI medical diagnostic system discussed in *Chapter 12*. An identified risk might be: "Algorithmic bias leading to misdiagnosis in minority patient groups":

- **Likelihood**: 4 (high – if training data is known to be imbalanced)
- **Impact**: 5 (catastrophic – leads to patient harm, legal action)
- **Risk score**: 4*5=20 (high priority)

The required mitigation plan would then mandate immediate action, such as retraining the model with balanced data and enforcing an HITL review for all affected demographic results.

Elements commonly included in an ethical risk assessment checklist might involve questions related to the following:

- **Data bias**: Does the training data reflect the target user population? Are there known limitations or biases in the data that could lead to unfair outcomes?
- **Model architecture bias**: Is the chosen model architecture or design complexity appropriate for the task, or does it inherently lead to systematic under- or over-prediction in certain scenarios?
- **Performance mitigation**: If the model's output is consistently flawed (such as underpredicting demand), are there clear operational procedures for a human reviewer to override the prediction, and is that process documented?
- **Model explainability and transparency**: How understandable is the AI system's decision-making process to end users (e.g., doctors or business leaders)? Are model cards and system cards in place to document design and limitations?
- **System reliability and safety**: What are the potential failure modes? Are there clear HITL safeguards to prevent catastrophic or harmful outputs?
- **Accountability and responsibility**: Is there a clear process for auditing system decisions? Who is explicitly responsible if the AI causes harm or issues an incorrect decision?
- **Prompt injection risk**: For Generative AI models (LLMs), has the system been tested against prompt injection and other adversarial attacks that could force the AI to violate its safety alignment or leak sensitive information?

- **Privacy and data security**: Is personal data handled in compliance with privacy regulations? Are anonymization and robust security measures in place to prevent data breaches?

- **Potential for harm and misuse**: What are the potential negative consequences or unintended uses of the AI system? What safeguards are in place to prevent harm?

- **Fairness and equity**: Does the AI system treat all individuals and groups equitably? Have fairness metrics been considered and evaluated?

- **Inclusiveness and accessibility**: Have the needs of diverse user groups been considered in the design and deployment of the AI system? Is it accessible to all intended users?

By integrating frameworks such as the RAI governance committee and utilizing tools such as ethical risk assessment checklists, organizations can establish a proactive and systematic approach to ethical AI governance, moving beyond ad hoc considerations to embed responsibility at the core of their AI initiatives. This structured approach not only mitigates potential risks but also fosters greater trust in AI systems among stakeholders and the wider public.

Beyond these overarching frameworks, establishing robust ethical governance also involves specific structures and practices. Ethical governance structures are pivotal as they involve establishing AI ethics committees, conducting regular reviews of AI projects, and assigning clear responsibility for AI outcomes. Furthermore, implementing logging and monitoring mechanisms provides essential visibility into AI system behavior, allowing for the detection of potential ethical issues. Maintaining comprehensive documentation, including data lineage, model development processes, and decision-making logic, is crucial for accountability, auditability, and traceability. Similarly, using data version control for model development helps establish reproducibility and the ability to track changes, which is vital for understanding and addressing any ethical concerns that may arise over time. These practices, alongside the broader governance frameworks, are critical steps to follow for achieving accountability, auditability, traceability, and transparency in AI systems.

Operationalizing transparency: model and system cards

Model cards and system cards are essential documentation tools that transform abstract ethical principles into practical checks within the AI life cycle, fulfilling the principles of transparency and accountability.

Model cards: documentation for the model

A model card is a structured document that provides key technical context and performance details for an ML model. It is the technical "nutrition label" intended for data scientists, developers, and auditors:

- **Key contents**: Model details, intended use, training data description (including known biases), technical performance metrics (especially fairness metrics across demographic groups), and ethical considerations (potential risks)

- **Purpose**: To provide technical transparency and detail a model's limitations before deployment, serving as a primary input for the system card

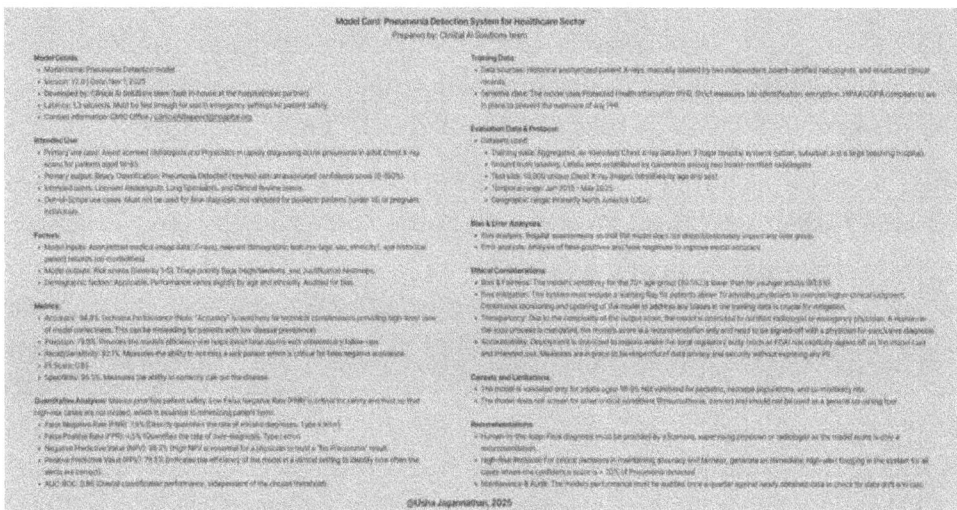

Figure 13.1: An overview of a model card template for a high-stakes medical diagnostic system

The Pneumonia Detection Model v2.0 model card presented here is intended purely as a sample template and a guide to RAI best practices. The results, metrics, and demographics provided are hypothetical and designed to illustrate the necessary level of detail for a high-stakes application in the healthcare sector. Specifically, the conversion and dual labeling of technical terms (e.g., recall/sensitivity) are best practices for aligning standard ML terminology with established clinical diagnostics. This document is not a real regulatory filing and should be used solely for educational and reference purposes.

System cards: documentation for the deployment

A system card is a comprehensive document that details the entire AI solution, which includes the ML model, the data pipelines, human oversight processes, and governance policies. It is the "user manual" and "governance plan" for business owners and legal teams:

- **Key contents**: System overview (how the model is integrated into the business process), risk assessment summary, operational procedures (who monitors the system and the HITL process), system maintenance schedule, and regulatory compliance status

- **Purpose**: For accountability needs, outlining how the complete AI system is intended to be used, its operational risks, and the clear lines of responsibility for the business owners

Integration in the life cycle

The operational function of these cards is to serve as mandatory gate checks. Both the model card and the system card are reviewed and signed off by the RAI governance committee as a mandatory step before a system moves into production, validating that transparency and accountability are non-negotiable gates in the development life cycle.

While frameworks for ethical AI governance establish the internal foundations for responsible innovation, they must operate within the broader ecosystem of legal and regulatory requirements. In the next section, we examine regulatory compliance in a global context.

Regulatory compliance in a global context

Effective AI governance requires adherence to a multi-layered compliance structure, encompassing external government mandates and internal corporate standards. This is a critical operational challenge because regulations are highly fragmented and continuously evolving across different jurisdictions. Here's a look at the different regulations:

- **Global regulatory frameworks**: Organizations must be vigilant in complying with emerging, high-impact regulations, such as the EU AI Act (which establishes a risk-based approach to AI deployment), the **General Data Protection Regulation** (**GDPR**) (which heavily influences data handling for all AI systems), and various US state and federal guidelines. Compliance often requires maintaining strict data provenance records and implementing regional deployment policies.

- **Company-specific regulations (internal policies)**: Beyond external laws, many organizations create their own stringent internal codes of conduct, RAI policies, and data usage standards. These policies often set up a higher ethical bar than legal minimums, reflecting the company's specific values and commitment to brand reputation. The legal and compliance teams are responsible for translating these internal and external mandates into actionable technical requirements that the AI development teams must follow.

- **The role of documentation**: Tools such as the system card become essential compliance assets. They document the model's design, risk mitigation measures, and compliance status against specific regulatory requirements, providing clear proof of due diligence to auditors and regulators.

As organizations navigate this intricate web of global and internal compliance requirements, maintaining transparency, accountability, and traceability becomes paramount. Yet, even the most comprehensive governance frameworks rely on human judgment to guide responsible implementation and oversight. The next section explores how integrating human-in-the-loop approaches strengthens this connection between regulatory compliance and ethical AI practice.

Human-in-the-loop approaches

HITL approaches integrate human judgment into the AI decision-making process. It should always be the case that AI systems are guided by human expertise in every phase of the project and during continuous monitoring and integration, rather than just being automated. HITL approaches are particularly important in high-stakes decisions, where human oversight can help mitigate risks and yield ethical, responsible outcomes that users can rely on. A few examples include using HITL in healthcare diagnostics, financial services, and autonomous vehicles.

While the goal of many AI systems is automation, the integration of human judgment through HITL approaches is crucial for achieving ethical, responsible, and reliable outcomes, particularly in complex or high-stakes scenarios. HITL strategically incorporates human expertise at various stages of the AI life cycle, making sure that AI systems are not solely autonomous but are guided and validated by human understanding, values, and ethical considerations.

For instance, a human-as-a-safeguard role is essential for mitigating risks identified during the bias audit. This role is critical when facing model architecture bias (as mentioned in the ethical risk assessment checklist: quantifying risk), such as a model that systematically underpredicts risk. In these cases, the human reviewer's primary duty is to override the biased low-risk prediction to prevent systemic harm, thereby correcting the model's architectural flaw in the operational environment. This section explores where and how HITL can be effectively implemented.

Here are the key stages and applications of HITL:

1. **Data collection and labeling**: Humans play a vital role in maintaining the quality, accuracy, and fairness of the data used to train AI models. This includes the following:

   - **Data labeling and annotation**: Human experts provide accurate labels and annotations for training data, especially in complex tasks such as medical image analysis or natural language understanding, where nuanced interpretation is required.

   - **Data validation and quality control**: Humans review and validate AI-labeled data to identify and correct errors, ensuring the model learns from reliable information and mitigating potential biases introduced during the labeling process.

   - **Bias detection and mitigation in data**: Human oversight is essential in identifying potential biases embedded within datasets that might not be apparent to automated systems. This involves analyzing data distributions and understanding the social and historical contexts that could lead to unfair representations.

2. **Model development and evaluation**: Human expertise is valuable in guiding the design and evaluating the performance of AI models, especially from an ethical standpoint:

   - **Feature engineering and selection**: Domain experts can provide insights into which features are most relevant and ethically sound for the model to consider, helping to avoid the use of proxies for protected attributes

   - **Model review and approval**: Ethics boards or domain experts can review the model's architecture, training process, and evaluation metrics to align with ethical guidelines and identify potential risks before deployment

   - **Adversarial attack testing and robustness evaluation**: Humans can design and oversee tests to evaluate the model's resilience to adversarial inputs, confirming it doesn't produce harmful or unreliable outputs under unexpected conditions

3. **Model deployment and monitoring**: Continuous human oversight is critical for verifying AI systems function as intended and do not lead to unintended negative consequences in real-world applications:

   - **Exception handling and intervention**: When AI systems encounter edge cases or ambiguous situations or make uncertain predictions, HITL allows for human intervention to make the final decision or guide the AI's response. This is particularly important in safety-critical applications such as autonomous vehicles or medical diagnosis.

- **Real-time monitoring and anomaly detection**: Human analysts can monitor AI system performance and logs for unusual behavior or unexpected outcomes that might indicate ethical breaches, bias amplification, or system failures.

- **Auditing and explainability review**: Humans can review the explanations provided by **Explainable AI (XAI)** techniques to verify that they are accurate, understandable, and ethically sound. This helps build trust and facilitates accountability.

4. **High-stakes decision-making**: In scenarios where AI decisions have significant consequences for individuals or society, HITL is often indispensable:

   - **Healthcare diagnostics and treatment recommendations**: While AI can provide valuable insights, human doctors retain the final decision-making authority, considering the patient's overall context and ethical considerations

   - **Financial services (loan approvals and risk assessment)**: Human loan officers or risk analysts can review AI-driven recommendations, especially for marginalized groups or in complex cases, to promote fairness and prevent algorithmic bias

   - **Criminal justice (sentencing and parole)**: While AI might assist in risk assessment, human judges and parole boards must ultimately make decisions, considering legal and ethical principles

   - **Autonomous weapons systems (if ever deployed)**: The ethical debate around autonomous weapons heavily emphasizes the need for human control over lethal force decisions

5. **Implementing HITL effectively**: Successful implementation of HITL requires careful consideration of the following:

   - **Defining clear roles and responsibilities**: Specifying when and how human intervention should occur and who is responsible for oversight

   - **Designing user-friendly interfaces**: Providing intuitive tools and information for human reviewers to understand AI outputs and make informed decisions

   - **Establishing escalation procedures**: Defining clear pathways for escalating complex or ethically sensitive cases to human experts

   - **Providing adequate training**: Verifying that human reviewers have the necessary domain expertise and understanding of the AI system

   - **Continuously evaluating and refining HITL processes**: Regularly assessing the effectiveness of HITL workflows and making adjustments as needed

By strategically integrating human intelligence and ethical judgment into the AI life cycle, HITL approaches can significantly enhance the responsibility, reliability, and trustworthiness of AI systems, particularly in applications with significant societal impact.

However, let's also discuss the cost and trade-offs of HITL approaches. While highly effective for high-risk domains, implementing an HITL system involves a critical trade-off. Organizations must account for the added costs of human labor, the potential for increased latency in the decision process, and the risk of human fatigue or bias overriding correct AI recommendations. Therefore, HITL must be deployed strategically, focusing on high-risk, high-impact decisions where the reduction in ethical and financial risk justifies the operational cost.

Metrics for RAI

The RAI governance committee establishes the policy requiring performance monitoring. However, effective monitoring is dependent on tangible data. Therefore, the next crucial step in operationalizing RAI is to define and monitor a comprehensive set of RAI metrics that allow the AIOps teams to continuously track model performance against the standards set by the committee.

While the RAI governance committee focuses on policy oversight and strategic review, the execution of day-to-day model performance monitoring falls to the AIOps teams and data scientists. These teams use automated tools to continuously track data drift, fairness metrics, and overall model performance against the standards set by the committee.

Optimizing ML models for RAI requires a comprehensive evaluation using various metrics that quantify alignment with ethical principles. Key metrics include the following:

- **Accuracy and precision (quantify performance)**: These are fundamental for evaluating model performance; for example, in healthcare, high accuracy and precision are highly important for diagnosing diseases.

- **Fairness metrics (quantify fairness)**: These are essential for preventing discrimination and promoting equitable treatment. Metrics such as **Statistical Parity Difference** (**SPD**), disparate impact, and equal opportunity difference help to assure fairness in hiring algorithms and loan approval systems.

- **Explainability metrics (quantify transparency)**: These metrics help enhance understanding of model decisions and build trust. Tools such as LIME and SHAP, along with counterfactuals, provide insights into model predictions, helping explain credit scoring decisions such as in the financial services domain.

- **Accountability metrics (quantify accountability):** These include measurable aspects of governance and oversight, such as the frequency and thoroughness of impact assessments and regular audits, the clarity of responsibility assignments for AI outcomes, and the documented responsiveness to identified ethical breaches. For example, in autonomous vehicles, the documented processes for safety incident review and updates serve as accountability metrics.

- **Privacy metrics (quantify privacy):** Warranting that the output of a model does not reveal sensitive PII. Differential privacy, often quantified by a "privacy budget," protects patient data in healthcare while allowing for valuable insights.

- **Safety metrics (quantify safety):** These metrics help conduct reliability and safety assessments to minimize potential harm. Examples include the mean time between failures, the severity of potential failure modes identified in safety assessments, and the effectiveness of implemented safety mechanisms. In fields such as industrial automation, safety is the topmost concern, and metrics evaluation keep in check that AI systems do not cause harm.

- **Robustness metrics (quantify reliability and safety):** These metrics evaluate the model's stability and reliability under various conditions, including noisy data, adversarial attacks, and distributional shifts. Examples include the model's accuracy on perturbed datasets or its resilience to specific adversarial attacks.

By integrating these metrics into the evaluation process, data scientists and AI practitioners can confidently say that their models are not only optimized for performance but also demonstrably aligned with ethical standards and societal values.

Best practices for implementing RAI

Implementing RAI is not a one-time task but an ongoing commitment that requires embedding ethical considerations deeply into the fabric of AI development and deployment. The following expanded best practices offer a more granular guide for organizations striving to build ethical, transparent, and accountable AI systems.

Strategic governance and policy

As we know, effectively embedding RAI begins at the strategic level with clear mandates from executive leadership. The foundational best practice is the establishment of the RAI governance committee. This cross-functional body defines the organization's ethical principles and sets the non-negotiable thresholds for risk and bias. Every AI initiative must start with a comprehensive ethical risk assessment checklist, where potential harms are quantified using the risk score (likelihood * impact). This initial step ensures that resources are immediately prioritized for high-risk systems (such as our medical diagnostic model) before any code is written.

Key takeaways: strategy and governance

Let's look at the critical insights gained:

- **Executive mandate**: Establishes that RAI is driven from the top down and is viewed as a business imperative, not just a compliance function
- **Establish oversight**: Formalize an RAI governance committee to define policy and review high-risk deployments
- **Quantify risk**: Use an ethical risk assessment checklist to quantify risk (likelihood * impact) and prioritize mitigation efforts based on the resulting risk score
- **Multi-jurisdictional compliance**: Proactively translate global laws (e.g., EU AI Act, GDPR, CCPA, and HIPAA) and internal ethical codes into clear, technical requirements for developers

Ethics by design

Best practices in the development life cycle require adopting an ethics-by-design approach. This means that ethical considerations are to be built into the system design, not retrofitted later. Developers must rigorously audit training data for bias and evaluate the model architecture itself, so that the design does not create systematic errors (e.g., constant under-prediction). Transparency is operationalized through documentation. Model cards are mandatory for technical detail, and system cards (or AI agent cards) are mandatory for operational and governance details. Approval of both cards by the RAI governance committee serves as a deployment gate-check.

Key takeaways: development and documentation

Below are the key insights:

- **Embed design checks**: Audit not just the data but the model architecture itself for sources of systemic bias
- **Mandatory documentation**: Implement model cards (for technical transparency) and system cards (for operational accountability) as non-negotiable steps in the development pipeline
- **Gate-check**: Use the approval of the model and system cards by the RAI governance committee as the mandatory gate to production deployment

- **Guard against LLM threats**: For GenAI, implement specific defenses against prompt injection and other adversarial attacks as part of the system design

Operational monitoring and recourse

Once deployed, best practices focus on continuous, real-world vigilance. This falls under the domain of AIOps teams. Monitoring must move beyond simple business metrics to track comprehensive RAI metrics such as SPD and other fairness measures. High-risk systems require robust HITL protocols, such as using a human as a final safeguard to override biased or unsafe AI decisions. A final requirement is a clear, functional mechanism for user recourse, allowing affected individuals to appeal decisions or report harm.

Key takeaways: monitoring and recourse

Here are the key takeaways:

- **Continuous monitoring**: Shift day-to-day oversight responsibility to AIOps teams for continuous tracking of technical, ethical, and fairness metrics
- **Strategic HITL**: Use HITL systems strategically, prioritizing high-risk areas (such as medical diagnosis) where the cost of human labor is justified by the reduction in harm
- **Recourse mechanism**: Establish a clear, accessible, and timely process for users to report harm, seek explanations, and request recourse or appeal automated decisions

Cultural integration

The most sustainable best practice is integrating RAI into the organizational DNA. This requires executive leadership to constantly reinforce the "tone at the top," demonstrating that ethical conduct is valued alongside profit. Cross-functional training is mandatory for engineers learning fairness metrics to legal teams understanding model limitations. Ultimately, success is defined by a culture that prioritizes proactive responsibility over reactive compliance, making every employee an active stakeholder in the RAI framework.

Key takeaways: cultural integration

- **Leadership buy-in**: Guarantees the executive team actively champions RAI, linking ethical performance to career advancement and resource allocation
- **Universal training**: Implement mandatory, role-specific training across all departments (legal, development, and product) to foster a shared understanding of risk and responsibility

- **Accountability**: Define clear, non-overlapping lines of accountability so that every stakeholder (from developers to product owners) understands their specific ethical duties in the AI life cycle

By implementing these actionable best practices, organizations can move beyond aspirational goals and build truly RAI systems that are ethical, transparent, and accountable in practice. We need to remember that this is an ongoing process that requires continuous learning, adaptation, and a strong commitment from all levels of the organization.

Real-world applications of RAI

RAI is being applied across various industry verticals, showcasing its potential to drive ethical and effective outcomes. In healthcare, AI systems are used for disease diagnosis and treatment recommendations, taking into utmost consideration protecting patient privacy and fairness through robust ethical governance structures.

Financial services leverage AI for fraud detection and anti-money laundering, integrating HITL approaches to enhance decision-making and maintain accountability.

In retail, AI models predict customer churn and personalize marketing strategies while adhering to transparency and fairness principles. Surveillance systems utilize AI for security and monitoring, with continuous monitoring and improvement to prevent biases and uphold ethical standards.

In the context of conflict minerals, smartphone manufacturing companies have implemented stringent ethical sourcing practices to warrant that the minerals used in their products do not fund armed conflict, child labor, or human rights abuses. This approach can be extended to AI procurement, where ethical sourcing safeguards that AI systems are developed and deployed responsibly, considering the environmental and social impact of the materials and processes involved.

In education, AI is transforming learning experiences by personalizing educational content, automating administrative tasks, and providing support for students with diverse needs. AI-driven tools such as intelligent tutoring systems and adaptive learning platforms enhance the educational process while maintaining fairness, inclusivity, and accessibility to all.

In policing, AI is used for crime analysis, facial recognition, and predictive policing, helping law enforcement agencies to allocate resources more effectively and improve public safety. However, it is crucial to validate that these AI applications are transparent and unbiased and respect individuals' privacy rights.

In manufacturing, AI is used for predictive maintenance, quality control, and supply chain optimization. RAI practices uphold that these applications are transparent, fair, and accountable, reducing operational risks and improving efficiency. By integrating ethical guidelines, manufacturers can enhance productivity while maintaining high ethical standards.

Real-world examples of ethical governance structure

To illustrate the diverse ways organizations are approaching ethical AI governance, the following examples are provided for consideration.

Example 1: Meta — a specific company's approach to LLM safety and ethical governance

Meta addresses AI ethics through a multifaceted system, not a single board, integrating the following:

- **Internal teams**: Dedicated RAI teams collaborate cross-functionally to address fairness, transparency, accountability, and safety throughout the AI life cycle, using a risk-based approach
- **External oversight**: The oversight board reviews content moderation decisions involving AI, and Meta engages with external experts and the public for diverse perspectives
- **Key principles**: Meta emphasizes transparency (e.g., open sourcing), accountability, fairness, privacy safeguards, and a layered approach to safety (e.g., Llama Guard) in its AI development and deployment

This structure combines internal responsibility, external input, and core ethical principles to guide Meta's AI practices.

A key aspect of Meta's ethical AI governance is its approach to safety in LLM development, which is implemented through a layered strategy:

- **Model-level safety**: Safety is addressed during data preparation and model training
- **System-level safety**: Safeguards are implemented at the input and output stages, utilizing tools such as Llama Guard 4 for content filtering
- **Transparency and reporting**: Efforts are made to provide transparency and establish feedback mechanisms for ongoing safety improvements

This multi-layered approach is a core component of their broader ethical governance framework, designed to mitigate risks throughout the LLM life cycle. Check out Meta AI's *Responsible Use Guide* (`https://ai.meta.com/static-resource/responsible-use-guide/`) and public blog posts on their LLM development (e.g., Llama 3.2 safety evaluations).

Example 2: A major enterprise software provider — building a culture of AI ethics for organizations

Beyond the critical focus on safety, particularly in LLMs, establishing a strong culture of AI ethics encompasses a wider range of ethical principles. To build a sustainable culture of AI ethics, a company must go beyond policy to embed ethical considerations into daily engineering practices.

This provider exemplifies this by treating RAI as a core product feature, not just a compliance obligation. They established the **Aether Committee** (an acronym for **AI and Ethics in Engineering and Research**) to advise leadership and drive innovation. Crucially, they developed and enforced the RAI standard, translating their six core RAI principles (fairness, reliability and safety, privacy and security, inclusiveness, transparency, and accountability) into actionable requirements and tooling for every AI project across the company. This clearly shows that responsibility is owned by the teams building the technology.

Establishing a strong culture of AI ethics involves several key elements, according to MIT Sloan:

- **Leadership commitment**: Strong support and visible commitment from senior leadership are essential for prioritizing ethical considerations across all AI initiatives

- **Clear ethical guidelines**: Developing and communicating clear principles and guidelines for AI development and deployment, addressing issues such as fairness, privacy, and accountability, in addition to safety

- **Education and training**: Providing comprehensive training to employees on AI ethics and RAI practices, fostering a shared understanding of ethical responsibilities

- **Cross-functional collaboration**: Fostering collaboration between technical teams, ethicists, legal experts, and other stakeholders to maximize the consideration of diverse perspectives in ethical decision-making

- **Transparency and accountability**: Establishing mechanisms for transparency and accountability in AI decision-making processes, enabling scrutiny and redress

- **Continuous monitoring and evaluation**: Regularly monitoring and evaluating the ethical implications of AI systems and making adjustments as needed, adapting to evolving ethical standards and societal expectations

Example 3: Unilever — a structured and actionable process for ethical governance

Unilever's journey in implementing AI ethics includes a structured approach to ethical governance:

- **Establishing an AI ethics board**: A cross-functional team responsible for setting ethical guidelines and reviewing AI projects, providing oversight and guidance

- **Developing an AI ethics framework**: A structured framework for assessing the ethical risks and impacts of AI applications, facilitating a systematic evaluation of ethical considerations

- **Implementing ethical risk assessments**: Conducting thorough risk assessments for each AI project, considering factors such as fairness, transparency, and accountability, in addition to safety

- **Training and awareness programs**: Educating employees on AI ethics and RAI practices, building ethical awareness and competence

- **Monitoring and reporting**: Continuously monitoring the performance and impact of AI systems and reporting on ethical considerations, promoting accountability and continuous improvement

You can read more about Unilever's AI assurance process in the article published in the MIT Sloan Management Review, *AI Ethics at Unilever: From Policy to Process* (https://sloanreview.mit.edu/article/ai-ethics-at-unilever-from-policy-to-process/).

Example 4: Deepfake voice impersonation and financial fraud — governance failure in proactive risk assessment

This case study demonstrates the high cost of a governance structure failing to mandate and enforce a risk assessment focused on the misuse of AI-generated synthetic media (deepfakes):

- **Context of the failure**: A deepfake audio of a senior executive's voice was used to authorize a fraudulent wire transfer from a financial institution, bypassing standard verbal security checks. The synthetic media was generated using readily available AI tools and publicly sourced audio of the executive.

- **The governance failure**: The failure resulted in a violation of financial regulations (security/fraud and KYC/AML failure in digital identity) and not having robust internal security policies in place. This exposure represented a significant liability due to the failure to assess and mitigate risks associated with synthetic media (supply chain risks in using third-party AI).

The following are the lessons learned for RAI governance (with actionable fixes):

- **Failure to assess new threats**: The governance structure did not require an audit of identity verification methods against modern synthetic media threats, violating the principle of proactive risk assessment. (Actionable fix: Mandatory Synthetic Media Risk Assessment (SMRA) for identity verification systems)

- **Lack of new guardrails**: The governance body failed to implement a policy to update security protocols to account for advancements in easily accessible deepfake technology. (Actionable fix: Mandate multi-modal authentication and implement real-time acoustic analysis for voice deepfake detection)

- **Insufficient supply chain oversight**: The failure to control the inputs (publicly available audio) and the potential outputs (fabricated instructions) demonstrates a lapse in digital supply chain risk management. (Actionable fix: Establish a clear crisis communications protocol for deepfake incidents)

The financial institution ultimately bore the loss, highlighting that ethical failures and governance gaps related to new AI threats lead to severe financial and reputational costs.

These examples demonstrate that building ethical AI systems requires a multifaceted approach. While safety is paramount, especially in the context of powerful technologies such as LLMs, a comprehensive ethical governance framework also encompasses broader principles, organizational culture, and structured processes.

Building upon its foundational commitment to RAI across sectors, InnovAIte LLC has made significant strides in implementing an ethical governance structure. Initially focused on its healthcare AI system, the company recognized the need for scalable governance practices and established an AI ethics committee, conducted impact assessments, performed regular bias audits, and maintained comprehensive documentation. They used data version control for model development and recorded data lineage and transformations to promote accountability and reproducibility across all AI projects. Policymakers provided guidelines for the ethical use of AI in healthcare, affirming InnovAIte LLC's system complied with relevant regulations. Last-mile vendors packaged and deployed the AI system, implementing safety mechanisms and conducting regular audits. End users provided feedback, further refining the system's reliability and ethical soundness.

By integrating HITL approaches and using metrics for RAI, InnovAIte LLC not only cemented the trustworthiness of its healthcare AI but also developed a governance framework applicable to its expanding AI initiatives. This proactive approach fostered trust, mitigated risks, and supported innovation as InnovAIte LLC grew into a leading AI-driven enterprise.

Summary

In this chapter, we explored the crucial elements of implementing RAI frameworks. We discussed the importance of establishing robust ethical governance structures, incorporating HITL approaches for oversight, and utilizing comprehensive metrics to evaluate AI models. By prioritizing these elements and integrating RAI best practices throughout the AI development life cycle, businesses can be sure that their AI systems are not only optimized for performance but also aligned with ethical standards and societal values. While the hypothetical example of InnovAIte LLC helped illustrate the setup of an ethical governance structure, real-world examples offer crucial, practical lessons: these include successful process implementations like Meta's approach to LLM safety and Unilever's structured ethics process, alongside the need for robust organizational change demonstrated by a major enterprise software provider's focus on culture, and the critical warnings gleaned from governance failure related to deepfake voice impersonation and financial fraud.

Building upon the foundational principles and governance structures discussed in this chapter, the next chapter delves into the specific ethical considerations and practices essential for the development of trustworthy LLMs. With the increasing capabilities and potential impact of LLMs, a focused examination of their unique ethical challenges and the strategies for building trust is critical.

Join us in the next chapter to explore key aspects, such as bias mitigation, transparency, explainability, and robust safety mechanisms for AI systems.

14

Building Trustworthy LLMs and Generative AI

Large language models (LLMs) have revolutionized the field of AI and are a cornerstone of the rapidly advancing field of **generative AI (GenAI)**. These models demonstrate remarkable capabilities in generating text, images, and videos, as well as in translation and code completion. These models, such as GPT-5 and now the newer models constantly emerging in the market, have vast potential across a wide array of applications. However, this immense potential comes with significant challenges that necessitate responsible deployment and auditing. LLMs are known to produce outputs that are factually incorrect or illogical, often referred to as **hallucinations**. Furthermore, due to their training on extensive datasets reflecting societal biases, they can generate biased and unfair content. This chapter explores ethical considerations and best practices for creating trustworthy AI applications in an enterprise environment.

GenAI, a rapidly advancing field, goes beyond analyzing existing data to create new content. GenAI technologies, including LLMs and **generative adversarial networks (GANs)**, learn patterns from vast datasets to create new, realistic data. LLMs, specifically designed for **natural language processing (NLP)**, excel at various language tasks, significantly advancing machine understanding and generation. While **retrieval-augmented generation (RAG)** offers a mechanism to improve the factual accuracy and coherence of LLM outputs by integrating information retrieval, the fundamental ethical considerations remain paramount.

The responsible use and evaluation of LLMs and GenAI are crucial, requiring a careful balance between innovation and ethical responsibility. This chapter delves into the key ethical considerations for developing the trustworthiness of these powerful models, including transparency, explainability, bias mitigation, privacy, and data security. Our goal is to explore best practices that promote the responsible and ethical application of LLMs and GenAI technologies.

We will cover the following key topics in this chapter:

- Transparency and explainability – a key to trustworthy LLMs
- Addressing biases and maintaining fairness in LLM outputs
- Privacy and data security in LLMs
- Guidelines for developing responsible LLMs

Transparency and explainability – a key to trustworthy LLMs

LLMs present unique challenges, including the potential for generating inaccurate or biased outputs. Transparency and **Explainability** (**XAI**) are therefore indispensable for building trust in AI applications. While traditional machine learning models are often complex, the scale of LLMs (with billions of parameters) presents an exponentially greater "black box" challenge.

For high-stakes enterprise applications, understanding *how* and *why* an AI system arrives at a specific conclusion, especially if that conclusion is inaccurate, biased, or harmful, is a mandatory requirement for accountability and compliance. Crucially, for LLMs, XAI focuses primarily on attributing the output to the input (prompt and context) and not on interpreting the internal weights of the foundational model, which is infeasible and out of scope for application governance.

LLM explainability – the shift to local attribution

Traditional XAI techniques (such as those providing feature importance or partial dependence plots) were designed for simpler models. For LLMs, these methods are adapted to provide local, token-level attribution, which is a necessary shift that aligns with the needs of application governance:

- **Token-level explanation**: XAI for LLMs focuses on explaining why a specific token or span of input text contributed to the final generated output, rather than attempting to explain the entire model's behavior. This ability to pinpoint influential inputs is critical for debugging biased outputs.

- **CoT and attention weights**: The most critical output of these XAI methods in the LLM context is the **Chain-of-Thought (CoT)** reasoning or attention weights. These mechanisms indicate the internal processing path of the model and are the primary evidence used in AI auditing and governance to identify the exact prompt tokens that led to a biased or incorrect response.

Let's now understand why XAI is essential for LLM application and governance:

1. **Compliance and auditability**: Regulatory frameworks, such as the EU AI Act, impose stringent requirements for transparency on high-risk AI systems. XAI provides the necessary audit trails to prove that an LLM decision was not based on protected or biased attributes.

2. **Bias investigation and remediation**: XAI tools are deployed during the evaluation and fine-tuning phases (pre-deployment). If an audit reveals an LLM is exhibiting unfair behavior (e.g., denying credit based on location proxies), XAI helps developers pinpoint the specific tokens or patterns in the input that are driving the bias, allowing for targeted fine-tuning to correct the model.

3. **Trust and user adoption**: Providing a justification alongside an LLM's output significantly increases user trust. If an LLM summarizes a complex legal document, knowing which source paragraphs were weighted most heavily in the summary is essential for human validation.

By focusing on local attribution and CoT outputs during LLM evaluation, auditing, and real-time inference, enterprises can enhance trust and transparency in LLM applications, fulfilling the crucial requirement of accountability within their governance frameworks.

Rigorous evaluation for trustworthy AI applications

To achieve true business value optimization, the evaluation of AI applications must extend beyond traditional ML metrics. While models used for classification and regression can be adequately assessed using scores like F1-score or AUC, these metrics fail completely when measuring the safety, reliability, and trustworthiness of GenAI outputs.

For responsible and optimized deployment of LLM and GenAI systems, a rigorous human-centric evaluation framework is mandatory, focusing on three core criteria:

1. **Groundedness (or faithfulness)**: Groundedness is a measure of factual accuracy, and it measures whether the response is based completely on the context. It is a critical metric for mitigating the risk of LLM hallucinations. This indicates that all factual claims made by the LLM can be directly attributed and verified against the provided source material (e.g., documents retrieved via RAG) or a known corpus of truth.

A high groundedness score, therefore, validates that the output is truthful, preventing the application from generating misleading information that could lead to severe business or legal consequences. Grounded outputs are transparent outputs.

2. **Utility (or helpfulness/relevance)**: Utility measures the extent to which the AI application fulfills the user's need and provides tangible value. Utility assesses whether the generated output is relevant, comprehensive, and ultimately useful to the human user in the specific business context (e.g., does the summary capture the main point? Does the generated code solve the problem?

    An AI application with high utility drives positive business value, reduces human effort, and maximizes impact.

3. **Safety and toxicity**: Safety metrics are the guardrails, measuring compliance with ethical and policy boundaries. This assesses whether the output contains harmful, biased, toxic, or non-compliant content. This evaluation is critical for preventing harm and maintaining trust with the public.

    A zero-tolerance policy for unsafe outputs must be enforced, often requiring **human-in-the-loop (HITL)** review for high-risk domains and automated filtering for all others.

These evaluation techniques are vital for establishing a continuous auditing loop, allowing organizations to quantify and manage the unique risks associated with LLM deployment and making certain that the pursuit of GenAI innovation is always anchored in responsibility and measurable positive impact.

Addressing biases and maintaining fairness in AI application outputs

Bias and fairness are among the most difficult ethical challenges in Responsible AI application development. Since AI systems learn patterns from the data they are trained on, they inevitably reflect and often amplify existing societal biases. This can lead to unfair or discriminatory outcomes in high-stakes decisions, such as loan applications, hiring, or medical diagnosis. To build trustworthy AI applications, organizations must proactively address bias throughout the entire lifecycle. Below, we discuss some bias mitigation techniques:

*   **Data-centric methods**: Verifying the training datasets for LLMs (and other foundational models) are diverse, representative, and audited for harmful proxies of protected attributes.

*   **Model-centric methods**: Using debiasing algorithms like adversarial learning or re-weighting techniques during the LLM training and fine-tuning process.

- **Application-centric methods**: Implementing guardrails and human review of final AI application outputs to check for discriminatory language or decisions before they reach the user.

Fairness is not a single metric, but a multidimensional concept requiring continuous auditing and intervention throughout the lifespan of the AI application. Organizations must define clear fairness metrics (e.g., demographic parity, equal opportunity, explained below) tailored to the specific context of their AI system.

The importance of fairness in LLMs

Fairness in LLMs is not merely an ethical ideal; it is a crucial requirement for building trustworthy and responsible AI systems. Biased LLM outputs can result in the following:

- **Discrimination**: LLMs may generate content that discriminates against individuals or groups based on sensitive attributes such as race, gender, religion, sexual orientation, or disability. This can perpetuate harmful stereotypes and limit opportunities for marginalized communities.

- **Erosion of trust**: When LLMs produce biased or unfair outputs, users lose trust in the technology, hindering its adoption and acceptance.

- **Legal and ethical consequences**: Biased AI systems can lead to legal challenges and reputational damage for organizations that deploy them.

The potential for discrimination, erosion of trust, and legal consequences highlights the critical importance of actively promoting fairness in all LLM applications.

Fairness metrics for LLMs

Fairness metrics provide quantifiable measures to assess and compare the performance of LLMs across different groups. These metrics are different from traditional LLM quality metrics like BLEU or ROUGE, which measure linguistic similarity to a reference text. Fairness metrics are task-agnostic measures of impact and harm. It's important to note that no single metric is universally applicable, and the choice of metric depends on the specific use case and the type of bias being addressed:

- **Demographic parity**: This metric checks whether the LLM's outputs are statistically independent of sensitive attributes. In simpler terms, it aims to support that different groups receive positive outcomes at similar rates. For example, in a loan application LLM, demographic parity would mean that loan approval rates are roughly the same across racial groups. However, demographic parity can sometimes lead to unfairness if the groups have different underlying distributions of qualifications.

- **Equalized odds**: This metric focuses on balancing error rates (false positives and false negatives) across different groups. It validates that the LLM performs equally well for all groups in terms of both accuracy and the types of errors it makes. For instance, in a hiring LLM, equalized odds would mean that the LLM has similar rates of false positives (incorrectly predicting someone will succeed) and false negatives (incorrectly predicting someone will fail) for male and female candidates.

- **Calibration and consistency**: Calibration assesses whether the LLM's predicted probabilities reflect the true likelihood of an event. A well-calibrated LLM will be correct 80% of the time when it states its confidence is 80%. However, modern LLMs are often miscalibrated and prone to overconfidence, a phenomenon where they claim high certainty even when incorrect. Also, studies indicate that the probabilistic predictions of LLMs are inconsistent, especially when the model is explicitly prompted to generate a numerical probability. This explicit probability is often unreliable due to the model's limitations in numerical reasoning. To address this, trustworthy LLM systems should utilize more robust methods for uncertainty estimation:

  - **Implicit probability**: Wherever possible, developers should use the model's internal implicit probability for fixed choice tasks, as this is typically more reliable.

  - **Consistency-based calibration**: For general or open-ended generation, confidence can be derived from consistency by generating the response multiple times and measuring the degree of agreement across the samples. When there is higher consistency, it correlates with higher reliability.

  - **Temperature scaling**: This post-processing technique can be applied to the model's output scores to mathematically adjust for overconfidence and improve overall calibration.

  - **Hallucination rate**: A key task-agnostic metric for LLMs, hallucination rate measures the frequency of generated content that is factually incorrect, nonsensical, or unfaithful to its source context (specifically in RAG). This is a critical measure of trustworthiness and is often evaluated using HITL or by comparing the LLM output against trusted knowledge sources.

The discussion of bias must extend beyond single attributes (e.g., gender or race) to address intersectional bias. Intersectional bias occurs when an LLM portrays unique discrimination toward individuals characterized by the combination of multiple attributes (e.g., black women and older women, and men).

These biases are often non-additive, meaning the harm is not just the sum of the individual biases but a distinct pattern of disadvantage. For example, in studies of LLM-based resume scoring, models awarded lower assessment scores to black male candidates compared to white male candidates with similar qualifications, even while other marginalized groups received higher scores. This demonstrates how the intersection of race and gender creates a specific discriminatory outcome not captured by analyzing race or gender in isolation. In addition, models may exhibit uncertainty or low confidence when reasoning about doubly-disadvantaged identities, leading to a harm of omission or unreliability.

By using these metrics, developers can quantify and evaluate the performance of LLMs across different groups, which is essential for identifying and addressing biases. For the fair evaluation of LLM outputs, a rigorous approach to testing is essential. To accurately measure and analyze the various model bias metrics (such as disparate impact or equal opportunity), it is of utmost importance to have a diverse golden dataset (such as a test set). This dataset must not only be large but also be explicitly designed to represent all relevant demographic and intersectional groups (including combinations of race, gender, age, disability, etc.) that the model will interact with. The golden dataset must include ground truth labels or expected responses for a wide array of prompts, allowing developers to generate and compare the model's outputs against an unbiased standard. This step confirms that fairness is evaluated comprehensively across all subgroups, and not just for the majority population.

These metrics are just one part of a broader, multi-faceted approach to mitigating bias in LLMs, which we will now explore.

Strategies to mitigate bias in LLMs

Mitigating bias in LLMs requires a multi-faceted approach that addresses potential sources of bias at various stages of the development lifecycle. Since most organizations utilize pre-trained foundational LLMs, the focus shifts from complex and expensive pre-training bias mitigation to post-training techniques that address bias in application and inference:

- **Regular bias audits**: Conducting frequent and systematic bias audits is crucial for identifying and quantifying biases in LLMs. These audits should involve evaluating the model's performance on diverse datasets and using a variety of fairness metrics. Bias audits should be an ongoing process, as biases can emerge or evolve over time.

- **Prompt engineering for neutrality (inferencing mitigation)**: The most practical, application-level mitigation strategy is to craft detailed system prompts that instruct the LLM to provide balanced, neutral, and non-stereotypical responses. For example, instructing the model to "Avoid all gender-specific or race-specific terminology unless explicitly requested" or "Validate that outputs are equally respectful regardless of the input's presumed demographic." This technique is highly effective for addressing inferencing bias directly at the point of use.

- **Fine-tuning for alignment and fairness (leveraging LLMs to mitigate bias)**: Instead of large-scale pre-training data diversification, organizations focus on fine-tuning the LLM using a small, high-quality, explicitly fair dataset. This process, often part of **Reinforcement Learning from Human Feedback (RLHF)**, teaches the LLM to prioritize fair and helpful responses over biased or toxic ones, effectively aligning the model with the organization's ethical standards.

- **Algorithmic adjustments**: Several algorithmic techniques can be used to mitigate bias during or after LLM training:

  - **Adversarial debiasing**: Training the LLM to minimize its ability to predict sensitive attributes. In reality, what this method does is use a second, adversarial network to reduce bias during training. The primary LLM is trained to perform its task correctly while simultaneously fooling the adversary, whose only job is to predict a sensitive attribute (such as race or gender) from the LLM's internal state. This forces the LLM to learn predictions that are independent of the sensitive attribute, thereby reducing reliance on it. This technique is highly resource-intensive and primarily used by foundational model developers; application developers should focus on fine-tuning and prompting.

  - **Fine-tuning for fairness**: Fine-tuning the LLM on a dataset specifically designed to promote fairness.

Therefore, by integrating these strategies, from prompt engineering to specialized fine-tuning and auditing, enterprises can proactively address potential biases in their AI applications and governance.

Practical examples of fairness in LLM applications

The following examples illustrate the importance of fairness in various LLM applications:

- **Content moderation**: Fairness metrics are crucial to verify that LLMs used for content moderation do not disproportionately flag or remove content from specific demographic groups. For example, an LLM should not be more likely to flag comments written in **African American Vernacular English (AAVE)** as offensive compared to standard English. Bias audits should be conducted to identify and address such disparities.

- **Customer service automation**: In customer service LLMs, fairness is essential to all customers receiving equitable and respectful treatment, regardless of their background. For instance, the LLM should provide the same level of helpfulness and empathy to customers with different accents or dialects. Training data should be diverse and representative of the customer base.

- **Healthcare chatbots**: Fairness is paramount in healthcare LLMs, as biased outputs can have serious consequences for patient well-being. LLMs providing medical information should be carefully evaluated to assess whether they perpetuate racial or gender disparities in diagnosis or treatment recommendations. Datasets used to train these LLMs must be comprehensive and unbiased, reflecting the diversity of patient populations.

These examples demonstrate that fairness is a domain-specific and continuous challenge that requires careful consideration of the context and potential societal impact. Next, we will explore the compounding nature of bias.

Addressing intersectional bias

It is crucial to recognize that biases can intersect and compound. For example, an LLM might exhibit bias against women of color, where the bias is greater than the sum of the individual biases against women and people of color. Intersectional bias is a particularly complex challenge that arises when multiple forms of bias intersect and compound, disproportionately affecting individuals at the intersection of various social identities.

Addressing intersectional bias requires careful consideration of multiple sensitive attributes and the development of fairness metrics and mitigation strategies that account for these complex interactions. This is an area of ongoing research and development.

As we have addressed the complexities of bias, we will now turn our attention to another critical ethical consideration: protecting user privacy and data security.

Privacy and data security in LLMs

As highlighted earlier, LLMs present unique privacy challenges, including the risk of unintentionally leaking sensitive information from their training data. This section addresses these concerns, focusing on protecting user data and preventing the generation of private information in LLM outputs.

Security risks with customer-facing LLM applications

While LLMs bring immense functional value, their public-facing nature introduces unique and significant security risks that demand explicit mitigation. Key threats include the following:

- **Prompt injection:** This is a major attack vector where users or external data sources embed deceptive instructions (e.g., "Ignore all previous instructions") to bypass the model's safety safeguards. Prompt injection can be direct (overwriting the system prompt, also known as **jailbreaking**) or indirect, where the malicious prompt is hidden in an external source such as a web page or in a document that the LLM is asked to process.

- **Insecure output handling:** This occurs when the responses generated by the LLM are not properly validated or sanitized before being sent to other systems or displayed to a user's browser. This is where the application treats the LLM's raw text output as safe. Attackers replace the LLM output with their own and can control what is shown to the customer. This is often achieved through **tag spoofing**, a type of prompt injection that mimics the application's internal delimiters (e.g., XML tags or special tokens) to hijack the model's output to inject code (such as HTML or JavaScript) that executes a **cross-site scripting (XSS)** attack when the application renders the raw response. Developers must therefore sanitize all LLM output before processing or displaying it. Continuous penetration testing and security health monitoring are paramount to deter such attacks.

- **Sensitive information disclosure:** LLMs trained on vast datasets can inadvertently reproduce confidential data, proprietary information, or **personally identifiable information (PII)** from the corpus of training data, especially when overfitting or given similar prompts.

- **Model denial of service (DoS):** Attackers can force the LLM to run resource-heavy operations by crafting complex or recursive inputs, aiming to degrade service quality for legitimate users or drive up operational costs.

Privacy risks in LLM development and deployment

Privacy risks are inherent in the development and deployment of LLMs, primarily due to the vast amounts of data they are trained on. These risks include the following:

- **Data leakage from training data:** LLMs are trained on massive datasets, which may contain PII or other confidential data. There is a risk that LLMs, even without being explicitly programmed to do so, could memorize and reproduce this sensitive information in their generated outputs. This is known as data leakage or model inversion.

- **Generation of sensitive information**: LLMs can be prompted to generate text that reveals PII or other sensitive details, even if that information wasn't directly present in the training data. This could happen if the LLM learns patterns that allow it to infer sensitive information based on other cues.

- **Use of customer data in model training**: When LLMs are fine-tuned or adapted for specific applications, they may be trained on customer data. This raises significant privacy concerns, as organizations must verify that this data is used ethically and in compliance with privacy regulations.

These risks highlight the critical importance of a proactive and systematic approach to privacy and data security throughout the LLM life cycle, which we will now explore.

Strategies for protecting privacy and data security in LLMs

To counter the privacy risks discussed in the previous section, a range of strategic approaches and technical safeguards are essential for protecting user data and maintaining security throughout the LLM life cycle. These strategies include the following:

- **Data anonymization and pseudonymization**: Before training, datasets should be carefully anonymized or pseudonymized to remove or replace PII. Techniques such as k-anonymity and differential privacy can be used to reduce the risk of re-identification.

- **Privacy-preserving training techniques**: Explore and implement **privacy-preserving machine learning (PPML)** techniques, such as federated learning or secure multi-party computation, which allow models to be trained on decentralized data without directly exposing the data itself.

- **Output filtering and sanitization**: Implement robust filtering mechanisms to prevent LLMs from generating sensitive information. This might involve techniques such as regular expression matching, **named entity recognition (NER)**, and content moderation models.

- **Access controls and data governance**: Implement strict access controls to limit who can access and use LLMs and the data they are trained on. Establish clear data governance policies that outline how data will be collected, used, and protected.

- **Transparency and user consent**: Be transparent with users about how their data is being used to train and fine-tune LLMs. Obtain explicit consent when using personal data.

- **Compliance with privacy regulations**: Uphold compliance with relevant privacy regulations, such as **General Data Protection Regulation (GDPR)**, **California Consumer Privacy Act (CCPA)**, and **Health Insurance Portability and Accountability Act (HIPAA)**. Understand the specific requirements of these regulations as they apply to LLMs.

- **Regular security audits**: Conduct regular security audits to identify and address potential vulnerabilities in LLM systems.

The following examples highlight how privacy and data security are critical in specific, high-stakes domains:

- **Healthcare**: LLMs used to generate medical summaries or patient reports must be carefully designed to prevent the disclosure of sensitive patient information. To protect patient data, techniques such as differential privacy can be used to add noise to the output while preserving its utility.

- **Finance**: LLMs used for fraud detection or risk assessment must be trained and deployed in a way that protects customer financial data. Access controls and data masking techniques are essential to limit access to sensitive information.

- **Legal**: LLMs used to generate legal documents must be carefully vetted to prevent unintentional disclosure of confidential information. Implementing robust output filtering and sanitization mechanisms in the application design is critical to avoid data leakage.

While foundational models are built with general safety measures, the specific application of LLMs requires additional safety measures. In the next section, we will review the guidelines that need to be implemented at the application level to promote responsible deployment.

Guidelines for developing responsible AI applications

Developing responsible AI applications requires careful consideration of the unique challenges posed by these models. LLMs, due to their ability to generate human-like text, can amplify biases, produce misleading information, or inadvertently violate privacy when integrated into real-world applications. To mitigate these risks and encourage ethical deployment, developers must implement specific guidelines at the application level. This also requires active engagement with stakeholders, including users, domain experts, and regulatory bodies, to work towards the comprehensive addressing of ethical considerations. These guidelines aim to help developers navigate the complexities of building AI-powered systems that are fair, transparent, accountable, and respectful of privacy.

Let us explore the key guidelines for responsible AI applications:

- **Content filters**: Content filters are the first line of defense in preventing the generation of harmful, offensive, or inappropriate content. This involves using a combination of techniques to implement robust content filters, such as the following:

- **Keyword filtering**: Blocking specific words or phrases
- **Toxicity detection models**: Identifying and flagging toxic language
- **Bias detection models**: Detecting and mitigating biased language patterns
- **Adaptability**: Filters should be adaptable and continuously updated to address evolving forms of harmful content

- **User disclosures**: Providing clear and transparent disclosures to users is a key part of building trust and accountability. Clearly disclose to users when they are interacting with AI-generated content. This promotes transparency and allows users to make informed decisions about how to use the application. Methods for disclosure include the following:

  - **Explicit labeling**: Clearly stating **AI-generated content** or **Powered by AI**
  - **Watermarking**: Embedding subtle markers in the generated text
  - **Interface design**: Using visual cues to indicate AI interaction

- **Continuous monitoring of outputs**: Even after deployment, continuous monitoring is vital for detecting and addressing potential issues in real time. This can involve the following:

  - **User feedback mechanisms**: Allowing users to report problematic content
  - **Automated anomaly detection**: Identifying unusual patterns in the generated output
  - **Regular audits**: Periodically reviewing outputs for bias, toxicity, or other ethical concerns

- **Contextual awareness**: Designing AI applications to be sensitive to the context of their use is crucial for responsible deployment. This includes the following:

  - Understanding the potential risks and harms associated with the specific use case
  - Tailoring the application's behavior and safeguards to the context

- **Human oversight**: In high-stakes scenarios, human oversight is an indispensable safeguard. This can be achieved through the following:

  - Incorporating human oversight into critical decision-making processes involving AI applications
  - In scenarios where errors or biases can have significant consequences, such as for business-critical solutions
  - Using HITL approaches to provide a balance between automation and human judgment

These guidelines are not just theoretical concepts; they are practical measures that must be implemented at the application level to guide the ethical and responsible deployment of AI systems.

Why do application-level guidelines matter?

The need for these application-level guidelines is particularly acute in finance. So, to find out the answer, we will discuss an example from the financial sector. LLM applications used for tasks such as risk management, fraud detection, and customer service must be carefully designed to do the following:

- Avoid biased decision-making that could discriminate against certain customers
- Protect sensitive financial data
- Provide accurate and reliable information
- Maintain transparency and accountability

Therefore, financial institutions must implement robust content filters, provide clear user disclosures, and continuously monitor the outputs of their AI applications for ethical and responsible use.

By carefully implementing these guidelines, financial institutions can harness the power of LLMs while protecting their customers, complying with regulations, and maintaining public trust. The following case study further illustrates the importance of these guidelines in practice.

Ethical LLM deployment — case study and best practices

This case study demonstrates that a proactive, collaborative, and human-centric approach is essential for the ethical deployment of AI applications in sensitive domains. We have used a hypothetical example to further explore the roles and processes involved in ethical AI deployment.

Deploying AI applications ethically in sensitive domains requires careful planning and execution. A compelling example of this is OpenAI's collaboration with a medical provider to develop an AI symptom checker. In this case, key ethical considerations included the following:

- **Addressing biases**: OpenAI and the medical provider worked diligently to identify and mitigate potential biases in the LLM's output by making sure that it provided equitable and accurate information across diverse patient populations. This involved training the LLM on a comprehensive and representative dataset of medical information, as well as rigorously evaluating its performance for different demographic groups.

- **Safeguarding patient privacy**: Protecting patient privacy was paramount. The system was designed to handle patient data securely and confidentially, adhering to relevant privacy regulations (e.g., HIPAA). This likely involved techniques such as data anonymization, access controls, and secure data storage.

- **Building trust**: By prioritizing ethical considerations and demonstrating a commitment to patient well-being, OpenAI and the medical provider fostered trust in the AI symptom checker among both healthcare professionals and patients.

Building on its experience in **responsible AI** (**RAI**) development, InnovAIte LLC expanded its AI solutions to customer service by deploying an LLM for automation. Demonstrating its commitment to ethical AI practices, InnovAIte LLC established an ethics committee to oversee the project and foster alignment with evolving ethical guidelines. AI developers conducted thorough impact assessments, evaluating the LLM's potential effects on customer interactions. Business leaders allocated resources for RAI initiatives and actively engaged with stakeholders, including customers, customer service representatives, and regulators, to gather diverse perspectives.

Policymakers provided guidelines for the ethical use of AI in customer service, which InnovAIte LLC diligently followed to adhere to regulatory compliance. Last-mile vendors carefully packaged and deployed the AI application, implementing robust safety mechanisms and conducting regular audits to maintain ethical standards. End users provided valuable feedback, contributing to the AI application's ongoing improvement.

By integrating HITL approaches and employing comprehensive metrics for RAI, InnovAIte LLC bolstered the AI application's ethical soundness and trustworthiness. These practices reinforced stakeholder trust, effectively mitigated risks, and fostered an environment of innovation, further solidifying InnovAIte LLC's reputation as a leader in responsible AI deployment.

Summary

This chapter has explored the critical ethical considerations and best practices for developing and deploying trustworthy AI applications. We began by outlining the unique challenges presented by LLMs, including their propensity for hallucinations (generating factually incorrect information), amplifying biases present in training data, and the potential for data leakage. We then explored key strategies for mitigating these risks and fostering responsible LLM development, focusing on transparency and explainability, bias and fairness, and privacy and data security. As noted, the development of trustworthy AI requires a fundamentally new approach to quality assurance, emphasized in rigorous evaluation for trustworthy AI applications. Because traditional ML metrics (such as accuracy, F1-score) cannot evaluate the quality of the new content generated by LLMs, evaluation needs to be human-centric. This shift establishes the necessity of measuring trustworthiness and business utility, specifically through criteria such as groundedness (factual accuracy) and utility (business relevance) for responsible deployment.

The chapter also emphasized the crucial role of implementing specific guidelines at the application level for responsible AI deployment, including content filters, user disclosures, and continuous monitoring of outputs. To illustrate successful ethical AI deployment, we presented a real-world case study, highlighting OpenAI's collaboration with a medical provider to develop an AI symptom checker. This example demonstrated the importance of addressing bias and privacy concerns to build trust in AI applications. We further explored the key roles and processes involved in ethical AI deployment through the hypothetical example of InnovAIte LLC. By adhering to these principles and best practices, developers and organizations can harness the immense potential of LLMs and GenAI while mitigating ethical risks and building trustworthy AI systems.

In the next chapter, we will explore the critical legal and regulatory frameworks for responsible AI, examining how different countries are approaching governance and how organizations can implement effective compliance strategies.

Subscribe for a free eBook

New frameworks, evolving architectures, research drops, production breakdowns—AI_Distilled filters the noise into a weekly briefing for engineers and researchers working hands-on with LLMs and GenAI systems. Subscribe now and receive a free eBook, along with weekly insights that help you stay focused and informed.

Subscribe at `https://packt.link/80z6Y` or scan the QR code below.

15

Regulatory and Legal Frameworks for Responsible AI

The increasing emphasis on **Responsible AI (RAI)** is not simply a passing trend; it reflects a growing necessity for ethical and responsible use of this powerful technology. We are at a critical juncture where aligning AI development and deployment with evolving ethical considerations and legal requirements is paramount. This journey goes beyond merely adopting AI; it requires embedding ethical principles and compliance mechanisms into the very fabric of AI systems. The rapid proliferation of AI technologies necessitates the development of robust governance and regulatory frameworks that promote responsible innovation, mitigate potential risks, and adapt to the dynamic nature of the AI field. Understanding and navigating this evolving regulatory landscape is crucial for organizations seeking to leverage AI's benefits while upholding ethical standards and adhering to legal compliance.

This chapter explores the key legal and regulatory frameworks governing AI and provides actionable strategies for implementing compliance within an organization.

We will cover the following key topics in this chapter:

- Comparing global AI regulatory approaches
- Implementing effective AI compliance strategies
- Addressing regulatory challenges – case studies

To provide a cohesive and actionable guide to RAI governance, this chapter follows a three-part structure designed to take you from the high-level global landscape down to practical organizational execution:

1. **Global regulatory approaches**: We first establish the external landscape by comparing the core philosophical and legal models (e.g., the EU's risk-based approach, the US's sectoral approach) shaping AI governance worldwide. This provides the necessary foundational context.

2. **Organizational compliance (KYAI framework)**: We then pivot to the internal action required by introducing the **Know Your AI** (**KYAI**) system. This section is dedicated to translating abstract global principles into a structured, practical internal framework for risk assessment, classification, and compliance control within an organization.

3. **GenAI risks, accountability, and case studies**: Finally, we address the unique, high-stakes challenges posed by GenAI and provide a clear framework for accountability. This material is then grounded through concrete, real-world case studies that illustrate how successful organizations have managed these regulations and risks in practice.

Comparing global AI regulatory approaches

While the need for RAI is globally recognized, different regions are adopting distinct approaches to regulation.

This section compares the frameworks of several key players:

- **EU – a risk-based and comprehensive approach**: The EU AI Act represents a pioneering effort to establish comprehensive AI regulation. It employs a risk-based approach, categorizing AI systems based on their potential to cause harm.

  Here are its key features:

  - Defines "AI system" broadly, encompassing systems that operate autonomously or semi-autonomously, adapt after deployment, and generate outputs that impact digital or physical environments

  - Prohibits high-risk applications deemed unacceptable (e.g., social scoring or real-time facial recognition in public spaces)

  - Imposes stringent requirements on high-risk systems, including transparency, data governance, and human oversight

  - Addresses **General-Purpose AI** (**GPAI**) models with specific transparency obligations

- Enforcement includes significant fines (up to €35M or 7% of global annual revenue)

Comparative perspective: The EU's approach is notable for its broad scope and emphasis on protecting fundamental rights. It sets a high bar for AI development and deployment.

- **United States – a sectoral and principles-based approach**: The US takes a more sectoral approach, with different agencies regulating AI in specific domains. It also emphasizes ethical principles.

Here are the key features of the US approach:

- The AI Bill of Rights outlines principles for safe and effective systems, algorithmic discrimination protections, data privacy, transparency, and accountability.
- Sector-specific regulations exist in areas such as healthcare (**Food and Drug Administration**, or **FDA**), finance (various agencies), and employment (e.g., New York City's **Automated Employment Decision Tools**, or **AEDT**). State-level laws, such as the **California Consumer Privacy Act** (**CCPA**), address data privacy related to AI.

It's important to note that while the US primarily adopts a sectoral approach to AI regulation, a degree of decentralization exists, with various state and local laws complementing federal guidelines.

Comparative perspective: The US approach is characterized by its flexibility and focus on innovation within specific sectors. However, it can lead to a fragmented regulatory landscape.

- **China – a government-led and control-oriented approach**: China's AI regulation is heavily influenced by government priorities and emphasizes control and social stability.

Here are its key features:

- Regulations focus on areas such as GenAI services, algorithmic recommendations, and deep synthesis technologies
- Emphasis on transparency, non-discrimination, data protection, and content control
- Government plays a significant role in guiding AI development and deployment

Comparative perspective: China's approach prioritizes government oversight and social control, which contrasts with the EU's focus on individual rights and the US's emphasis on innovation.

- **Other notable approaches:**

  - **India:** Focuses on policies such as "AI for all" and ethical frameworks but lacks a strong enforcement mechanism
  - **Australia:** Emphasizes AI ethics principles centered on human well-being, fairness, and transparency
  - **Singapore and Canada:** Promote principles-based governance frameworks to guide RAI development
  - **Japan:** Relies on industry self-regulation and guidelines from the AI Strategy Council to foster ethical AI development by aiming to enhance data handling, security, and transparency among AI operators

It's important to note that while the US primarily adopts a sectoral approach to AI regulation, a degree of decentralization exists, with various state and local laws complementing federal guidelines.

The following table provides a comprehensive comparison of global AI regulatory approaches, outlining key features such as their scope, enforcement, and focus:

Feature	EU	US	China	Other notable examples
Regulatory approach	Risk-based and comprehensive	Sectoral, principles-based, with elements of decentralization (state and local laws)	Government-led, control-oriented, and innovation-focused	Principles-based: Singapore (Model AI Governance Framework) and Canada (AI Principles) Ethics-focused: Australia (AI Ethics Principles) Developing: India (AI for All), Brazil (developing AI framework)

Feature	EU	US	China	Other notable examples
Scope	A broad definition of AI, categorized by risk	Specific sectors (healthcare, finance, law enforcement, etc.), principles for critical sectors	Focus on specific AI applications (GenAI, recommendations)	Varied, often focused on ethical guidelines or specific AI uses
Enforcement	Strong, with significant fines	Varies by sector and state/local level, indicating some decentralization	Strong government oversight and enforcement	Developing or less centralized enforcement mechanisms in some cases
Key focus	Protecting fundamental rights, managing high-risk AI	Promoting innovation while addressing specific risks (bias, privacy)	Social stability, government control, technological advancement	Ethical considerations, guiding principles, adapting to global trends
Notable regulations	EU AI Act	US notable regulations: AI Bill of Rights (principles), CCPA (state privacy law), NY Local Law 144 (local employment law), FDA guidelines (federal sectoral), FTC (consumer protection), NIST AI (risk management framework)	Measures for the Management of Generative AI Services, Algorithmic Recommendation Management. China's regulations are evolving rapidly.	Model AI Governance Framework (Singapore), AI Principles (Canada), AI Ethics Principles (Australia)

Table 15.1: Comparison of global AI regulatory approaches

This comparative analysis demonstrates the varying global priorities for AI regulation, highlighting the importance of a nuanced and comprehensive approach to compliance.

Navigating cross-border AI compliance

For multinational organizations, achieving AI compliance is complicated by conflicting jurisdictional demands, primarily concerning data localization and data transfer. While some regions (e.g., China and India) impose data localization requirements that restrict data processing to within national borders, others (e.g., the EU) rely on strict **Standard Contractual Clauses (SCCs)** or adequacy decisions to permit cross-border data flows. This forces companies to adopt a "highest common denominator" compliance standard, where the most stringent regulatory requirement (e.g., GDPR's privacy rules) must often be applied globally to avoid deploying multiple, segregated AI instances. The key challenge lies in maintaining this harmonized policy while the underlying laws rapidly change.

Next, we will explore the practical strategies organizations can implement to navigate this complex landscape.

Implementing effective AI compliance strategies

Organizations today must proactively address AI compliance to mitigate the risks of penalties, legal challenges, and reputational damage. This requires not only staying informed about evolving AI regulations but also establishing robust AI governance frameworks. A crucial component of such frameworks is the KYAI process, which provides a structured approach to identifying and managing AI systems in accordance with regulatory requirements.

The KYAI process empowers organizations to systematically navigate AI compliance. It involves the following key steps:

1. **Identification**: Determine whether a system qualifies as an "AI system" under applicable regulations. This often involves assessing whether the system achieves the following:

    -   Operates with some level of autonomy (autonomously or semi-autonomously). It has the capacity to adapt its behavior after deployment.

    -   Generates outputs that can significantly impact digital or physical environments.

    Practical guidance: Maintain a comprehensive inventory of all AI systems within the organization, documenting their functionalities and potential impact.

2. **Risk assessment**: Evaluate the potential risks associated with each AI system and determine whether it falls into any "high-risk" categories defined by relevant regulations. Common high-risk areas include the following:

    -   Healthcare

    -   Financial services

- Critical infrastructure
- Law enforcement
- Employment decisions
- Public safety

Practical guidance: Conduct thorough risk assessments, considering potential harm to individuals, society, and the organization itself. Use risk assessment frameworks provided by regulatory bodies where available.

3. **Compliance implementation**: Identify and implement the specific compliance measures necessary for each AI system to adhere to regulatory requirements. These measures may include the following:

   - Implementing safety and security mechanisms
   - Maintaining data quality and governance
   - Providing transparency and explainability
   - Establishing human oversight and intervention protocols
   - Maintaining detailed documentation and audit trails
   - Conducting regular audits and impact assessments

Practical guidance: Develop a detailed compliance plan for each AI system, assigning responsibilities and timelines.

Beyond the KYAI process, organizations can employ additional compliance strategies to strengthen their overall AI compliance posture:

- **Continuous regulatory training and awareness**:

  - Provide ongoing training and education to employees on AI regulations and ethical considerations
  - Foster a culture of responsibility and vigilance regarding AI compliance

Practical guidance: Establish a system for monitoring regulatory changes and disseminating updates to relevant personnel. Note: The team is solely responsible and will evaluate downstream changes and share relevant updates, as not all information is applicable for all verticals or **Business Units (BUs)** within an organization.

- **Independent audits and certifications:**

  - Engage independent third-party auditors to assess AI systems for compliance and ethical soundness

  - Pursue certifications from recognized bodies to demonstrate commitment to RAI practices.

  Practical guidance: Select reputable auditors with expertise in AI governance and relevant industry regulations.

- **Regulatory Technology (RegTech) solutions:**

  - Leverage RegTech tools to automate compliance tasks, monitor regulatory developments, and manage compliance documentation efficiently

  - Reduce the burden of manual compliance efforts and minimize the risk of errors

  Practical guidance: Carefully evaluate RegTech solutions to align with the organization's specific needs and regulatory requirements.

By adopting a proactive approach and implementing these strategies, organizations can effectively navigate the evolving AI regulatory landscape, embed ethical AI practices into their operations, and cultivate trust with stakeholders.

Implementing the KYAI system – registration template

The KYAI framework is only effective if every deployed AI model is formally registered and classified. The following template is to be used as a starting point for your organization's internal model registry and defines the steps for building an AI system inventory:

Field	Purpose	Example
System name	Unique, internal project identifier.	Customer_Sentiment_Analyzer V2.0
System owner	The product owner holds accountability for the system's performance, risk, and compliance.	VP of customer success
Model type	Classification of the technology (e.g., traditional ML, LLM/GenAI, RAG, simple heuristic).	GenAI (LLM)

Field	Purpose	Example
Primary use case	A simple, clear description of the system's function and the decision it supports.	Summarize customer feedback and auto-generate draft help documentation
Data scope	What kind of data does the model ingest? (PII, financial, protected health information, public)	Customer support transcripts (contains PII)
Regulatory scope	Which regulations apply? (GDPR, HIPAA, AI Act, sectoral regulations)	GDPR (data minimization), AI Act (transparency)
Initial risk score (1–5)	A quick, initial self-assessment of the system's potential to cause harm (1=Low, 5=High).	4 (high, due to PII and customer-facing nature)
Control priority	Which areas need immediate focus? (Fairness, security, explainability)	Security (prompt injection), fairness (bias in summaries)

Table 15.2: The KYAI system registration template

The checklist shared in the next section is the **AI Impact Assessment** (**AIIA**). This is a critical tool used when the KYAI system flags a model as *high risk*.

AI Impact Assessment (AIIA) checklist template

The AIIA provides a granular, mandatory review of high-risk AI systems. This template is designed so that all regulatory and ethical domains are explicitly reviewed and mitigated before deployment:

Risk domain	Assessment question	Status (Y/N/NA)	Required mitigation/ Action owner
Fairness and bias	Is the model's performance equitable across all identified sensitive subgroups (e.g., race, gender, age) based on testing metrics?		
Transparency	Is there a clear, non-technical explanation of the model's core function and its impact provided to end users (e.g., a model card)?		

Risk domain	Assessment question	Status (Y/N/NA)	Required mitigation/ Action owner
Data governance	Is all training and deployment data legally sourced, accurately labeled, and compliant with all privacy regulations (e.g., GDPR and CCPA)?		
Robustness and security	Has the system been tested for resilience against adversarial attacks, including prompt injection and data poisoning?		
Accountability	Are clear human oversight and intervention mechanisms defined for all decisions where the system operates as "high risk"?		
Testing and validation	Have independent third parties (or a distinct internal validation team) verified the system's compliance and risk mitigation controls?		
Approved for deployment	Has the system been formally approved for deployment by the internal AI governance board or a designated executive owner?		

Table 15.3: AIIA checklist

Your organization's AI governance process can be formalized using these templates as a starting point. Use the KYAI registration template for your model registry and initial risk assessment. Once KYAI identifies a system as high risk, deploy the AIIA checklist template to conduct the required detailed risk analysis and structured review process. These tools work in tandem, providing a necessary control loop for RAI deployment.

As we have explored practical compliance strategies, we will now delve into the broader challenges of navigating the complexities of AI regulation.

Navigating the complexities of AI regulation

The AI regulatory landscape is rapidly evolving, presenting organizations with a complex web of challenges. The journey toward comprehensive AI governance is fraught with systemic difficulties inherent to regulating rapidly evolving, cross-sectoral technology. Understanding these challenges is crucial for organizations building resilient compliance programs:

- **The pace of innovation versus the pace of regulation**: Regulatory frameworks are slow by nature, often taking years to draft, debate, and enact. In contrast, new AI models, capabilities, and risks (such as new jailbreaks or model attacks) can emerge in months or even weeks. This fundamental mismatch means laws risk becoming obsolete before they are even enforced, creating a continuous game of regulatory catch-up.

- **The challenge of technology neutrality**: Regulators strive for technology-neutral laws that govern the *impact* of an AI system rather than the *specific technology* used. However, the unique properties of GenAI (its opacity, its scale, and its tendency to "hallucinate") constantly challenge this neutrality, requiring specific, prescriptive rules (such as those targeting foundation models) that can quickly become outdated.

- **Regulatory fragmentation and overlap**: Unlike other regulated industries, AI systems are subject to overlapping rules from multiple jurisdictions (e.g., GDPR, CCPA, sector-specific laws such as HIPAA for the US healthcare industry). For multinational organizations, complying with this diverse patchwork of often conflicting global, national, and state-level requirements presents an enormous hurdle in achieving a harmonized corporate standard.

- **The unprecedented scale of risk**: AI systems introduce risk at a scale that traditional software does not. A single flawed LLM deployed globally can instantly affect millions of users, leading to brand damage, market volatility, and massive regulatory fines. This forces organizations to move from reactive compliance (checking boxes) to a proactive, risk-first culture where the potential for catastrophic failure must be modeled and mitigated before deployment.

The ongoing evolution of AI regulation presents a continuous challenge for enterprises. By adopting a strategic and adaptable approach to governance, organizations can not only mitigate risks but also build a foundation of trust that fosters long-term success.

Liability, accountability, and risk management in the age of GenAI

As AI systems become more autonomous and capable of generating novel content, the question of responsibility is no longer theoretical. The development of powerful LLMs and multimodal GenAI models necessitates a clear understanding of who is responsible when these systems cause harm. The legal and ethical landscape for AI is rapidly evolving to address the crucial concepts of liability, accountability, and risk management.

What's at stake: defining the core concepts

Let's delve into the foundational ideas shaping the legal and ethical aspects of AI:

- **Liability**: In the context of AI, liability is the legal responsibility for harm or damage caused by an AI system. This can range from a chatbot providing incorrect medical advice to a GenAI model producing content that infringes copyright. Unlike traditional software, the unpredictable and emergent nature of GenAI makes assigning liability particularly challenging.

- **Accountability**: The obligation to explain and justify the actions and decisions of an AI system. With complex "black-box" models, this means an organization must establish clear lines of responsibility for the AI's design, development, and deployment, by always making sure there is a human or a team that can answer the system's behavior.

- **Risk management**: This is the proactive process of identifying, assessing, and mitigating potential harms before they occur. For modern GenAI, this involves addressing new risks such as the creation of convincing deepfakes, the spread of hate speech at scale, or the unintentional generation of malicious or biased content.

New risks from advanced GenAI

The proliferation of advanced GenAI, including multimodal models capable of generating images, video, and code, introduces a new category of risks that go beyond traditional AI concerns. These risks require a more nuanced approach to security and governance.

The adoption of GenAI in businesses has grown exponentially, especially in the last two years, transforming industries and accelerating innovation. On average, organizations are using about 66 GenAI applications, with 10% of these classified as high risk, significantly increasing the potential attack surface (Hendren, 2025).

Enterprise risks

These are threats that impact an organization's operations, data, and reputation. The unsanctioned use of GenAI by employees, a phenomenon known as "Shadow AI," is a primary concern. When employees use unapproved third-party models, it can lead to unintentional data leakage and intellectual property exposure (Safe Security, 2025).

A significant risk is the unauthorized use of GenAI tools, which can expose confidential corporate data to third-party services and models (Oswal, 2025). This can lead to security vulnerabilities and compliance issues.

GenAI capability risks

These risks stem from the inherent behaviors and limitations of the models themselves, which can compromise the integrity and reliability of their outputs:

- **Hallucinations and misinformation**: The newest, more sophisticated models still generate "hallucinations," factually incorrect or illogical outputs that are highly convincing and difficult to detect. This was demonstrated in a real-world case where Air Canada faced a lawsuit due to its chatbot providing incorrect information.

- **Prompt injection**: This is a form of adversarial attack where a user's input manipulates the model into bypassing its security controls or performing unintended actions.

Adversarial AI risks

These are risks associated with malicious actors using GenAI to execute more sophisticated and large-scale attacks:

- **Deepfakes and social engineering**: Advanced generative models can create hyper-realistic deepfakes and personalized social engineering attacks, such as highly convincing phishing emails, that are difficult to distinguish from authentic content (UK Government, 2025)

- **Insecure AI-generated code**: Models that write code can introduce vulnerabilities or security flaws, making the resulting software a new attack vector (PwC, 2024)

Regulatory and governance risks

There are broader, systemic risks that affect the wider economy and society, often resulting from the lack of established legal frameworks:

- **Erosion of trust**: The widespread availability of synthetic media, including deepfakes and hyper-realistic bots, can erode public trust in information (Center for AI Safety, 2024).

- **Evolving legal landscape**: The legal and regulatory landscape is rapidly changing. For example, enforcement under the EU AI Act could result in significant fines, up to €35M or 7% of global annual revenue (Article 99: Penalties. EU AI Act, 2025), highlighting the severe consequences of non-compliance.

- **Lack of transparency in risk appetite**: The absence of a publicly clear risk appetite, which is the level of risk an organization is willing to accept with AI development, makes it difficult for regulators and the public to trust companies. Making these risk frameworks more "legible" is essential for building public confidence and driving RAI development (CDT Insights, 2025).

Next, let's explore some best practices for navigating these risks.

Building an accountability framework — best practices for enterprises

To navigate the new risks and the evolving regulatory landscape, organizations must proactively build a robust accountability framework based on several key practices:

- **Conducting AIIAs**: These assessments are a proactive measure to identify, evaluate, and mitigate potential risks and harms of an AI system before and during its deployment. AIIAs help define the system's purpose, identify affected stakeholders, map relevant laws, and assess potential benefits and risks.

- **Establishing AI governance boards**: Enterprises should create dedicated governance boards or committees with diverse expertise (legal, technical, ethical, and business) to oversee AI strategy, risk management, and compliance. These boards ensure that AI initiatives are aligned with the company's values and that clear roles and responsibilities are assigned for accountability.

- **Prioritizing human oversight**: For high-risk AI applications, meaningful human oversight is critical. This means empowering humans with the ability to understand, monitor, and, most importantly, override or correct a system's output. Training for human reviewers is essential to ensure they can interpret AI decisions and maintain a healthy skepticism toward automation bias.

RAI is a journey of continuous adaptation and innovation. By embedding ethical principles and a proactive accountability framework, organizations can move from merely leveraging AI's technical capabilities to upholding a higher standard of ethical responsibility. This not only mitigates risks but also builds the trust necessary to achieve sustainable business excellence in an AI-driven future.

Building on the best practices for establishing an accountability framework, the following section on case studies will explore how organizations have practically applied these principles to address real-world risks and comply with evolving regulatory landscapes.

Addressing regulatory challenges — case studies

Real-world scenarios highlight the importance of proactive AI compliance and the consequences of non-compliance. They also illustrate how addressing regulatory needs can yield positive outcomes. The following table gives a consolidated view of real-world incidents, the specific regulatory issues they raised, and the organizational or technical solutions required to prevent recurrence:

Case study/ incident	Situation/problem (immediate failure)	Regulation/compliance issues (the "why")	Solution/change needed (actionable fixes)
Air Canada chatbot (hallucination)	The customer service chatbot provided a non-existent bereavement policy, leading to customer harm and financial liability.	Accountability failure (model was an agent of the company); LLM03: Lack of grounding (OWASP Top 10).	Technical: Mandate RAG/ grounding; Implement safe/fallback responses. Governance: Establish AI content administrator role; define human-in-the-loop thresholds.
Meta's ad targeting (bias)	The ad delivery system showed job or housing ads unevenly by demographic, reinforcing bias.	Discrimination/fairness (violation of equal opportunity laws); AI Act: High-risk (used for employment services).	Technical: Apply in-processing debiasing (e.g., adversarial debiasing). Governance: Mandatory AIIA on disparate impact; implement fairness audits.
Google Gemini image gen (inaccuracy)	The model generated historically inaccurate images due to the over-correction of existing bias controls.	Transparency/trust erosion (lack of control over content guardrails); KYAI failure (misclassification of cultural/historical harm risk).	Technical: Tweak RLHF policies; implement output validation filters for sensitive categories. Governance: Establish an RAI review board for sensitive content.
OpenAI ChatGPT (data breach)	A temporary software bug caused user chat histories and payment information to be exposed to other users.	Privacy and security (violation of GDPR/ CCPA data security requirements); LLM04: Denial of Service (system became unreliable). (OWASP Top 10).	Technical: Implement robust multi-tenant separation logic; conduct frequent security penetration testing. Governance: Mandatory Data Protection Impact Assessment (DPIA); formal breach response plan.

Case study/ incident	Situation/problem (immediate failure)	Regulation/compliance issues (the "why")	Solution/change needed (actionable fixes)
Microsoft Bing/Copilot (toxic output)	The model was jailbroken to generate abusive, manipulative, or emotionally harmful text during long, unmonitored sessions.	Safety and harms (violation of acceptable use policies); LLM01: Prompt Injection/ Jailbreak (OWASP Top 10).	Technical: Implement stronger guardrails and content filters; enforce turn limits and conversation resets. Governance: Define acceptable use policy; implement continuous monitoring of harmful outputs.
Apple Siri (privacy review)	User voice recordings were stored and manually reviewed by third-party contractors without fully explicit user consent.	Data governance/privacy (violation of GDPR/ CCPA consent and data processing principles).	Technical: Implement differential privacy (data anonymization); introduce client-side processing. Governance: Update privacy policy with explicit review consent; implement mandatory data minimization protocol.
Pragya Prasun & Ors. v. Union of India (Supreme Court of India)	Government digital KYC program requiring blinking/ facial gestures led to automatic rejection for acid attack survivors and visually impaired persons, denying access to essential services (e.g., bank accounts and telecom services).	Fairness/bias (Violation of the Fundamental Right to Life – Article 21) and Violating the Rights of Persons with Disabilities (RPwD) Act, 2016, failing to provide reasonable accommodation.	Technical: Mandate alternative, non-biometric alternatives (e.g., in-person verification) for users who cannot meet the biometric requirement. Governance: Require human-assisted review for accessibility-related rejections and establish inclusivity audits and design for reasonable accommodation during the system architecture phase.

Table 15.4: Summary of AI governance failures and actionable compliance fixes

These case studies collectively illustrate that regulatory and legal challenges are a continuous reality in the AI landscape. Proactive compliance, robust governance, and a commitment to ethical design are essential for mitigating risk and fostering public trust. We have examined the key legal and regulatory frameworks governing AI and explored practical strategies for achieving compliance. We will now conclude this chapter with a summary of the key takeaways and a look ahead at future trends.

Summary

The challenge of RAI governance is that it is a dynamic, continuous process, not a static destination. By establishing a robust, immediate compliance structure such as the KYAI system and standardized post-incident review through an AIIA, organizations can confidently meet current global legal requirements. However, the regulatory landscape will continue to be fundamentally reshaped by rapid technological progress. The next chapter will focus on the strategic imperative of looking forward, examining the emerging technical trends (such as scaling laws, quantum computing, and agentic AI) and the profound societal impacts (including sustainability and equitable AI) that will define the AI-driven enterprise of 2030.

References

- Artificial Intelligence Act (EU) 2024/1689. (2025, August). *Article 99: Penalties.* EU Artificial Intelligence Act. https://artificialintelligenceact.eu/article/99/

- Center for AI Safety (CAIS). (2024). CAIS 2024 impact report. *An Overview of Catastrophic AI Risks.* https://safe.ai/ai-risk

- Chin-Rothmann and Robison, *How AI bots and voice assistants reinforce gender bias.* Brookings. https://www.brookings.edu/articles/how-ai-bots-and-voice-assistants-reinforce-gender-bias/

- Department for Science, Innovation & Technology – GOV.UK. (2025, April). *Safety and security risks of generative artificial intelligence to 2025 (Annex B).* https://www.gov.uk/government/publications/frontier-ai-capabilities-and-risks-discussion-paper/safety-and-security-risks-of-generative-artificial-intelligence-to-2025-annex-b

- Hendren, W. (2025, January 8). *5 Generative AI Risks Your Business Must Resolve to Tackle in 2025.* Safe Security. https://safe.security/resources/new-year-new-ai-5-generative-ai-risks-your-business-must-resolve-to-tackle-in-2025/

- Lanka, S. N., & Zaidi, I. M. (2025, May 26). *When KYC Becomes a Barrier: Supreme Court's Stand for Digital Inclusion.* Internet Freedom Foundation (IFF). https://internetfreedom.in/when-kyc-becomes-a-barrier-supreme-courts-stand-for-digital-inclusion/

- Microsoft. (2023, February 18). Bing. `https://blogs.bing.com/search/february-2023/The-new-Bing-Edge-Learning-from-our-first-week`

- Oswal, A. (2025, June 5). *GenAI's impact – Surging Adoption and Rising Risks in 2025*. Palo Alto Networks Blog. `https://www.paloaltonetworks.com/blog/2025/06/genais-impact-surging-adoption-rising-risks/`

- Pollina, E., & Armellini, A. (2024, December 20). *Italy fines OpenAI over ChatGPT privacy rules breach*. `https://www.reuters.com/technology/italy-fines-openai-15-million-euros-over-privacy-rules-breach-2024-12-20/`

- PricewaterhouseCoopers. (2024). *Managing the risks of generative AI*. PwC. `https://www.pwc.com/us/en/tech-effect/ai-analytics/managing-generative-ai-risks.html`

- Raghavan, P. (2024, February 23). *Gemini image generation got it wrong. We'll do better*. Google. `https://blog.google/products/gemini/gemini-image-generation-issue/`

- Ribera, T., & Virkkunen, H. (2025, April 23). *Commission finds Apple and Meta in breach of the Digital Markets Act*. European Commission. `https://ec.europa.eu/commission/presscorner/detail/en/ip_25_1085`

- Wang, M. (2025, August 27). *Beyond High-Risk Scenarios: Recentering the Everyday Risks of AI* – Center for Democracy and Technology. `https://cdt.org/insights/beyond-high-risk-scenarios-recentering-the-everyday-risks-of-ai/`

- Wilson, S., & Dawson, A. (2024, November 18). *OWASP Top 10 for LLM Applications 2025*. `https://genai.owasp.org/resource/owasp-top-10-for-llm-applications-2025/`

- Yagoda, M. (2024, February 23). *Airline held liable for its chatbot giving passenger bad advice – what this means for travellers*. BBC News. `https://www.bbc.com/travel/article/20240222-air-canada-chatbot-misinformation-what-travellers-should-know`

16

The Future of AI Optimization: Trends, Vision, and Responsible Implementation

This book has explored the transformative power of **artificial intelligence** (**AI**) and the critical importance of optimizing its development and deployment. We have emphasized that true AI innovation is not solely about maximizing efficiency or pushing technological boundaries; it is also about making sure that AI systems are developed and used responsibly and ethically. As we reach the conclusion of our exploration, it is essential to look ahead to the future of AI.

This final chapter will not only examine the emerging trends that will shape AI optimization in the coming years but also underscore the enduring significance of the responsible implementation of AI in navigating this ever-evolving landscape. By envisioning the AI-driven enterprise of 2030, we aim to inspire a future where AI's potential is fully realized in a way that benefits both businesses and society at large.

In this chapter, we will cover the following key topics:

- Emerging trends in AI optimization and responsible implementation
- The societal impact of AI – people and sustainability
- Visionary outlook – the AI-driven enterprise of 2030

Emerging trends in AI optimization and responsible implementation

The future of AI will be shaped by several key trends, from computational power to autonomous systems, that not only promise to enhance AI's capabilities but also necessitate a renewed focus on responsible implementation. This section will explore these emerging trends, including breakthroughs in scaling laws, the rise of quantum computing, the evolution of agentic AI and **explainable AI (XAI)**, and the critical role of AI in cybersecurity. Each of these advancements emphasizes the need for proactive ethical governance to secure and harness AI's power for the betterment of society.

Scaling laws and the future of compute

The continuous advancement of AI is fundamentally linked to scaling laws, which describe how increasing the scale of model size, dataset size, and compute power generally leads to enhanced AI performance (NVIDIA, 2023; AI Safety Book, 2024). As NVIDIA CEO Jensen Huang has explained, these scaling laws are not one-dimensional but rather operate across three key stages of AI development: pre-training (like foundational learning), post-training (specialization in specific domains), and test-time scaling (reasoning for high-quality output).

AI models grow in three key dimensions, known as scaling laws: pre-training, post-training, and test-time scaling. This concept can be illustrated with a graph showing "intelligence" on the y axis and "compute" on the x axis. As computational resources increase, so too does intelligence, moving through three stages: pre-training, where models gain foundational knowledge; post-training, where they specialize in specific domains; and test-time scaling, where they engage in "long thinking" for high-quality output.

This inherent demand for more compute power is a primary catalyst for the ongoing development and widespread deployment of specialized AI chips, such as GPUs and TPUs, designed for efficient AI processing and acceleration of these scaling processes. As AI models grow larger and more capable, the need for robust AI governance and explainability becomes paramount. Implementing transparency and accountability in these complex systems is of prime importance for building trust and mitigating potential risks.

Key technological drivers of future AI

Quantum computing is emerging as a transformative technology with the potential to solve problems that are currently intractable for classical computers. Here are some real-world examples:

- **Pharmaceuticals and materials science**: The field of drug discovery is already leveraging quantum computing to accelerate the process of finding new medications and creating new materials. For example, quantum computers can simulate molecular interactions at a level of complexity that is currently impossible for conventional supercomputers, which could lead to breakthroughs in medicine and material development, such as creating self-healing materials.

- **Financial services**: Quantum computers have the potential to solve complex financial modeling problems. They can be used to optimize investment portfolios by quickly analyzing vast amounts of data and identifying patterns that are too subtle for classical computers. This could lead to more efficient markets and better risk management.

- **Fundamental physics and science**: Companies such as Google are using quantum processors to simulate fundamental interactions in particle physics. This type of research could lead to a deeper understanding of the universe's most basic laws, such as the behavior of particles and the "hidden strings" that connect them.

- **Supply chain and logistics**: The immense computational power of quantum computers can be applied to optimization problems, such as managing complex supply chains. By finding the most efficient routes and schedules, quantum computing could significantly reduce costs and environmental impact.

- **AI and quantum computing**: The convergence of AI and quantum computing could unlock unprecedented computational power, as quantum processors can dramatically accelerate the training and development of even more powerful AI models. This synergy has the potential to drive further innovation across multiple industries.

Let's look at quantum computing in some detail.

Quantum computers are being developed to perform tasks that would be very difficult, if not impossible, for traditional digital computers. They are uniquely suited to solving complex problems such as finding the prime factors of large numbers, searching vast databases, and simulating quantum systems. While significant scientific and engineering challenges still need to be overcome, the potential of this technology is immense.

What is a qubit?

A **qubit** (short for **quantum bit**) is the basic unit of information in quantum computing. Unlike a classical bit, which is either 1 (on) or 0 (off) and can hold one piece of information at a time, a qubit is like a switch that can be on, off, and both simultaneously, which is referred to as superposition.

Because one qubit can represent many possibilities at once, quantum computers can process a massive number of variables and potential solutions in parallel. This is why they promise to solve specific, complex problems (such as optimizing global supply chains or modeling new drug molecules) exponentially faster than any traditional supercomputer.

To help you learn more about the leaders in this space, here are some resources from the companies at the forefront of quantum computing:

- **Google**: Google's Quantum AI team is focused on superconducting qubits and has achieved "quantum supremacy" with its Sycamore processor. They are actively working on building an error-corrected, logical qubit system. For those interested in their work, you can explore the Google Quantum AI educational resources page (`https://quantumai.google/resources`) or the Cirq open source framework (`https://quantumai.google/cirq`).

- **Microsoft**: To put this into context, Microsoft is taking a different, long-term approach with topological qubits. The goal of this method is to create qubits that are inherently more stable and resistant to decoherence, which could dramatically simplify the error correction process.

  The challenge of error correction is that qubits are extremely fragile and their stored information is instantly corrupted by environmental noise, ruining calculations. Therefore, **Quantum Error Correction (QEC)** is essential: it requires bundling hundreds or thousands of unstable physical qubits together to create just one stable, reliable logical qubit. To learn more about topological quantum computing, visit the Microsoft Research page on topological quantum computing. (`https://www.microsoft.com/en-us/research/project/topological-quantum-computing/`)

- **Pasqal**: Pasqal's approach uses neutral atoms manipulated by lasers, a technology rooted in Nobel Prize-winning research. This method offers the potential for high qubit counts and flexible configurations. The need for a high qubit count is necessary for two reasons:

  - **Error correction**: As noted, it takes hundreds or thousands of physical qubits to create a reliable logical qubit

- **Problem size**: The complexity of the real-world problems that quantum aims to solve (e.g., drug discovery, materials science) is so vast that it requires hundreds or thousands of logical qubits to run the necessary algorithms

To learn more, you can explore Pasqal's neutral atom technology overview and their white papers (`https://www.pasqal.com/neutral-atoms/`).

Data storage and accessibility

The ever-increasing data demands of AI necessitate advanced storage solutions. **Non-Volatile Memory Express** (**NVMe**), the industry standard for SSDs, offers significant benefits over traditional storage by streamlining deployments, reducing latency, and enabling direct GPU-to-storage access, which is crucial for efficient AI model training and inference (Cisco, 2025). This technology improves power efficiency and scalability for AI infrastructure.

The greatest bottleneck for training massive AI models is often not the GPU's speed but how quickly data can be fed to it. Direct GPU-to-storage access is a hardware optimization that allows the GPU to bypass the CPU and system memory and pull data directly from high-speed storage. This radically speeds up the data flow, so the powerful GPUs spend less time waiting and more time processing, which is crucial for achieving true scalability and cost-efficiency with large models.

Scalable cloud storage solutions provide the capacity and cost-efficiency needed to manage vast datasets. Complementing these advancements, confidential computing can help move the needle that encrypts data in use, providing a secure foundation for scaling AI initiatives, establishing the security of AI data and models during processing by creating **Trusted Execution Environments** (**TEEs**) (Guan, 2025). This protects sensitive information from unauthorized access, facilitates secure collaboration, supports compliance, and fosters trust in AI deployments. Emerging trends such as hybrid storage models and quantum storage hold the potential to further optimize data storage and accessibility for AI applications. AI-powered personalization is expanding, moving towards hyper-personalized experiences.

Agentic AI and the next wave of automation

Agentic AI systems, which can act autonomously, make decisions, and carry out tasks without constant human intervention, represent a significant leap forward in AI capabilities. Recent projections indicate the rapid growth of this trend. By 2028, it is anticipated that 33% of enterprise software will feature agentic AI. This will empower AI to autonomously manage a substantial portion of digital storefront interactions, estimated at 20%, as well as handling 15% of daily work decisions (Gartner, 2024). These systems have the potential to automate complex tasks across various industries, increasing efficiency and productivity. However, the development and deployment of agentic AI necessitate careful ethical considerations and the establishment of clear guidelines for responsible use.

XAI for trust and transparency

As AI systems become more intricate, the importance of XAI grows. XAI aims to make AI decisions transparent and understandable to humans. XAI is essential for building trust in AI systems, promoting accountability, and enabling their responsible adoption, particularly in critical sectors such as healthcare and finance. Let's look at its applications in more detail:

- **Healthcare**: XAI is being used to enhance diagnostic accuracy and trust. For instance, AI-powered cancer detection systems can generate detailed heatmaps that highlight suspicious regions in mammograms, providing doctors with visual explanations for a diagnosis. XAI also helps medical professionals and patients understand treatment recommendations by explaining which specific data points, such as genetic markers or clinical history, influenced the AI's suggestion.

- **Finance**: XAI provides critical transparency in high-stakes financial decisions. When a loan application is denied, XAI can provide the applicant with clear reasons, such as recent late payments or high credit utilization, empowering them to take corrective action. Similarly, in fraud detection, XAI allows banks to identify and explain suspicious patterns, such as a large transaction from an unusual location, helping them balance security with customer experience.

However, transparency and trust are meaningless if the underlying models and data are compromised. Therefore, the next critical frontier for optimization is leveraging AI to counter increasingly advanced digital threats.

AI-driven cybersecurity

We are all witnessing how AI is transforming the field of cybersecurity by enhancing threat detection, predicting vulnerabilities, and automating responses to attacks. While AI offers powerful tools for cybersecurity, it is crucial to acknowledge the potential for malicious use of AI by cybercriminals. Ethical AI development and deployment are paramount so that AI strengthens cybersecurity rather than undermines it.

AI is revolutionizing threat detection and response. Companies such as Darktrace use AI to learn the "normal" behavior of a network and then detect and flag any anomalies that might signal an unknown or "zero-day" threat. IBM's Watson for Cybersecurity automates responses by analyzing vast amounts of security data and taking actions such as quarantining a detected phishing email. In the realm of insider threats, some large tech companies use AI to analyze user activity logs to detect and prevent data exfiltration (the unauthorized transfer of data out of a network or system) before it happens.

The trends in AI optimization from the raw power of quantum computing to the ethical imperatives of XAI are redefining what is possible. While these technological advancements promise unparalleled efficiency and innovation, they must be paired with a steadfast commitment to responsible implementation. As we continue to push the boundaries of AI, it is crucial that we consider not only the technical feasibility of our solutions but also their broader human and societal impact. We will explore this vital topic in the next section.

The societal impact of AI — people and sustainability

Beyond its technical capabilities, AI is poised to have a profound impact on society, influencing how we live, work, and interact with the world around us. It is crucial to proactively address the societal implications of AI, making sure that its benefits are shared broadly and its potential risks are mitigated.

Transforming work and industries

The AI revolution represents a fundamental shift in humanity's relationship with technology, potentially reshaping economic and social structures as profoundly as the agricultural revolution. AI's impact on employment is complex, with the potential to displace jobs while also creating new ones, though AI may also compete for these new jobs. PwC projects that AI technologies will increase productivity and GDP by 1.5% by 2035, building a permanent increase in the level of economic activity (Amon & Paulson, 2025). The analysis projects that AI's strongest boost to annual productivity growth will occur in the early 2030s. This growth is underpinned by the fact that approximately 40% of the current GDP could be substantially affected by Generative AI tools.

AI-powered automation, hyper-personalization, and predictive analytics are already reshaping industries, driving increased efficiency and innovation. As AI continues to advance, it will transform the future of work by automating routine tasks and creating new opportunities for human-AI collaboration. To prepare for this shift, it is essential to invest in workforce reskilling and upskilling initiatives, ensuring that individuals can adapt to the changing demands of the AI-driven economy.

AI and human values

Integrating human-centric values into AI systems is paramount. This includes prioritizing fairness, inclusivity, transparency, and privacy to foster trust in making AI benefit all members of society. In healthcare, AI offers the potential to enhance disease diagnosis, personalize treatment recommendations, and improve patient care. However, it is crucial to address ethical considerations related to data privacy, algorithmic bias, and equitable access to AI-driven healthcare solutions.

AI is also transforming transportation, enabling the development of autonomous vehicles and smart transportation systems. Ethical considerations in this domain include ensuring the safety of autonomous systems, addressing liability issues, and mitigating potential job displacement. In education, AI can personalize learning experiences and automate administrative tasks. However, it is important to maintain fairness and inclusivity, ensuring that AI tools support students with diverse needs and do not exacerbate existing inequalities.

AI for a sustainable future

AI can be a powerful tool for promoting sustainability across various industries. AI-driven solutions can optimize energy consumption, improve resource management, and enhance climate modeling, contributing to a more environmentally friendly future. However, it's crucial to acknowledge the significant energy footprint of the infrastructure supporting AI. McKinsey & Company projects that data centers in the US will consume 11 to 12% of the nation's total power by 2030, a substantial rise from the current 3 to 4% (Noffsinger, 2025). This clearly emphasizes the importance of developing energy-efficient algorithms, sustainable storage solutions, and green data centers to minimize the environmental impact of AI itself.

Visionary outlook — the AI-driven enterprise of 2030

We have so far explored the key technological and societal trends shaping the next decade from quantum computing and deep autonomy to responsible governance and AI-driven sustainability. It is essential to synthesize these elements into a tangible vision. The true measure of AI optimization is not in individual pilot projects, but in the creation of a fully evolved, AI-driven enterprise.

The following fictional case study of InnovAIte LLC will illustrate how a modern company will transition from the challenges of today into the fully realized AI enterprise of 2030.

By the year 2030, AI will no longer be a separate department or a collection of tools; it will be the very fabric of successful enterprises. The AI-driven enterprise of 2030 operates with a seamless integration of AI across all its functions, fostering unprecedented levels of efficiency, innovation, and ethical responsibility.

Quantum computing is emerging as a transformative technology with the potential to solve problems that are currently intractable for classical computers. Industries such as pharmaceuticals are already leveraging quantum computing for applications such as drug discovery. The convergence of AI and quantum computing could unlock unprecedented computational power and intelligence, driving further innovation.

Companies such as IBM and Google are at the forefront of this revolution, racing to launch commercial quantum services by 2025. The significant investment in quantum computing demonstrates the industry's commitment to this technology. In both 2022 and 2023, quantum computing startups secured over $1.27 billion in capital, confirming the sustained, high-level funding necessary to drive the next decade of research and development. For comparison, investments in quantum communication and quantum sensing were significantly lower, with both seeing a decrease from 2022 to 2023. Simultaneously, the rise of agentic AI systems is predicted to disrupt the fundamental structure of knowledge work across industries by 2030 (Heim, 2025), automating complex tasks and requiring a re-evaluation of human roles in the workplace.

AI will transform human resources by aiding talent acquisition and personalized development for equitable opportunities by creating a dynamic and inclusive workforce. Research and development will harness AI's predictive power to accelerate scientific breakthroughs, design sustainable solutions, and anticipate future market needs with remarkable accuracy. Operations will be optimized by AI-powered automation, predictive maintenance, and intelligent supply chains, leading to unprecedented efficiency and resource utilization. Marketing and sales will employ hyper-personalized AI to understand customer needs deeply, build lasting relationships, and deliver tailored solutions with exceptional precision. Even finance and legal departments will benefit from AI's analytical capabilities, enhancing risk management, adhering to regulatory compliance, and streamlining complex processes.

The key characteristic of the AI-driven enterprise of 2030 is its unwavering commitment to responsible AI. Ethical considerations are not an afterthought but are deeply embedded in every stage of AI development and deployment. Transparency is paramount, with clear explanations of AI decision-making processes fostering trust among employees, customers, and stakeholders. Robust governance frameworks in place promote accountability, and continuous monitoring systems proactively identify and mitigate potential biases or unintended consequences.

This future enterprise will understand that the true power of AI will lie not just in its ability to optimize processes and drive innovation but in its potential to create a more sustainable, equitable, and prosperous future for all. By prioritizing ethical considerations and human-centric values, the AI-driven enterprise of 2030 will set out a new standard for business excellence in the age of intelligent machines.

InnovAIte LLC — AI-driven enterprise embodiment

Moving forward from the foundation of responsible AI principles established in earlier chapters, InnovAIte LLC will have consistently prioritized transparency, fairness, accountability, and safety in its AI solutions. By 2030, this commitment will culminate in InnovAIte LLC becoming a compelling illustration of the AI-driven enterprise, fundamentally transforming its operations and culture to achieve a powerful synergy of innovation, efficiency, and ethical integrity.

Here is a timeline of its responsible AI innovation:

- **Early 2020s: Healthcare AI foundation and ethical framework**: InnovAIte LLC begins its journey with a focus on developing AI-driven diagnostic tools for healthcare, establishing its core ethical principles and governance structures.

- **Mid-2020s: Proactive regulatory compliance and scalable governance**: Recognizing the increasing importance of AI regulation, InnovAIte LLC prioritizes building agile and adaptable AI systems that can meet evolving compliance requirements. The company expands its ethical governance framework to enable scalability across its AI initiatives, including healthcare and finance.

- **Late 2020s: Agentic AI and human-AI collaboration**: The focus will shift to specialized, semi-autonomous agents that execute multi-step, complex tasks (e.g., initial research, code generation, and drafting legal documents). Organizations such as InnovAIte LLC will begin prioritizing the governance and ethical implications of these agents, as they will still require human-in-the-loop validation for high-stakes decisions.

- **Early 2030s: Highly autonomous enterprise AI agents**: AI agents will reach a state of deep autonomy, becoming capable of managing complex, end-to-end business workflows with minimal human intervention. This level of autonomy is characterized by human-in-the-loop governance, where the agents execute tasks independently and only flag exceptions or critical decisions to human monitoring for final validation. Examples include fully autonomous contracting, dynamic resource allocation in supply chains, and self-optimizing security protocols that require only human oversight, rather than intervention. This level of autonomy unlocks the projected exponential productivity gains and drives the organizational overhaul to achieve the 2030 enterprise vision.

As an AI-driven enterprise of 2030, InnovAIte's AI-driven solutions will span various fields, from financial services to healthcare, showcasing its commitment to applying responsible AI principles across all sectors. Here is what will they have achieved:

- **Pioneering ethical governance and transparency**: By 2030, InnovAIte LLC will have established a leading-edge ethical governance framework. AI ethics committees will be deeply integrated into every stage of AI development, to be in alignment with ethical guidelines and regulatory requirements. The company will publish detailed transparency reports, openly explain AI decision-making processes, and foster trust with all stakeholders.

- **Championing continuous monitoring and improvement**: InnovAIte LLC will excel in its commitment to continuous monitoring and improvement. Advanced AI-powered systems will proactively detect and mitigate biases, so that AI models remain fair, accurate, and aligned with evolving ethical standards. Regular updates and stakeholder feedback loops will drive ongoing refinement of AI systems.

- **Embracing stakeholder engagement and inclusivity**: InnovAIte LLC will actively engage with a diverse ecosystem of stakeholders. Through workshops, surveys, and collaborative forums, the company will incorporate a wide range of perspectives, making sure that its AI solutions are both innovative and socially responsible.

- **Driving AI-powered transformation across industries**: InnovAIte LLC will exemplify the transformative power of AI across multiple sectors. This rapid, multi-sector expansion will not be based on traditional infrastructure (which would make it overly optimistic) but on highly generalized AI agents and modular foundational models. The core business model of the 2030s AI firm will enable this speed because the fundamental AI function will be transferable. For instance, the same self-optimizing, resource allocation agent developed for healthcare supply chains can be easily fine-tuned and redeployed to entirely different sectors: optimizing traffic flow in sustainable transportation or managing energy grid balancing in smart cities. This generalizability of function will allow AI-first firms to scale vertically across disparate domains with unprecedented speed, validating the enterprise vision for 2030.

- **Leading the way in sustainable AI**: InnovAIte LLC will be a trailblazer in sustainable AI practices. The company will prioritize energy-efficient algorithms, operate carbon-neutral data centers, and develop AI-driven solutions that address climate change and promote environmental stewardship.

- **Scaling AI with responsibility and agility**: InnovAIte LLC will have mastered the art of scaling AI solutions responsibly. By leveraging MLOps and robust governance frameworks, the company will efficiently deploy and manage AI systems at scale, for both innovation and ethical compliance purposes.

InnovAIte LLC's journey will provide an inspiring glimpse into the future of business. It will demonstrate that by embedding responsible AI into their core strategy, organizations will unlock AI's full potential to drive not only business success but also a more equitable and sustainable world.

Summary

As we conclude this exploration of the future of AI, one central message emerges with unwavering clarity is that the path to unlocking AI's transformative potential lies in the inseparable pairing of innovation and responsibility. AI optimization, in its pursuit of enhanced efficiency and ground-breaking capabilities, including those enabled by the convergence of AI and quantum computing, must be guided by a steadfast commitment to ethical principles and human-centric values.

This chapter has illuminated the exciting trends that will shape the coming years, from the scaling of AI models and the evolution of data storage to the rise of increasingly autonomous agentic AI systems and the imperative of XAI. We have also emphasized the profound societal impact of AI, its power to reshape industries, and the critical importance so that its benefits are shared equitably and sustainably. The vision of the AI-driven enterprise of 2030 serves as an inspiring reminder of what is possible when organizations prioritize both innovation and responsibility, creating a future where AI empowers human progress and drives positive change.

Ultimately, the future of AI is not predetermined. It is a future that we actively shape through the choices we make today. By embracing responsible AI innovation and fostering ongoing dialogue and collaboration to address the evolving ethical and societal implications of advanced AI, such as agentic systems and quantum-enhanced AI, we can navigate the challenges and harness the opportunities that lie ahead, building a world where AI serves as a force for good, enriching lives and creating a brighter tomorrow.

References

- Artificial Intelligence Act (Regulation (EU) 2024/1689. (2025, August). *Article 99: Penalties.* EU Artificial Intelligence Act. https://artificialintelligenceact.eu/article/99/

- Amon, A., & Paulson, M. (2025, September 8). *The Projected Impact of Generative AI on Future Productivity Growth.* Penn Wharton Budget Model. https://budgetmodel.wharton.upenn.edu/issues/2025/9/8/projected-impact-of-generative-ai-on-future-productivity-growth

- Briski, K. (2025, February 12). *How Scaling Laws Drive Smarter, More Powerful AI.* NVIDIA Blog. https://blogs.nvidia.com/blog/ai-scaling-laws/

- Center for AI Safety (CAIS). (2024). AI risks that could lead to catastrophe – CAIS 2024 impact report. *An Overview of Catastrophic AI Risks.* https://safe.ai/ai-risk

- Cisco. (2025, April 10). *What is NVMe?.* Cisco. https://www.cisco.com/c/en/us/solutions/computing/what-is-nvme.html#~benefits-of-nvme

- Department for Science, Innovation & Technology – GOV.UK. (2025, April). *Safety and security risks of generative artificial intelligence to 2025 (Annex B).* https://www.gov.uk/government/publications/frontier-ai-capabilities-and-risks-discussion-paper/safety-and-security-risks-of-generative-artificial-intelligence-to-2025-annex-b

- Gartner. (2024, October 21). *Gartner Identifies the Top 10 Strategic Technology Trends for 2025.* https://www.gartner.com/en/newsroom/press-releases/2024-10-21-gartner-identifies-the-top-10-strategic-technology-trends-for-2025

- Guan, L. (2025, April 14). *Securing the future of gen AI with confidential computing.* Accenture. https://www.accenture.com/us-en/blogs/data-ai/securing-future-gen-ai-confidential-computing

- Heim, A. (2025, May 5). *Meet the companies racing to build quantum chips.* TechCrunch. https://techcrunch.com/2025/05/05/meet-the-companies-racing-to-build-quantum-chips/

- Hendren, W. (2025, January 8). *5 Generative AI Risks Your Business Must Resolve to Tackle in 2025.* Safe Security. https://safe.security/resources/new-year-new-ai-5-generative-ai-risks-your-business-must-resolve-to-tackle-in-2025/

- Hendrycks, D. (2024, December 31). AI safety, ethics, and society textbook. https://www.aisafetybook.com/

- The Official Microsoft Blog. (2022, June). *Microsoft Responsible AI Standard, v2.* https://msblogs.thesourcemediaassets.com/sites/5/2022/06/Microsoft-Responsible-AI-Standard-v2-General-Requirements-3.pdf

- Mucci, T., & Stryker, C. (2024, October 10). *What is AI governance?*. IBM. https://www.ibm.com/think/topics/ai-governance

- Noffsinger, J. (2025, February 26). *Re-think: How to provide the power the digital future demands*. McKinsey & Company. https://www.mckinsey.com/~/media/mckinsey/email/rethink/2025/02/2025-02-26e.html

- Oswal, A. (2025, June 5). *GenAI's Impact – Surging Adoption and Rising Risks in 2025*. Palo Alto Networks Blog. https://www.paloaltonetworks.com/blog/2025/06/genais-impact-surging-adoption-rising-risks/

- PricewaterhouseCoopers. (2024). *Managing the risks of generative AI*. PwC. https://www.pwc.com/us/en/tech-effect/ai-analytics/managing-generative-ai-risks.html

- Rao, A. S., & Verweij, G. (2017, June). PWC's global artificial intelligence study: *Sizing the prize*. PwC. https://www.pwc.com/gx/en/issues/analytics/assets/pwc-ai-analysis-sizing-the-prize-report.pdf

- Wang, M. (2025, August 27). *Beyond High-Risk Scenarios: Recentering the Everyday Risks of AI* – Center for Democracy and Technology. https://cdt.org/insights/beyond-high-risk-scenarios-recentering-the-everyday-risks-of-ai/

Subscribe for a free eBook

New frameworks, evolving architectures, research drops, production breakdowns—AI_Distilled filters the noise into a weekly briefing for engineers and researchers working hands-on with LLMs and GenAI systems. Subscribe now and receive a free eBook, along with weekly insights that help you stay focused and informed.

Subscribe at https://packt.link/80z6Y or scan the QR code below.

17

Unlock Your Exclusive Benefits

Your copy of this book includes the following exclusive benefit:

- ⟲ Next-gen Packt Reader
- 🄿 DRM-free PDF/ePub downloads

Follow the guide below to unlock them. The process takes only a few minutes and needs to be completed once.

Unlock this Book's Free Benefits in 3 Easy Steps

Step 1

Keep your purchase invoice ready for *Step 3*. If you have a physical copy, scan it using your phone and save it as a PDF, JPG, or PNG.

For more help on finding your invoice, visit `https://www.packtpub.com/unlock-benefits/help`.

> **Note**
> If you bought this book directly from Packt, no invoice is required. After *Step 2*, you can access your exclusive content right away.

Step 2

Scan the QR code or go to `packtpub.com/unlock`.

On the page that opens (similar to *Figure 17.1* on desktop), search for this book by name and select the correct edition.

Figure 17.1: Packt unlock landing page on desktop

Step 3

After selecting your book, sign in to your Packt account or create one for free. Then upload your invoice (PDF, PNG, or JPG, up to 10 MB). Follow the on-screen instructions to finish the process.

Need help?

If you get stuck and need help, visit
`https://www.packtpub.com/unlock-benefits/help`
for a detailed FAQ on how to find your invoices and more. This QR code will take you to the help page.

> **Note**
>
> If you are still facing issues, reach out to `customercare@packt.com`.

Index

‹packt›

packtpub.com

Subscribe to our online digital library for full access to over 7,000 books and videos, as well as industry leading tools to help you plan your personal development and advance your career. For more information, please visit our website.

Why subscribe?

- Spend less time learning and more time coding with practical eBooks and Videos from over 4,000 industry professionals

- Improve your learning with Skill Plans built especially for you

- Get a free eBook or video every month

- Fully searchable for easy access to vital information

- Copy and paste, print, and bookmark content

At www.packtpub.com, you can also read a collection of free technical articles, sign up for a range of free newsletters, and receive exclusive discounts and offers on Packt books and eBooks.

Other Books You May Enjoy

If you enjoyed this book, you may be interested in these other books by Packt:

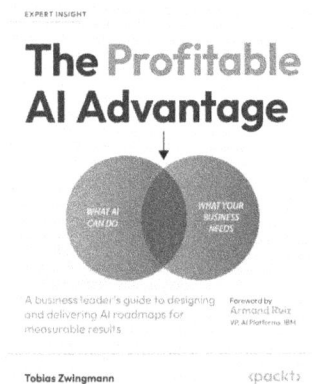

The Profitable AI Advantage

Tobias Zwingmann

ISBN: 978-1-83620-589-0

- Identify and leverage AI opportunities in your business
- Create actionable AI roadmaps and implement them incrementally
- Scale AI operations to enhance business functions
- Design and evaluate AI use cases through feasibility assessments
- Recognize AI trends to quickly prototype and iterate AI solutions
- Manage AI projects and teams effectively without deep technical skills
- Understand fundamental concepts of modern AI, including Generative AI, LLMs, and predictive models

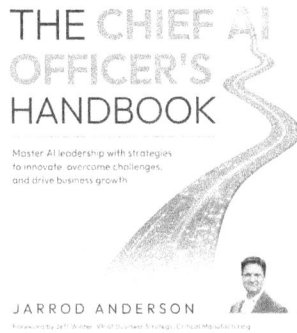

The Chief AI Officer's Handbook

Jarrod Anderson

ISBN: 978-1-83620-085-7

- Develop and execute AI strategy as a CAIO, ensuring ethical compliance
- Master agile AI project management from ideation to deployment
- Apply deterministic and probabilistic AI concepts through case studies
- Design and implement AI agents for autonomous system optimization
- Create human-centered AI systems using proven design principles
- Enhance AI security through data privacy and model protection measures

Packt is searching for authors like you

If you're interested in becoming an author for Packt, please visit `authors.packtpub.com` and apply today. We have worked with thousands of developers and tech professionals, just like you, to help them share their insight with the global tech community. You can make a general application, apply for a specific hot topic that we are recruiting an author for, or submit your own idea.

Share your thoughts

Now you've finished *The AI Optimization Playbook*, we'd love to hear your thoughts! Scan the QR code below to go straight to the Amazon review page for this book and share your feedback or leave a review on the site that you purchased it from.

`https://packt.link/r/1806115115`

Your review is important to us and the tech community and will help us make sure we're delivering excellent quality content.

Join our Discord and Reddit space

You're not the only one navigating fragmented tools, constant updates, and unclear best practices. Join a growing community of professionals exchanging insights that don't make it into documentation.

Stay informed with updates, discussions, and behind-the-scenes insights from our authors. Join our Discord space at `https://packt.link/z8ivB` or scan the QR code below:	Connect with peers, share ideas, and discuss real-world GenAI challenges. Follow us on Reddit at `https://packt.link/0rExL` or scan the QR code below: